D0498543

PLUTOCRATS UNITED

RICHARD L. HASEN

Plutocrats United

CAMPAIGN MONEY, THE SUPREME COURT,

AND THE DISTORTION OF AMERICAN ELECTIONS

Yale UNIVERSITY PRESS

NEW HAVEN & LONDON

Yale University Press books may be purchased in quantity for
educational, business, or promotional use. For information, please e-mail
sales.press@yale.edu (U.S. office) or sales@yaleup.co.uk (U.K. office).

Set in Scala type by Integrated Publishing Solutions,
Grand Rapids, Michigan.
Printed in the United States of America.

ISBN 978-0-300-21245-7 (cloth : alk. paper)
Library of Congress Control Number: 2015940942

A catalogue record for this book is available from the British Library.

This paper meets the requirements of ANSI/NISO Z39.48-1992
(Permanence of Paper).

10 9 8 7 6 5 4 3 2 1

For Lori,
a life partner whose love, wisdom, beauty, and support
are far more than I could have imagined or deserve

CONTENTS

ACKNOWLEDGMENTS

I have been thinking and writing about campaign finance law and policy for more than twenty years. This book is a culmination of my work in this area, but I see it as more of a collaborative effort. My scholarship has been possible only because of how much I have learned from others in the field who came before me and from those who write in dialogue on these issues. I cite and discuss many of my fine colleagues' work in this book.

Bob Bauer, Bruce Cain, Erwin Chemerinsky, Yasmin Dawood, David Ettinger, Ned Foley, Paul Horwitz, Steve Kay, Sarah Lawsky, Tom Mann, Ken Mayer, Bob Mutch, Jake Rowbottom, John Sides, Nick Stephanopolous, Marty Wattenberg, Sonja West, and Adam Winkler read and provided detailed comments on significant portions of the manuscript. Others read portions of the manuscript or provided important information or feedback, including: Tim Bartlett, Keith Ewing, Dave McBride, Jeff Milyo, Nate Persily, Rick Pildes, Chris Rhodes, and Irit Samet.

A group of colleagues at the University of California, Irvine, read the manuscript and met to discuss it, providing me with wonderful feedback as the book was being written. Thanks to Erwin Chemerinsky, Sarah Lawsky, Jack Lerner, Greg Shaffer, Bob Solomon, Ann Southworth, and Colleen Taricani for stimulating conversations. I also learned a great deal from presenting a portion of this manuscript at talks or workshops at Bucknell, Cal Poly San Luis Obispo, Kings College, Oxford, UCLA, and at the Yale University Freedom of Expression Scholars Conference.

Law students Emily Cross and Tara Schonhoff provided exemplary research assistance, and Emily (whose work on this project was probably much more than she thought she was signing up for) was joined by Justin O'Neill for meticulous cite-checking work and Nassim Alisobhani and Francis Yao for proofreading. UC Irvine's law librarians Betty Lim, Jessica Pierucci, Dianna Sahhar, and Christina Tsou were indispensable in assisting me with my arcane research queries, joined by Annette Buckley of the business school library when research took me into the world of potato chip marketing. Erwin Chemerinsky, dean of the UC Irvine School of Law, generously supported my scholarship. Robert Medeiros and Stacy Tran provided cheerful and professional administrative support.

Bill Frucht at Yale University Press made this a considerably better book. Aside from being an excellent editor and pushing me on my arguments, he has remarkably good judgment and instincts. Jaya Chatterjee of the Press graciously eased the way for my manuscript to sail through the many stages of review and editing, and Phil King helped my prose flow more effortlessly. I have been lucky to have the wise counsel of my agent, John Wright, a person of uncommon integrity, good sense, and smarts.

Finally, I owe a great debt to my wife, Lori. Her support, encouragement, and love made this book—and all I do—possible; this book is dedicated to her.

In the course of writing this book, I relied upon some of my earlier writings on related topics. I reprint with permission, in somewhat altered from, material appearing originally in the following publications:

Citizens United *and the Illusion of Coherence,* 109 Mich. L. Rev. 581 (2011)
End of the Dialogue? Political Polarization, the Supreme Court, and Congress, 86 S. Cal. L. Rev. 205 (2013)
Lobbying, Rent-Seeking, and the Constitution, 64 Stan. L. Rev. 191 (2012)
The Nine Lives of Buckley v. Valeo *in* First Amendment Stories (Richard Garnett & Andrew Koppelman eds., 2012)
Campaign Finance Laws and the Rupert Murdoch Problem, 77 Tex. L. Rev. 1627 (1999)
Three Wrong Progressive Approaches (and One Right One) to Campaign Finance Reform, 8 Harv. L. & Pol'y Rev. 21 (2014)

PLUTOCRATS UNITED

Introduction

A New American Plutocracy?

THE CHRIS CHRISTIE STORY WAS JUST TOO good for progressives to pass up, even though it obscured larger truths about the influence of money in American politics.

In the spring of 2014, a group of Republican presidential hopefuls, including Governor Christie of New Jersey, converged on the Venetian Hotel in Las Vegas to speak before the Republican Jewish Coalition and its key board member, the billionaire casino mogul and Venetian hotel owner Sheldon Adelson. It was a big moment for Christie, who was trying to get past a controversy over the closing of lanes on the George Washington Bridge allegedly in retaliation because Fort Lee's mayor, a Democrat, did not support Christie's reelection bid.

The speakers, the former Florida governor Jeb Bush, Ohio governor John Kasich, Wisconsin governor Scott Walker, and Christie, fell all over themselves to flatter Adelson and to announce their support for a continued strong relationship between the United States and Israel, Adelson's signature issue. Walker, according to a *New York Times* story, "brought up his father's trip to Israel, and said he puts 'a menorah candle' next to his Christmas tree. The name of his son, Matthew, actually comes from Hebrew, he pointed out."[1]

But Christie stepped in it. In his speech to the group, he "warmly recalled a trip he took with his family to Israel, calling it an extraordinary personal experience. But he touched off disapproving whispers from the

crowd when he described flying over the 'occupied territories' where Pal-
estinians live." To conservative supporters of Israel, who believe Israel has
a right to sovereignty over the West Bank and other areas captured in the
Six-Day War in 1967, it was a faux pas to call them "occupied territories."
Christie quickly apologized in a private meeting with Adelson.[2]

Progressives denounced the "line to kiss Sheldon Adelson's boots" (or
perhaps a bit higher up), the candidates' "prostrat[ing] themselves, seeking
Adelson's stamp of approval and cash," and Christie's apology to Adelson
for describing the disputed regions with a term regularly used by U.S. presidents and the U.S. government.[3]

Who could blame these candidates for participating in the "Sheldon primary" or for their obsequiousness? Adelson and his wife had contributed
an astounding $98 million to $150 million (thanks to holes in our campaign disclosure laws we are not sure exactly how much) to help elect Republican candidates during the 2012 election, including giving more than
$15 million to a "Super PAC" called "Winning Our Future" that seemed to
single-handedly keep the former speaker of the House Newt Gingrich in
the 2012 race for the Republican presidential nomination. The Adelsons
later gave tens of millions more to support Mitt Romney's run against President Barack Obama in the general election. The 2016 presidential hopefuls wanted Adelson's support and, more importantly, his money.[4]

But if the lesson progressives drew from the Chris Christie story was
that big money is "buying elections," the claim was off the mark. Instead,
Adelson's money bought Gingrich's 2012 presidential campaign only a second (and third and fourth) look from Republican primary voters, but those
voters ultimately rejected him. Romney beat Gingrich in the primary, but
then, even with significant support from Adelson, lost to Obama in a campaign where each candidate and his party raised around a billion dollars.[5]

So we can begin our consideration of the problem of money in American
politics by rejecting the crass common liberal refrain that money simply
buys elections. The eBay entrepreneur Meg Whitman's $140 million in
self-financed cash did not allow her to beat Jerry Brown to be California's
governor in 2010; the more she spent on her election ads, the less voters
seemed to like her. Similarly, the environmentalist Tom Steyer's efforts to
keep a Democratic majority in the U.S. Senate failed in the 2014 elections

despite spending nearly $74 million. And in an electoral earthquake in 2014, Dave Brat, an unknown college professor with two full-time staffers, beat Eric Cantor, the House majority leader, in a Virginia congressional primary race. Cantor's campaign spent more at steakhouses than his more conservative opponent spent on his entire campaign. The relationship between money and politics is the United States is more complicated than mere vote buying.[6]

We can also reject the claim progressives sometimes make that campaign money "bribes" politicians. Take the group United Republic/Represent Us, backed by such reformers as Trevor Potter, a prominent campaign finance lawyer who helped form the comedian Stephen Colbert's "Americans for a Better Tomorrow, Tomorrow" Super PAC. Represent Us backs the proposed American Anti-Corruption Act. The website supporting the legislation is headed: "Get Money Out of Politics: Stop lobbyist bribery, End secret money & Empower voters." Its first point for why the legislation is necessary: "Stop Politicians from Taking Bribes."[7]

But as Harvard professor and campaign reformer Lawrence Lessig explains, most members of Congress are not taking bribes, and that cash-for-votes corruption likely is as rare as it has ever been in Congress. Sure, there are the occasional stories: Republican Randy "Duke" Cunningham of California went to jail for getting a yacht and other goodies from defense contractors, and Democrat William Jefferson of Louisiana was caught in an FBI bribery sting in which he was arrested with $10,000 of literally cold cash in his freezer. But neither man was bribed by *legal* campaign contributions. Federal candidates legally can take no more than $5,400 from an individual across a two-year campaign cycle and just $5,000 from a political action committee. Who in Congress could be bought so cheap?[8]

Super PACs such as the one supporting Gingrich cannot give their large sums directly to the candidates. But they can raise unlimited funds so long as they do not violate federal rules against "coordination" with candidates. The few members of Congress who take bribes are not taking them primarily through legal campaign contributions (at least not yet).

But reformers and reform groups Common Cause and Democracy 21 use the language of "corruption" all the time. Lessig, for example, has talked of the need for new laws to staunch "dependence corruption," in which the "system" is corrupted by politicians dependent upon campaign funders to remain in office rather than on "the people alone."[9]

It is hard for reformers to avoid the corruption talk. To begin with, "corruption" resonates with the general public—a poll commissioned by Represent Us saw support jump from 60 to 72 percent of Americans when a campaign finance reform bill is packaged as an anticorruption measure. Using the term broadly, corruption can mean anything deviating from some perfect state of nature. But there's another, stronger reason why those in the election-reform business talk so much about "corruption" in American politics, a reason that has distorted Americans' thinking and talking about money in politics for decades.[10]

The Supreme Court.

☑

In 1976, the Court decided *Buckley v. Valeo*, upholding some parts of a 1974 federal campaign finance law and striking down others. *Buckley* held that campaign finance limits complied with the United States Constitution's First Amendment guarantee of freedom of speech and association only if they could be justified by the government's interest in preventing "corruption" or the "appearance of corruption." The Court rejected the idea that the government could limit money in politics to promote political equality as "wholly foreign to the First Amendment."[11]

This singular focus on corruption explains the Supreme Court's constantly shifting approach to the constitutionality of campaign laws. Liberal justices read the term "corruption" broadly and vote to uphold many limits. Conservative justices read it narrowly and vote to strike down just about everything—witness the era of skepticism we are in right now. This is why a host of reformers and academics try to shoehorn a variety of reasons to limit money in politics under the label "corruption."

Justice Anthony Kennedy, writing for the Supreme Court in 2010 in *Citizens United v. Federal Election Commission*, explained that when large donors and spenders ingratiate themselves with elected officials to secure access to them, it is not corruption. "Ingratiation and access" or the appearance of ingratiation and access thus provide no basis for limiting money in politics. *Citizens United*, a 5–4 decision pitting the Court's conservatives against its liberals, opened a new era of corporate and union spending in federal elections and fueled the emergence of Super PACs and other outside spending groups.[12]

In a case decided in 2014, *McCutcheon v. Federal Election Commission,* Chief Justice John Roberts went even further, celebrating the idea of politicians responding to the wishes of big donors and spenders. Not only are "ingratiation and access" afforded those making large campaign contributions not corruption, Roberts explained. Donors "embody a central feature of democracy—that constituents support candidates who share their beliefs and interests, and candidates who are elected can be expected to be responsive to those concerns." In a democracy, Roberts tells us, we should *want* politicians to be responsive to big donors.[13]

The new *Citizens United* era is not full of corrupt politicians taking bribes or of elections going to the highest bidder. To claim it is so puts the public's spotlight in the wrong place, looking for elected officials to use large amounts of money for private gain. The more central problem of money in politics is something just as troubling but much harder to see: a system in which economic inequalities, inevitable in a free market economy, are transformed into political inequalities that affect both electoral and legislative outcomes. Without any politician taking a single bribe, wealth has an increasingly disproportionate influence on our politics. While we can call that a problem of "corruption," this pushes the limits of the words too far (certainly far beyond what the Supreme Court is going to entertain as corruption) and obscures the fundamental unfairness of a political system moving toward plutocracy. The political power of the wealthy is especially troubling in our current period of rising economic inequality, when those with great economic clout can use their increased political power to protect their economic position.

Most of the important money-in-politics action happens not in the glare of the television cameras at the Venetian in Las Vegas, but in steakhouses and on golf courses all around Washington, D.C., where lobbyists—often former senators, members of congress, or staffers—do their ingratiation and secure their access. There is a reason big business pays lobbyists so well, and it is not that lobbyists are information specialists who help create sound public policy. Lobbyists secure access both by bundling campaign contributions and by using personal connections. It should be no surprise that half of retiring senators become lobbyists, many with seven-figure salaries, and that lobbyists who used to work for a U.S. senator see their income fall by nearly a quarter when that senator retires.[14]

Money works especially well in the shadows. Lobbyists, like mushrooms, thrive in low light. A recent study about a one-time special tax rule passed as part of the American Jobs Creation Act of 2004 shows that ninety-three companies lobbied for its passage, spending a total of $282.7 million to obtain overall tax benefits of $298 billion, with savings of approximately $88 billion for those ninety-three companies.[15]

Money could not stop the passage of the Dodd-Frank bill, which regulated the securities industry against the industry's wishes: public outrage over the 2008 financial crisis was just too great to overcome. But once public attention faded, moneyed interests could work their magic, using influence to water down implementing legislation and regulations and stalling or stopping much of what Dodd-Frank promised to achieve.[16]

In the new era of Super PACs and non-disclosing "social welfare" groups spending millions of dollars on elections, it is no longer just access that matters. Money's *potentiality* is sometimes enough to cause a skew. Just the threat of large money being spent against an elected official sometimes seems enough to get that official to shift priorities, a point that former senators (but less often current ones) publicly acknowledge.[17]

The result is that money systematically skews U.S. public policy even if it does not buy elections. As Professor Martin Gilens of Princeton University and Benjamin Page of George Washington University recently demonstrated, public policy across a wide range of issues regularly skews toward the interests of the wealthy and well organized, and against the poor and disorganized. With the new wave of campaign finance deregulation giving the wealthy more chances to leverage their influence, there is every reason to believe the trend will accelerate.[18]

In the electoral realm, money matters even when it does not dictate the outcomes of elections. As we have seen, Newt Gingrich got a second (and third and fourth) shot at the Republican presidential nomination not because that was what most Republican voters wanted, but because it is what Sheldon Adelson wanted. Meg Whitman got her chance to convince Californians that she would be a better governor than Jerry Brown only because she had millions of dollars to burn on her campaign. No doubt thousands of other Californians were equally convinced they would be good governors, but they did not have $140 million to buy that chance.

Further, while advertising alone does not necessarily sway voters who are engaged and have strong political opinions, in a close election it could sway enough swing voters—generally the least informed and most easily persuadable voters—to affect the outcome.[19]

Lessig is exactly right that politicians depend on the funders, not only the people, for their jobs—there is a reason political scientists refer to the "money primary," which occurs before the actual primary. This raises a concern, however, not about corruption, but about wealthy donors' disproportionate influence over elections and policy.

Why not simply limit money in politics to promote a level playing field? Leveling the ability to contribute and spend money on politics would not create perfect equality in political power (and we would not want perfect equality even if we could get it), but it would be a reasonable step in that direction. Yet depending on how society writes and implements such laws, limits could have profoundly bad effects: censoring political activity, entrenching incumbents over challengers, or giving special treatment to media corporations. These are not trivial concerns, and any argument to limit money in politics cannot simply sweep them aside in the name of important social interests. Most reformers simply ignore the hard arguments; in this book I confront these challenges head on.

Courts grapple with these issues when opponents of regulation challenge campaign laws as violating the First Amendment. That amendment provides, among other things, that "Congress shall pass no law . . . abridging the freedom of speech." The words of the First Amendment are not self-defining, and ever since *Buckley* the Supreme Court has vacillated over how to strike a balance between individual rights and society's interests.

In the past, it sometimes upheld limits on corporate money in politics essentially on political equality grounds (dressed up in anticorruption garb). These days, however, the conservative majority on the Court, over the strenuous objections of the more liberal justices, has embraced the First Amendment attack on campaign finance.

The First Amendment critique is serious, yet many Democrats ignore it.

In 2014, forty-three Democratic senators co-sponsored a proposed constitutional amendment to "overturn" the *Citizens United* decision. The amendment's text raised concerns about free speech and political competition that Democrats dismissed without making a serious response.[20]

Mostly, Democrats pay lip service to campaign finance reform. The former Senate majority leader Harry Reid has repeatedly attacked the libertarian Koch brothers and their network of supporters for funneling hundreds of millions of dollars into federal, state, and local elections, much of it without any disclosure of donors. Reid has claimed that Republicans are "addicted to Koch," and there is merit to his claim that Republicans increasingly depend on large donors for their campaigns. But Reid is a Koch addict too: he uses the brothers as a political foil to raise funds for Democrats. (Perhaps unsurprisingly, Reid did not say a word against his fellow Nevadan Sheldon Adelson, perhaps out of fear that Adelson would finance a Republican opponent for his Senate seat.) In any case Democrats too are increasingly dependent on large money, and money skews their priorities as well; the party has done a great job protecting the interests of Wall Street.[21]

Although Democrats in office tend to rail against *Citizens United* and the Supreme Court, some Democratic lawyers and politicos are secretly ecstatic about the brave new world of campaign finance the Supreme Court is creating. In the close 2014 race for control of the U.S. Senate, Democratic-leaning Super PACs outraised their Republican counterparts. Democrats in 2014 were the ones who engineered a congressional deal to vastly increase the contributions political parties could accept. President Obama has been a master of hypocrisy—castigating the Supreme Court for opening the floodgates of money but undermining the public financing system for presidential campaigns. He was the first candidate to decline public money in the general election, a perhaps reasonable choice at the time given the inevitability of the program's collapse, but he reneged on his promise to propose a fix for the future. Indeed, he became the first president to transform his presidential campaign committee into a "social welfare" group that can take unlimited and secret donations to support his agenda. The group, now called "Organizing for Action," is voluntarily disclosing the names of donors giving at least $250.[22]

While Democrats try to have it both ways on campaign finance, Republicans have united behind a deregulatory agenda. The John McCains of the party, who used to be leaders in supporting bipartisan reform efforts, have gone silent on the issue, while the Mitch McConnells, who have long fought limits but called for full and easy disclosure of donors' identities, now fight the disclosure laws they used to support. Senator Ted Cruz of Texas has grandstanded on the issue, declaring that "Senate Democrats are seeking unfettered power to regulate and stifle political speech."[23]

As with many other issues that now divide along party lines, the debate thus lacks nuance. Even on the merits, it has been hampered by the Supreme Court's insistence that any justifications for limits be phrased in anticorruption terms, and the willingness of activists and scholars to go along with this unhelpful framing.

This book proposes that we think of campaign finance limits differently, as a means of promoting and preserving political equality. First Amendment critics are right that limiting money in elections raises the risk of censorship, incumbency protection, and unfair preferential treatment of the media. The task, difficult but essential, is to develop a plan that both protects robust political speech in elections and guards against the rise of a plutocratic class that has too much influence over both the outcome of elections and what elected officials do once in office. I argue that under certain circumstances, campaign limits to promote political equality are constitutional. Promoting political equality is a compelling interest that can justify measures that do not squelch too much political speech or inhibit robust political competition.

Any system of limits on money in politics likely must include subsidies for political activity to ensure robust, competitive elections in which many voices are heard. We need to put campaign finance vouchers in the hands of all voters to fund and democratize our elections. In this book I propose a "voucher + limits" program in which we give each voter $100 in campaign finance vouchers per two-year congressional cycle, to donate to candidates, parties, and interest groups (such as the Sierra Club or the National Rifle Association). Further, no individual could contribute or spend in the aggregate more than $25,000 for any single federal election or $500,000 on all federal elections in a two-year election cycle. These rules will be supplemented by other ones, such as those that limit the campaign finance activities of lobbyists.

It is a careful balancing act, but this program is both constitutionally defensible and as central to fair elections as the "one person, one vote" principle, which says that no eligible voter should have more voting power than another. The $25,000 individual limit is a big compromise on political equality—it still gives one wealthy person 250 times more influence (or much more than that, if the person contributes or spends in multiple races) than someone who cannot afford to give beyond the voucher dollars. But this generous limit helps promote robust political speech, helps ensure competitive elections and multiple paths for challenging incumbents, and may insulate the program from court challenge.

This book has four parts: "Problems," "Solutions," "Objections," and "Changing the System." Part I, "Problems," explores the problems created by money in American politics. It explains how the Supreme Court's misguided focus on corruption has distorted our thinking about the problem of unequal economic power in a democracy and describes what we know about how money actually influences elections and politics. While money does not buy votes or elections, it is a key factor in determining the political viability of candidates. It also buys access to elected officials and their staffs. More important, money skews toward the interests of the wealthy the policy that government adopts.

Part II, "Solutions," argues that political equality is a compelling interest that can justify setting limits on political donations. I compare our current political system to a voting and policy lottery in which the wealthy get to buy extra tickets, and make the case for what I term an *equality of inputs* rationale for reform: that it is permissible for society to try to assure rough equality of wealth in influencing elections. This justifies both "leveling up" through campaign vouchers and "leveling down" through generous individual campaign spending limits.

Part III, "Objections," responds to the three key First Amendment objections to campaign money limits. Objectors include Chief Justice Roberts, Justices Antonin Scalia and Anthony Kennedy, Capital University law professor Bradley Smith, and the noted First Amendment lawyer Floyd Abrams. In separate chapters, I respond to the argument that campaign laws censor political speech or otherwise discriminate against the wealthy; that limits cannot deal with exemptions for the corporate-owned press, especially in the social media age where it is unclear who counts as the media; and that campaign laws are intended to—and actually do—protect incumbents. I also explore other potential unintended consequences of reform, such as increasing political polarization and weakening political parties. To assess these risks, I draw on the experiences of Canada and Great Britain, both of which impose strict limits on money in campaigns yet have robust elections in which there is no appreciable censorship.

Finally, Part IV, "Changing the System," asks how we can move to acceptance of political equality as a compelling interest that could justify campaign regulation. I start by looking at wrong paths. A constitutional amendment to overturn *Citizens United* is the most prominent wrong way to fix the problem, even if its supporters were not largely engaging in political theater. Such an amendment likely would be either too damaging to robust political speech or too full of holes to be effective. I also reject other ideas, such as those proposed by Lessig's Mayday PAC—the Super PAC to end all Super PACs—and the idea of progressives simply giving up on reform out of a belief that the role of money in politics is not so bad.

Instead, the answer to the problem of money in politics is political change. We need a Supreme Court that will accept political equality as a compelling interest that justifies reasonable campaign regulations, and to build the jurisprudence necessary for a new progressive Supreme Court. That Court cannot come until after the retirement of four older justices currently sitting on it, which would open up the potential for a new progressive majority.

This book sets out new thinking about how to rescue our politics from plutocracy. We need to move beyond a partisan world in which Chris Christie bows before Sheldon Adelson and in which Democrats propose futile amendments to "overturn *Citizens United*" while engaging in fundraising practices similar to Republicans. We should think through these issues before American democracy is too far skewed toward the interests of the wealthy, in the hope that some future Supreme Court proves willing to accept reasonable limits on money in politics. This book offers a way to advance the goal of political equality to resolve the inevitable tension between free economic markets and voter equality.

PART ONE

PROBLEMS

1

The Corruption Distortion

BENJAMIN BLUMAN AND ASENATH STEIMAN hardly seemed like threats to American democracy, but the lawsuit they filed in 2011, *Bluman v. Federal Election Commission,* could have allowed the Chinese government, a large Russian corporation, or Mexican billionaires to spend millions of dollars to get someone sympathetic to their interests elected to Congress, a governorship, or the presidency.[1]

Bluman is a Canadian citizen who went to law school on a student visa and then worked as an associate at a New York City law firm on a temporary work visa. In 2011, he wanted to contribute to three Democratic candidates including President Obama, print flyers supporting Obama's reelection bid, and distribute the flyers in Central Park. These days he is a lawyer in Vancouver.[2]

Steiman is a dual citizen of Israel and Canada who in 2011 was living in the United States on a temporary work visa as a medical resident. She wanted to contribute before the 2012 elections to Republican candidates including Oklahoma senator Tom Coburn and to the conservative group Club for Growth.[3]

Under federal laws limiting the campaign finance activity of foreign individuals, corporations, and governments, neither Bluman nor Steiman could contribute or spend money in U.S. elections. Congress had tightened up those laws after finding evidence that foreign citizens and the Chinese government had made donations to political parties during the 1996 campaign. Under current law, only foreign individuals with permanent residency status have the same right as citizens to contribute to candidates or spend money in U.S. elections.[4]

The *Bluman* lawsuit asking permission to engage in this spending was the brainchild of Yaakov Roth, a Canadian lawyer and Harvard Law School classmate of Bluman's who had clerked for Supreme Court justice Antonin Scalia and who went to work at Jones Day, one of the top law firms in Washington, D.C.[5] The suit followed both the playbook and the legal reasoning of the Supreme Court's 2010 case, *Citizens United v. Federal Election Commission,* but without the same success.

The playbook: find a sympathetic, small-potatoes plaintiff to mount a First Amendment challenge to a major federal campaign finance law, a challenge that if successful would open the door for much bigger political actors. Bluman told the press, "It seems nonsensical to me . . . that I am allowed to go to Central Park and tell every person I see why I think they should vote for Obama, but if I go to Kinko's and spend 50¢ to print out a piece of paper with the words 'Vote Obama' on it and then show that piece of paper to one American, I have committed a federal crime punishable by a fine of up to US$10,000 or five years in prison." Of course, campaign reformers were not really concerned about a Canadian law student spending fifty cents at Kinko's. They were worried that if he won the case, it would allow outside forces to spend millions of dollars to tilt the results of U.S. elections. With so much at stake, one did not have to be a xenophobe to distrust foreign influence over U.S. elections.[6]

Roth argued that spending money on ads independently of a candidate cannot corrupt the candidate and therefore, under the First Amendment, the government cannot limit such spending. The Supreme Court had accepted the same theory in *Citizens United* regarding the First Amendment rights of corporations to spend money in elections.

But *Bluman* failed. A three-judge panel of the federal district court in Washington, D.C., in an opinion by Court of Appeals judge (and likely Republican Supreme Court short-lister) Brett Kavanaugh, rejected the plaintiffs' arguments and upheld the ban on foreign spending. The case went to the Supreme Court under an obscure statutory appeal provision that made it very likely the Court would hear the case—but the justices did not bite.

Without argument or discussion, the Court simply affirmed the lower court ruling.[7]

☑

The question of foreign money in campaigns had dogged the Supreme Court since shortly after *Citizens United* was decided. Just six days later, in his 2010 State of the Union address, with some Supreme Court justices sitting in the audience, President Obama suggested that the decision opened the door to foreign money in elections: "Last week the Supreme Court reversed a century of law that I believe will open the floodgates for special interests—including foreign corporations—to spend without limit in our elections. Well I don't think American elections should be bankrolled by America's most powerful interests, and worse, by foreign entities. They should be decided by the American people, and that's why I'm urging Democrats and Republicans to pass a bill that helps to right this wrong."[8]

This was just too much for Justice Samuel Alito, one of the five conservative justices who voted for the *Citizens United* result, who was sitting in the audience. He was seen shaking his head and mouthing "not true," an action he later alluded to when he said he would make a bad poker player.[9]

In fact, Justice Kennedy's majority opinion in the case expressly stated that the Court was not addressing the constitutionality of the foreign money ban, but would leave that question for another day. It was Justice John Paul Stevens in his dissent who raised the specter of foreign campaign money and potential First Amendment protection for "Tokyo Rose," a World War II propagandist who had broadcast radio entreaties urging American soldiers to surrender.[10]

Citizens United considered only the right of domestic corporations to spend money in federal elections. Like *Bluman* it featured a small-potatoes plaintiff with an apparently compelling claim. And like *Bluman,* the case was a Trojan horse for getting big money into politics.[11]

Citizens United is a small conservative group based in Washington, D.C. When Hillary Clinton seemed to be a lock for the Democratic presidential nomination in 2008, Citizens United produced a ninety-minute documentary called *Hillary: The Movie.* It was deeply negative and intemperate, featuring such conservative personalities as Ann Coulter saying bad things about Clinton. One speaker said she was not fit to be commander-in-chief. Dick Morris earnestly claimed that "Hillary is the closest thing we have in America to a European socialist."[12]

Citizens United wanted to pay Comcast $1 million to make *Hillary* available as a free on-demand movie for its cable subscribers, but the Federal Election Commission said it could not do so. Commission rules, following a federal statute, said that corporations could not run certain election-related television or radio ads paid for out of the corporation's general treasury funds. Citizens United was a nonprofit corporation, but it took money from for-profit corporations to pay for its election-related activities.

Since 1907, a federal law known as the Tillman Act had barred business corporations from making direct contributions to candidates. In the 1940s, Congress expanded the law to prevent corporations from spending money independently on federal elections and to apply the same restrictions to labor unions. Eventually it allowed corporations and labor unions to set up political committees, more commonly known as political action committees, or PACs, to engage in election-related activities. Corporate PACs could raise money from the company's executives and shareholders; labor unions could raise money from union members (provided they gave the money voluntarily). PACs could take contributions of up to $5,000 from individuals and contribute up to $5,000 per candidate in each election, and they could also spend independently. But they could not take any funds from the corporation or the union's general accounts for political activities.[13]

Probably to set up a challenge to the existing campaign finance rules, Citizens United asked the Federal Election Commission for permission to take actions that could be seen as violating those rules. It did not want to use its PAC (even though it had one) to pay for the movie and, although it is a nonprofit, it took some money from for-profit corporations. This is how lawyers often work: engineer a test case by finding a sympathetic plaintiff and creating the right "vehicle" to get courts to make larger change in the law.

The gambit worked: the Supreme Court's eventual ruling not only freed nonprofits like Citizens United to air movies on cable TV; it decided that Exxon and Google and the AFL-CIO have a First Amendment right to spend unlimited amounts of money on thirty-second TV ads (something that, as we will see, they have done very little of so far).

✔

To understand Citizens United's argument before the Supreme Court, we have to back up to the 1970s.[14] Even before the Watergate scandal brought down the presidency of Richard Nixon, campaign finance reformers had succeeded in passing the Federal Election Campaign Act of 1971. Part of the reason for their success was that the legislation had a certain appeal to the self-interest of legislators: while reformers worried about corruption of elected officials, incumbents wanted to rein in the skyrocketing costs of campaigns. Opponents argued, with some force, that legislators were passing the campaign finance law to handicap their challengers.

The Watergate scandal brought significant amendments in 1974, which provided the first major regulation of money in politics in American history. Among the revised law's most important provisions were limits on the amount of money an individual could contribute to a federal candidate ($1,000 per election per candidate), and on the amount an individual could spend independently of a federal candidate (also $1,000 per election per candidate). The law additionally included important disclosure provisions, created the Federal Election Commission to regulate federal campaign financing, and established a voluntary public financing plan for presidential elections. It was a wide-ranging and ambitious law that likely would not have passed without the public outcry over corruption during the Watergate scandal.

The scandal had many facets, but the parts that concern us most here have to do with President Nixon and campaign money. The reform group Common Cause filed a lawsuit claiming that the Nixon administration had backed price supports for milk products after receiving $1 million from the milk producers' cooperative. Later investigations not only supported these allegations but revealed that things went much further. In spite of the long-standing prohibition on corporate contributions, major corporations had given sums of $100,000 or more to Nixon's 1972 presidential campaign. American Airlines pleaded guilty to contributing $55,000 in illegal corporate cash, funneled through a Lebanese agent and a Swiss bank, to the campaign. Others donated cash inside paper bags. The money was used for dirty tricks, such as breaking into the offices of rivals, planting spies with opposition campaigns, and attempts at bribery.[15]

In an effort to rehabilitate Americans' faith in the political system after Watergate, Congress agreed to serious limits on spending in electoral campaigns, and Gerald Ford, who became president when Nixon resigned, felt he had no choice but to sign the 1974 amendments. Opponents immediately challenged the law as unconstitutional. In spite of the federal government's defending the law before the Supreme Court, Ford's solicitor general, Robert Bork, eventually filed a second government brief strongly suggesting that key components of the law violated the First Amendment.

The challengers fell into two main camps. Some, like Senators James Buckley and Eugene McCarthy, believed that the campaign finance laws benefitted incumbents. Both of these senators had run campaigns that depended on large donors. McCarthy had challenged President Lyndon Johnson for the Democratic Party's presidential nomination in 1968, relying on money from the liberal philanthropist Stewart Mott. Although McCarthy did not win, many credited his campaign with pushing Johnson out of the race.

Others opposed to the 1974 amendments were concerned about government censorship. Led by the American Civil Liberties Union, these groups argued that the Nixon administration had interpreted earlier campaign finance laws against Vietnam War protestors as a government tool to stifle political speech.

This diverse group of plaintiffs came together in the case known as *Buckley v. Valeo*. The Buckley in the title was Senator Buckley, who not only opposed the 1974 law but also was responsible for inserting an amendment requiring direct and quick constitutional review of its provisions in the Supreme Court. The ACLU also sued. There were many other plaintiffs as well with different interests and arguments, including members of minor parties who believed that the part of the law offering more generous public financing to the major parties was unconstitutional. Valeo was Francis Valeo, the secretary of the Senate, who was sued in name only as a stand-in for the U.S. government.

The *Buckley* plaintiffs argued that the limits on contributions and spending contained in the Federal Election Campaign Act amendments of 1974 violated the First Amendment guarantees of freedom of speech and association. After a lower court upheld most of the challenged parts of the 1974 amendments, the Supreme Court rushed its consideration of *Buckley v. Valeo*, and in January 1976 issued a split, unsigned decision that turned out to have been drafted in pieces by different justices, a highly unusual procedure. The result created the framework for analyzing First Amendment challenges to campaign finance laws that still applies today.[16]

Even by Supreme Court standards, First Amendment legal doctrine on speech and association rights is complicated. Follow me on a brief excursion into the weeds of the Court's jurisprudence, because the course it sets for handling these cases is important for understanding the rest of this book.

The Constitution says very little about who and what the First Amendment protects, only that "Congress shall make no law . . . abridging the freedom of speech, or of the press. . . ." These words have led to lots of platitudes about how to apply First Amendment doctrine to campaign regulation.

Opponents of regulation proclaim that "no law" means no law. (Of course that interpretation would bar a law against falsely yelling "Fire!" in a crowded movie theater and would read "abridging" as a flat prohibition.) I love it when opponents, in a kind of selective textualism, make the "no law" point in cases involving *state* rather than *federal* campaign finance laws— after all, the provision says only that *Congress* shall make no law abridging the freedom of speech. The Court has long read First Amendment limitations on government to apply to state and local governments as well, not just to Congress. Opponents of campaign finance law also often, and quite reasonably, raise the First Amendment right of political association, even though the First Amendment does not actually mention association; this protection is the product of "activist" interpretation by the Supreme Court.[17]

Campaign finance reformers have their own sloganeering, beginning with the idea that "money isn't speech," it's property. I find the debate over whether money equals speech unedifying and unhelpful. I suppose the logic of this argument means the First Amendment should not apply at all to campaign finance laws. But as the First Amendment scholar Eugene Volokh has pointed out, flying on an airplane is not speech, but most of us would surely conclude that a law preventing someone from flying on an airplane to make a speech would be unconstitutional under the First Amendment's free speech guarantee. In other words, although money is not speech, money facilitates speech, and therefore laws limiting money in politics raise First Amendment concerns.

I find Volokh's point convincing, but some other reformers do not. For those unconvinced (because lots of things, such as education, can facilitate speech without being speech and getting extra constitutional protection), spending money on campaign contributions or ads are merely conduct that communicates speech. But even those who see spending money as mere conduct should recognize that it is conduct innately tied to political activity protected by the First Amendment. In short, whether or not money is speech is beside the point. There is no question the First Amendment is in play. That does not mean campaign finance laws are unconstitutional, but only that First Amendment claims need to be considered seriously.[18]

In campaign finance cases, the Supreme Court has said that courts must balance First Amendment rights against the government's interests. This balancing is the typical way the Court decides cases these days when someone challenges a law as violating a provision of the Bill of Rights.

To decide these cases the modern Supreme Court applies any of a number of balancing tests, depending on what is at stake. When the stakes are very high—when a law affects a "fundamental right," such as the right to vote, or when it discriminates in a bad way, such as on the basis of race—the Court applies a "strict scrutiny" test. Under this test, the challenged law is unconstitutional unless it is "narrowly tailored" to serve a "compelling" government interest. In contrast, for garden-variety laws that neither affect fundamental rights nor discriminate against a specially protected class of people, the Court applies a "rational basis" test, where the law is upheld so long as it is "rationally related" to a "legitimate" government interest.[19]

Think of strict scrutiny as a big thumb on the scale favoring challengers of a law and rational basis scrutiny as a big thumb on the scale favoring the government. Usually (but not always), strict scrutiny review leads a court to strike down a law, while rational basis review leads to upholding it. The reason for the thumb is the stakes. When the government takes an action that could impinge on something important or discriminate between people in a troubling way, a thumb for challengers seems appropriate. But if there were a thumb on the scale for challengers all the time, courts would have to throw out many normal laws, and the lawmaking process would be hobbled.

The ways these tiers of scrutiny play out across the broad swath of constitutional law fill many volumes of law reviews. There are arguments for "strict scrutiny lite," "rational basis with bite," and much in between. For our purposes, we can focus on how the Court applied these tiers of scrutiny in the campaign finance cases, beginning with *Buckley.*

The Court decided in *Buckley* to uphold the 1974 amendments' campaign contribution limits but to strike down its spending limits. While stating that any law regulating campaign finance was subject to the "exacting scrutiny required by the First Amendment," the Court chose different tiers of scrutiny for contributions as opposed to expenditures: spending limits got the tough strict scrutiny review while contributions received lesser "exacting scrutiny," a middle-level type of review that barely exists outside these campaign finance cases.[20]

The Court held that people spending money on elections were engaged in core political speech, but a limit on the amount of campaign contributions only "marginally" restricted a contributor's ability to send a message of support for a candidate. For constitutional purposes, it was the act of contributing, not the amount of the contribution, that mattered. (Try telling that to the candidates soliciting the contributions!) But in overall spending, the Court saw a core threat to free speech: the $1,000 spending limit would prevent a person from taking out an ad in the *New York Times* urging readers to vote for or against a candidate, and would leave only candidates, parties, and the media (which were exempt from these provisions) free to spend money on elections. Expenditures were thus entitled to greater constitutional protection than contributions.

When it came to the government's interests in regulating campaign financing, in *Buckley* the Court recognized only one justification for infringing on First Amendment rights: preventing "corruption" and the "appearance of corruption."

Large contributions raised the problem of corruption "to the extent that [they] are given to secure a political *quid pro quo* from current and potential officeholders." But truly independent expenditures do not raise the same danger, because a *quid pro quo* is more difficult if the politician and spender cannot communicate about the expenditure. At least, there was no evidence on the limited record in *Buckley* that such independent spending could corrupt.

The Court did not explain how far corruption might extend beyond a *quid pro quo* exchange. But it clarified that the concern went beyond bribery and could not be remedied simply by disclosing the identities of campaign contributors. "Laws making criminal the giving and taking of bribes deal with only the most blatant and specific attempts of those with money to influence governmental action. . . . Congress was surely entitled to conclude that . . . contribution ceilings were . . . necessary to deal with the reality or appearance of corruption inherent in a system permitting unlimited financial contributions, even when the identities of the contributors and the amounts of their contributions are fully disclosed."

The "appearance of corruption," meanwhile, was tied to public confidence in government: "Of almost equal concern as the danger of actual quid pro quo arrangements is the impact of the appearance of corruption stemming from public awareness of the opportunities for abuse inherent in a regime of large individual financial contributions. . . . Congress could legitimately conclude that the avoidance of the appearance of improper influence is . . . critical . . . if confidence in the system of representative Government is not to be eroded to a disastrous extent."

After the Court concluded that the government's interest in preventing corruption could not justify a limit on independent expenditures, it considered the alternative argument that spending limits were justified by "the ancillary governmental interest in equalizing the relative ability of individuals and groups to influence the outcome of elections."

But in a key—and controversial—paragraph, the Court rejected this rationale: "The concept that government may restrict the speech of some elements of our society in order to enhance the relative voice of others is wholly foreign to the First Amendment which was designed to secure the widest possible dissemination of information from diverse and antagonistic sources, and to assure unfettered interchange of ideas for the bringing about of political and social changes desired by the people." Here, the Court took a wrong turn.

☑

This brings us back to Benjamin Bluman's flyers and Citizens United's attempt to have Comcast offer its anti-Clinton movie. Why didn't *Buckley*'s holding that independent spending could not corrupt lead to a decision for both Bluman and Citizens United, at least to the extent that they wanted to spend money on election activities independent of the candidates they supported?

To begin with, the plaintiffs in *Buckley* did not argue that spending limits on corporations or non-citizens violated the First Amendment. *Buckley* applied only to (citizen) individuals and to candidates—the Court struck down not only the limits applying to ordinary American citizens but also overall spending limits that applied to congressional and Senate candidates, as well as limits on how much of a candidate's own funds she could spend on her campaign. It did not apply to the plaintiffs in either *Citizens United* or *Bluman*.

After *Buckley*, the Court's campaign finance cases swung for and against limits as different justices came and went. Sometimes justices read the term "corruption" quite broadly and upheld a variety of spending and contribution limits; other times they read it more narrowly and struck down or limited campaign laws. Despite these swings, the Court's general approach seemed to be to uphold campaign contribution limits, even if the evidence supporting their anticorruption benefits was weak (one case cited a newspaper editorial and the statement of a state senator to prove corruption was a problem in Missouri), but to strike down spending limits even in the face of more convincing evidence of corruption. The big exceptions to this pattern were limits on corporate spending in elections involving candidates for public office, which until *Citizens United* passed strict scrutiny review.[21]

First National Bank of Boston v. Bellotti was a 1978 case reviewing a Massachusetts limit on corporate spending on ballot measures. The state had passed a series of laws apparently intended to stop corporations from opposing a tax increase that the legislature supported. This was just the sort of case campaign finance opponents would point to as the reason legislatures should not set the rules for political competition. The Supreme Court struck down the Massachusetts law as a violation of the First Amendment. Applying strict scrutiny review to the spending limit, as required by *Buckley*, the Court held that the law could not be justified for anticorruption reasons: because the limit applied only to ballot measures, there were no candidates to corrupt (or to appear to corrupt).[22]

When you become a lawyer, especially one who deals with Supreme Court cases, you learn that sometimes the most important information is found in an opinion's footnotes. *Bellotti* included a hugely important footnote (number 26) explaining that its decision did not intend to call into question longstanding federal and state laws limiting corporate spending in *candidate* elections. "Our consideration of a corporation's right to speak on issues of general public interest implies no comparable right in the quite different context of participation in a political campaign for election to public office. Congress might well be able to demonstrate the existence of a danger of real or apparent corruption in independent expenditures by corporations to influence candidate elections." This was in deep tension with the idea the Court expressed in *Buckley* that independent spending could not corrupt candidates because the independence prevented any *quid pro quo.*

While this idea of corporate independent spending potentially causing *quid pro quo* corruption hung in the air, the liberals on the Court advanced a new theory to justify a ban on corporations spending money on elections from their general treasury funds. In *Federal Election Commission v. Massachusetts Citizens for Life*, the Court held that nonprofit ideological corporations (later known as "*MCFL* corporations"), such as the antiabortion group involved in the case, that do not take corporate or union money cannot be limited in spending their treasury funds in candidate elections.[23]

The Court held that the First Amendment does not permit limits on campaign spending by ideological groups that do not accept funding from for-profit corporations or labor unions. But the Court also suggested that the government could limit *for-profit* corporations' independent spending. It did not raise the *Bellotti* concern about large amounts of such spending leading to *quids pro quo*. Instead it suggested that the government might legitimately want to prevent corporate spending on campaigns that was out of proportion with the public's support for the corporations' political ideas.

Then, in the 1990 case *Austin v. Michigan Chamber of Commerce*, the Court relied on just this theory in upholding the constitutionality of limits on spending by for-profit corporations in candidate elections. If a Michigan corporation wanted to be involved in state candidate campaigns, it could set up a PAC for this purpose.[24]

The decision in *Austin* did not address the suggestion in *Bellotti*'s crucial footnote that Michigan's corporate limits might be justified to prevent corruption of candidates. Instead, building on the *Massachusetts Citizens for Life* case, the Court held that the law could prevent what Justice Thurgood Marshall termed a "different type of corruption in the political arena: the corrosive and distorting effects of immense aggregations of wealth that are accumulated with the help of the corporate form and that have little or no correlation to the public's support for the corporation's political ideas." The case drew outraged dissents from Justice Scalia and Justice Kennedy, who called Marshall's opinion "Orwellian" and the "rawest form of censorship."

The *Austin* court may have called these "distorting effects" a type of corruption, but its reasoning looked more like the equality rationale the Court seemed to reject in *Buckley*. Indeed one of Justice Marshall's clerks from that year, Elizabeth Garrett, acknowledged years later that *Austin*'s antidistortion interest was a kind of equality argument. The problem Marshall's opinion identified with large corporate wealth was not a *quid pro quo* or dollars for political favors but the oversized influence of wealthy corporations in candidate elections.[25]

In 2003, the Supreme Court faced a big showdown over whether *Austin* was going to survive. A year earlier, Congress had passed the Bipartisan Campaign Reform Act, more commonly known as the McCain-Feingold law (after its Senate co-sponsors), primarily because the Federal Election Campaign Act amendments of 1974 had sprung a few leaks in the 1990s.[26]

Individuals and groups started spending, and political parties started collecting, money for campaign ads that avoided words like "Vote for Smith" or "Vote Against Jones." These so-called "issue ads" were clearly campaign ads, but because they avoided words of express advocacy, they didn't count as election ads—a point the Supreme Court first acknowledged in *Buckley* when it expressed concern that the 1974 laws regulating spending "relative to" a clearly identified candidate for federal office were too vague.

Issue ads became big hits in the late 1990s and early 2000s. One of my favorite examples was an ad run against a Democratic candidate in a Montana congressional race, Bill Yellowtail. The ad accused Yellowtail of taking a swing at his wife and urged voters: "Call Bill Yellowtail. Tell him to support family values." The ads never said vote against Yellowtail. They didn't have to. Voters got the message, and likely few of them called Bill Yellowtail to express their opinions on family values.[27]

Corporations, labor unions, and wealthy individuals also gave money for these ads to the political parties, even though political parties were not allowed to accept large (or corporate or labor) contributions to fund election ads. The parties took the position that these "soft money" contributions for "issue ads" were not subject to limits.

The McCain-Feingold law did two things. First it prevented political parties from collecting this kind of soft money. Second, it provided that if a corporation or labor union ran a television or radio ad close to the election mentioning a candidate for federal office, that ad would be treated like a normal campaign ad even if it did not say "Vote for" or "Vote against" a candidate. That meant corporate or union treasuries could not be used to pay for the ads; the corporation or labor union had to use PAC funds.

The 2003 showdown over this law was called *McConnell v. Federal Election Commission*. On a 5–4 vote, the Court upheld these provisions; it endorsed *Austin* as good law, and extended its reasoning both to campaign "issue ads" and to labor unions. Opponents of McCain-Feingold, led by the Republican senator (and later majority leader) Mitch McConnell of Kentucky (who became the lead plaintiff in the litigation), argued for *Austin* to be overruled, but Justice Sandra Day O'Connor cast the deciding vote to reaffirm *Austin*. (Ironic, because Justice O'Connor had dissented in *Austin* along with Justices Kennedy and Scalia.)

The Court also upheld the limits on political party soft money, finding that the parties were selling access to elected officials (coffee with the president, golf with the speaker of the House) in exchange for big donations. Labor unions were favoring Democrats; corporations gave money to both sides but favored Republicans.

The Court in *McConnell* viewed soft money as creating a system of ingratiation and access, and it recognized this as a form of corruption. Here it followed a series of earlier cases in which the same five justices expanded the meaning of corruption and the appearance of corruption to include all kinds of influence and the appearance of influence. As the Court wrote in a 2001 case, which rejected the need for the government to show that large contributions can corrupt or create the appearance of corruption, "leave the perception of impropriety unanswered, and the cynical assumption that large donors call the tune could jeopardize the willingness of voters to take part in democratic governance."[28]

Despite being in considerable tension with *Buckley*'s claim that independent spending could not corrupt, *Austin* and *McConnell* would have seemed to put an end to attacks on corporate spending rules by the likes of Citizens United. But there was a huge difference between the Supreme Court in *McConnell*, which recognized a right to limit corporate spending and soft money, and the Supreme Court that reached the opposite conclusion in *Citizens United*.

Sandra Day O'Connor's retirement.

When Justice O'Connor retired and Justice Alito replaced her, campaign finance law turned 180 degrees. Since Justice Alito came on board, the Court has held unconstitutional or severely curtailed every campaign finance limit it has considered. Nothing seems to survive Court review these days but disclosure laws.

Let's pause on this point for a moment, because I will return to it in Part IV. In *Citizens United*, the Supreme Court decided that what had been constitutional under the First Amendment one day was unconstitutional the next. No one formally amended the Constitution. One justice, Sandra Day O'Connor, retired, and her replacement, Samuel Alito, had a different view about what government could do under the First Amendment. Similarly, when one of the five conservative members of the Supreme Court majority in *Citizens United* leaves the Court, we could see another reversal.

☑

Citizens United was an audacious opinion. To begin with, the Court had a number of ways in which it could have upheld the group's rights to show

its movie through Comcast video-on-demand without overruling its earlier precedents requiring corporations and labor unions to pay for election-
related activities through their PACs. It failed to follow a principle called
"constitutional avoidance," which cautions that the Court should look for
ways to read statutes that avoid rendering them unconstitutional.[29]

There were multiple grounds for avoidance. For example, the Court could
have interpreted the McCain-Feingold law to apply only to short ads, not to
ninety-minute movies. It could have said that Citizens United in showing
this movie was really engaged in press activities, and thus entitled to the
"press exemption" to spending rules. It could have said that even though
Citizens United took a little bit of for-profit corporate money, it was still
entitled to the exemption the Court had recognized for non-profit "*MCFL*
corporations" in the 1980s.

The Court did none of those things. Instead, rumor has it that a majority
of the justices were looking for a pretext to overrule *Austin* even though the
parties in *Citizens United* did not take that issue to the Court. What may
have spurred the conservatives' decision to go big in the case was a controversial debate over whether the government supported the banning of
books paid for with corporate money around the election—a claim I revisit
in detail later.

As *New Yorker* writer Jeffrey Toobin later revealed, Justice David Souter
had drafted a bitter dissent calling out the conservatives for judicial activism in overruling the *Austin* case without full briefing on the question. But
Justice Souter's dissent remained unpublished when the Court at the end
of the term set the case for additional briefing and a highly unusual second
oral argument, which was to focus on the question whether *Austin* and the
part of *McConnell* affirming *Austin* should be overruled.[30]

In a rare September argument (the Supreme Court's term usually begins
the first Monday in October), the new solicitor general, Elena Kagan, asked
the Court to let the government lose in the best way possible: "If you are
asking me, Mr. Chief Justice, as to whether the government has a preference as to the way in which it loses, if it has to lose, the answer is yes."[31]

But the government did not lose in a good way. The Court returned to
Buckley's idea that independent spending could not corrupt or create the
appearance of corruption, but now extended the principle to for-profit cor-

porations. In the face of evidence from the earlier *McConnell* case that large soft money donations were corrupting candidates through ingratiation and access, and an argument that large independent spending favoring or attacking a candidate could do the same, the Court severely narrowed its definition of corruption.

"When Buckley identified a sufficiently important governmental interest in preventing corruption or the appearance of corruption, that interest was limited to quid pro quo corruption," Justice Kennedy explained for the Court. He quoted his own dissent in the *McConnell* case: "The fact that speakers may have influence over or access to elected officials does not mean that these officials are corrupt." "Favoritism and influence" are unavoidable in representative politics, and a "substantial and legitimate reason" to cast a vote or make a contribution to one candidate or another "is that the candidate will respond by producing those political outcomes the supporter favors." Furthermore, "the appearance of influence or access . . . will not cause the electorate to lose faith in our democracy," and independent spending that is not coordinated with a candidate cannot create an appearance of corruption because the additional political speech simply seeks to persuade voters, who have "the ultimate influence over elected officials."[32]

As for footnote 26 in *Bellotti* suggesting that large independent spending could cause *quid pro quo* corruption, the Court rejected the possibility, saying the footnote was based on an ill-considered student law review article. A year later, in a case from Montana, the Supreme Court refused to consider any evidence that independent spending on elections could lead to *quid pro quo* corruption, despite the finding by the Montana Supreme Court that this had happened in Montana.[33]

As for the argument the Court made in *Austin* that corporate spending could impermissibly distort political outcomes, the *Citizens United* decision explained that antidistortion had nothing to do with anticorruption. Antidistortion was the rejected equality rationale, an unconstitutional basis on which to limit money in politics.

Citizens United marked a major change in the Court's approach to campaign finance—a change one would have thought should have benefited Benjamin Bluman and Asenath Steiman. After all, if *corporate* independent spending could not corrupt or create the appearance of corruption, and if we were not worried that corporations could distort the outcome of an election by spending money that might not represent the intensity of views of actual voters, why could we not say the same thing about money coming from these nice Canadian citizens? The law that applied to foreigners was even stricter than the one for corporations. Corporations could at least set up a PAC for political activity, but foreigners could not.

Benjamin Bluman was hardly going to corrupt the country's politics by spending fifty cents at Kinko's to print a "Vote for Obama" flyer. His First Amendment case looked at least as compelling as Citizens United's desire to spend $1 million to push an anti-Hillary documentary as an on-demand video.

Judge Kavanaugh's opinion for the three-judge lower court held that Citizens United left the issue of the foreign campaign spending ban open. Drawing on the dissent by Justice Stevens in Citizens United, which flagged the danger of foreign spending in elections, the lower court upheld the ban on foreign money in elections. It cited a series of cases upholding the government's ability to limit foreign individuals' participation in democratic processes of government.[34]

But if large independent spending from U.S. citizens, U.S. corporations, or U.S. labor unions could not corrupt the political process, how could small foreign money do so? How could small foreign spending cause the public to lose confidence in the fairness of the electoral process when large independent spending from American persons and entities could not? The Court in Citizens United repeatedly stressed that when it comes to the First Amendment, the corporate identity of the speaker does not matter. Why should corporate identity be any different from foreign identity? And if the public has a right to hear ideas about politics, why did it have the right to hear from IBM (which no doubt has many foreign shareholders) or the Service Employees International Union but not Mr. Bluman?

Having faced withering public criticism of its Citizens United decision, the Court demurred. Its "summary affirmance" of Judge Kavanaugh's ruling kept the foreign spending ban in place without requiring the Court to explain the conflict with the logic of Citizens United.

In the meantime, the genie Citizens United let out of the bottle started wreaking havoc. Using the small-potatoes model, a small conservative group, SpeechNow.org, filed a new lawsuit seeking to overturn the law imposing contribution limits on PACs. Anyone, not just corporations or labor unions, could set up a federal PAC to participate in federal elections. But the Federal Election Campaign Act amendments of 1974 limited the ability of PACs to both accept contributions and give contributions to federal candidates. PACs could accept contributions only from individuals, not corporations or labor unions, and these contributions were limited to no more than $5,000 per election. They could also contribute no more than $5,000 to a candidate per election.[35]

SpeechNow.org said its PAC did not want to contribute any money directly to candidates. Instead, it wanted the right to accept unlimited contributions from individuals to fund its independent spending.

The logic of SpeechNow's First Amendment argument flowed directly from *Citizens United:* if independent spending cannot corrupt, then contributions funding such spending cannot corrupt either. The United States Court of Appeals in Washington, D.C., agreed with this argument and struck down the contribution limit to independent PACs, citing *Citizens United* eleven times in its decision. The federal government wisely decided not to seek further review of the case before the Supreme Court, which could only have made things worse.

And so was born the "Super PAC": a political action committee that can accept unlimited contributions to fund independent ads supporting or opposing federal candidates. The *SpeechNow.org* case concerned only the right of individuals to contribute to these Super PACs, but the Federal Election Commission soon ruled that corporations and labor unions could give unlimited sums as well. A later court ruling said that every federal PAC could become a Super PAC, even those that made direct contributions to candidates, so long as they set up separate accounts for independent giving and candidate contributions.[36]

Perhaps the most interesting fact about the Super PAC phenomenon is that most Super PAC funding so far has come not from corporations or labor unions but from individuals. Even though individuals, since the *Buckley* case in 1976, have had the constitutional right to spend unlimited amounts independently in support of presidential campaigns, outside spending exploded only after *Citizens United* and *SpeechNow.org*.

The reason for this late explosion seems to be, at least in part, about campaign disclosure laws. Since the amendments to the Federal Election Campaign Act in 1974, campaign advertising must include a "disclaimer" telling viewers, listeners, or readers what person or group paid for the advertising. I do not know whether donors were shy about including their names on ads or if they thought their names would make the ads less effective in motivating voters than those sponsored by anodyne-sounding groups like "Restore Our Future" or "Priorities U.S.A."

Before the rise of Super PACs, big donors avoided spending money directly on ads when they could give money to a group. In 2004, for example, when the Democrat John Kerry faced President George W. Bush running for reelection, the liberal financier George Soros gave more than $20 million to outside groups supporting Kerry (who lost), claiming his contributions were not subject to the $5,000 limit because they lacked words of express advocacy. One such group, America Coming Together, later paid hundreds of thousands of dollars in fines for failing to spend money on election ads from its federal PAC with donations limited to $5,000. We did not see a flood of ads labeled "Paid for by George Soros."[37]

With the $5,000 contribution limit to PACs blown away by SpeechNow. org, money started flowing into Super PACs. In 2012 it led to such presidential campaign donations as Sheldon Adelson's major contributions to a Newt Gingrich Super PAC and then to one for Mitt Romney in the general election, and Foster Friess's large donations supporting Rick Santorum's presidential bid.[38]

But some donors wanted more anonymity. Super PACs eventually disclose their donations in reports that are searchable at sites like OpenSecrets .org. Karl Rove's group, American Crossroads, found a disclosure workaround. It created "Crossroads GPS," an affiliated nonprofit organized as a "social welfare organization"—or 501(c)(4) organization, after the relevant section of the tax code. Crossroads GPS got into the business of running election ads, along with other activities opposing the Obama administration, which it said showed its "social welfare" purpose. When the Internal Revenue Service did not stop the activity, other groups followed suit. Whether and how 501(c)(4) organizations are allowed to participate in politics is a big messy topic—it is what led to the outcry about the IRS targeting 501(c)

(4)s affiliated with the Tea Party—but one we can safely put aside for our purposes. The key point is that people who want to give money for election ads anonymously are doing it at increasingly high rates without any fear of breaking the law.[39]

✔

Meanwhile, back at the Supreme Court, the project of the five *Citizens United* justices to blow up campaign finance limits continues apace. The latest plaintiff to reach the Court was an Alabama business owner named Shaun McCutcheon. He filed suit to knock down limits on the total amount an individual can give to federal candidates in a single election. Federal law capped the *total* amount an individual may donate to *all* federal candidates for office during any single two-year election cycle at $48,600. It also limited to $74,600 the total amount an individual can give to political committees that make contributions to candidates and sets a cap of $123,200 for total contributions in any two-year cycle. McCutcheon wanted to give a series of $1,776 contributions to more congressional candidates than he was allowed.[40]

The Supreme Court in *Buckley* upheld an earlier $25,000 overall cap on contributions to federal candidates, but in 2014 the Roberts court saw things differently. In *McCutcheon v. Federal Election Commission,* the same five justices from the *Citizens United* majority held the federal aggregate cap unconstitutional.

The opinion by Chief Justice Roberts did not merely rule in Shaun Mc-Cutcheon's favor. It seemed to lay the groundwork for further challenges to the remaining campaign finance limits. Although *McCutcheon* side-stepped the question whether to raise the standard for review of contribution limits to "strict scrutiny," as Senator McConnell urged in a brief to the Court, the opinion defined *Buckley*'s lesser "exacting scrutiny" standard in a stricter way, making it easier for lower courts to strike more contribution limits.

The *McCutcheon* opinion also incorporated into the contributions cases the very stingy definition of corruption used in *Citizens United.* Roberts affirmed the *Citizens United* holding that ingratiation and access are not corruption. He seemed to go even further, celebrating donors who give the money and elected officials' responsiveness to them. Roberts also truncated the "appearance of corruption" concept. In *Buckley*, we saw a concern with "an appearance of improper influence" and "public awareness of the opportunities for abuse inherent in a regime of large individual financial contributions." But in *McCutcheon*, the Court reduced appearance of corruption to the appearance of actual bribery: "the Government's interest in preventing the appearance of corruption is equally confined to the appearance of *quid pro quo* corruption, [and therefore] the Government may not seek to limit the appearance of mere influence or access." Put together, these restrictive definitions give lower courts the tools to strike down more and more contribution limits.

Finally, Roberts suggested that Congress might not have the power to ban party soft money, even if parties were blatantly selling to the highest bidder access to elected officials like the president or the speaker of the House. "When donors furnish widely distributed support within all applicable base limits, all members of the party or supporters of the cause may benefit, and the leaders of the party or cause may feel particular gratitude. That gratitude stems from the basic nature of the party system, in which party members join together to further common political beliefs, and citizens can choose to support a party because they share some, most, or all of those beliefs. . . . To recast such shared interest, standing alone, as an opportunity for *quid pro quo* corruption would dramatically expand government regulation of the political process."

Benjamin Bluman still could not distribute his fifty cents' worth of "Vote Obama" flyers in Central Park. But U.S. citizens, corporations, and labor unions can now contribute and spend millions of dollars or more on political campaigns because the government cannot prove to a skeptical Supreme Court that limits are necessary to prevent *quid pro quo* corruption or its appearance, and because the Court has taken off the table real concerns about political inequality in a system of increasingly unlimited political money.

2

What Does Money Buy in Politics?

THE BATTLE BETWEEN POTATO CHIPS AND campaign spending took a major turn in 2012.

Back in 2001, Professor Bradley Smith (who later became the chairman of the Federal Election Commission) wrote that "Americans spend two to three times as much money each year on the purchase of potato chips" as they do on political campaigns. It is an oft-repeated line. The conservative columnist George Will in 2010 added comparisons to yogurt and Halloween candy, and to Procter & Gamble's advertising budget. Their point was that for all the talk of money flooding into politics, we actually spend very little on elections.[1]

But by 2012, campaign spending had overtaken potato chips. Total spending just on federal elections in the 2012 season was $7.1 billion, eclipsing the approximately $6 billion in potato chip sales for that year. That is not a completely fair comparison, as the $7.1 billion campaign figure covers a two-year election cycle and includes a presidential election, when campaign spending is higher; about $5.1 billion of that amount was actually spent in calendar year 2012. On the other hand, the $7.1 billion covers only *federal* campaign spending, not the billions more spent on state and local races. The National Institute on Money in State Politics estimates state and local election spending in the 2012 cycle at an additional $3 billion. Meanwhile, potato chip sales have suffered a long-term decline that was not helped by Michelle Obama's anti-obesity campaign.[2]

Even if we look only at federal money, the trend line is unmistakable:

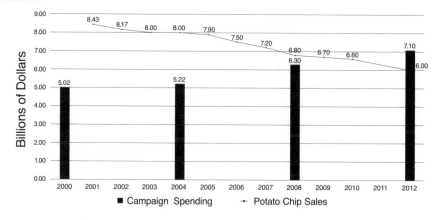

Federal Spending per Two-Year Presidential Election Cycle, Compared with Annual U.S. Sales of Potato Chips, 2000–2012 (in 2012 dollars)
Sources: Lowenstein, Hasen, and Tokaji, Election Law—Cases and Materials 642 (5th ed. 2012); Lowenstein, Hasen, and Tokaji, 2014 Supplement to Election Law—Cases and Materials 77 (2014); United States Potato Board Potato Sales & Utilization Estimates 2001–2010, at 14, www.uspotatoes.com/newsletters/down loads/2011USPB-SalesUtilizationEstimatesFINAL.pdf; United States Potato Board, Chip-Stock U.S. Market Long Range Plan 2012–2016, www.uspotatoes.com/down loads/Chips_and_Chipping_Potatoes-US_Market.pdf
Note: Inflation calculated using Inflation Calculator at http://www.bls.gov /data/inflation_calculator.htm

potato chip sales are falling while political spending is increasing with each presidential election cycle.

This appears to be good news for political consultants, television stations, and commercial websites, which receive much of that political spending in the form of campaign advertising and fees. It is less good for potato farmers. But what kind of news is it for the American people? To those who oppose campaign finance laws, we spend *only* $7 billion on political campaigns, a pittance of the United States gross domestic product, which was just under $16 trillion in 2012. But to campaign reformers, it is a whopping *$7 billion* in political spending![3]

The potato chip comparison is misleading and unhelpful. Professor Joshua Tucker of New York University crunches the differences:

- Potatoes do not have to spend time or effort soliciting donations so they can be converted to potato chips.

- Once purchased, people rarely lobby potato chips for favors in enacting preferential legislation.
- Potato chips rarely, if ever, face trade-offs between trying to please the individual who bought them, their constituents, and the country at large. They can just simply be oh-so-tasty.
- Anyone in the United States is allowed to buy potato chips, not just citizens. Indeed, even children and foreigners can purchase potato chips.
- Potato chips are accessible to all citizens, rich and poor alike (with the possible exception of people dealing with cholesterol issues).
- Sheldon Adelson doesn't purchase $15 million worth of potato chips for his own personal use (at least I hope not).[4]

I begin with the potato chip comparison not because it tells us something important about money and politics, but because it does not. As with potatoes, there are lots of ways to slice and dice campaign finance data, but much of what the public hears about money in American politics is misleading. It is impossible to evaluate the claim that $7 billion is too much, or too little, to spend on politics without a baseline more relevant than potato chip sales and a theory of what might be good or bad about that level of spending.

To understand anything about the relationship between money and politics, we need to ask the right questions and look at the data, and not rely on anecdotes or sound bites. Asking if the country spends the right amount on political campaigns by comparing its spending on a food product is not the right question. It is empty rhetoric, not analysis, just as when Smith ends his book arguing against campaign finance laws by reminding us that the First Amendment begins with "Congress shall make no law . . ."[5]

The three key sets of empirical questions on the role of money in U.S. politics are:

- *Money and electoral outcomes.* What is the relationship between money spent on campaigns and campaign outcomes? When does money matter? Do limits on money spent in elections skew campaign outcomes toward incumbents or in any other way?
- *Money and legislative influence.* What is the relationship between money spent on politics (or threatened to be spent on politics) and

governmental outcomes? To put it another way, why do people contribute and spend money on politics, what do they expect to get, and
what do they actually get?

- *Campaign laws and public confidence.* What is the relationship between the presence or absence of campaign finance limitations and
  public confidence in government and the electoral process? Can
  campaign finance limits promote public confidence in the fairness
  of the electoral process?

Much controversy, and a lot of misinformation and reasoning by anec-
dote, surround the answers to these questions. Here I will try to make sense
of what we know, and do not know, about money in politics. The truth turns
out to be neither what campaign reformers or their opponents claim, and
political science may not be able to fully resolve all of the empirical questions. We therefore also need to consider what to do when empirical evidence on the role of money in politics is inconclusive.

☑

How does campaign money influence campaign outcomes? This seems
like a straightforward question that one could answer simply by comparing
the amounts spent on the campaigns of winners versus losers. A headline
from *Business Insider* in 2012 appears to tell the story: "House Candidates
Who Spent More Money Won Their Elections 95% of the Time." In 2012 the
average House seat winner spent three times as much on his or her campaign (about $1.5 million) than the average House loser (about $500,000).[6]

The problem with this correlation between spending and winners (besides the fact that it ignores campaign spending controlled by parties and
outside groups, an ever growing amount) is that causation may run in
both directions. Money may follow the winner, the winner may follow the
money, or both. Are incumbents attracting money that causes them to win,
or are they attracting money because they are already likely to win, or are
they attracting money for other reasons?

It is hard to separate cause from effect. House incumbency reelection
rates have been sky high for some time: ninety percent of House members who ran for reelection in 2012 were reelected. An incumbent running

for reelection has all sorts of advantages, from name recognition and easy media access to free mailing privileges from Congress (with the "franking" rules stopping only the most blatant campaigning). It is not clear how much the money matters in these races, although it may affect the amount by which candidates win.[7]

Further, a money advantage does not always translate into electoral advantage. Meg Whitman's disastrous run for California governor, where she outspent Jerry Brown $177 million to $36 million, and Dave Brat's primary win over Eric Cantor are only the most noteworthy examples. Cantor not only outspent Brat, roughly $5 million to $206,000, he also had much better name recognition and a national media platform.[8]

Analysts offered after-the-fact explanations for these aberrant races: Brown had higher name recognition, was savvy, and husbanded his campaign funds to achieve some parity in television advertising during the final four weeks of the campaign. Cantor was out of touch with his district, did not focus on constituent services, and miscalculated the primary voters' strong anti-Washington sentiment. But if money always determined campaign outcomes, these explanations would not have been necessary.[9]

We also know that the "quality" of candidates sometimes matters. In the 2012 elections, pundits pegged Claire McCaskill, a U.S. senator from Missouri, as among the most vulnerable Democrats up for reelection in a state trending red. But she handily beat her Republican opponent, Todd Akin, after Akin made controversial comments about "legitimate rape." It did not hurt that McCaskill outspent Akin $21 million to $6 million (plus $9 million in outside spending for McCaskill compared to $3.8 million helping Akin). The funding disparity was probably caused by Akin's disastrous campaign, not the other way around: donors are much less likely to give their money to a candidate who clearly appears on his way to losing, especially when he commits a boneheaded gaffe like the "legitimate rape" remark.[10]

The examples show that we cannot predict outcomes simply by looking at the amount of money each side spends. Things are much more complicated. Political scientists have had a longstanding debate over whether campaign money helps challengers more than incumbents, and they have come to some nuanced conclusions about the role of money in contemporary U.S. campaigns.

They seem to agree that money can matter to election outcomes in close races. Money can be used to sway low-information voters who are more likely to split their tickets and to lack strong party allegiances. Professor Lynn Vavreck of UCLA writes: "It is tempting to think that something as important as control of the Senate lies in the hands of voters who carefully pick and choose which candidates to vote for in each race on the ballot, but this seems unlikely. It is more likely that split-ticket voters are buffeted by idiosyncratic factors, like incumbency status, recent campaign advertising, and the tone and share of news coverage candidates receive. . . . All of this makes the quality of the campaigns and the fund-raising it takes to wage them very important."[11]

Campaign expenditures can also mobilize supporters to show up to vote. Especially in the intensely polarized partisan competition in today's U.S. political system, money can make a difference in a close election when campaigns get their supporters to the polls, even though having more money does not guarantee electoral success. But while money is not a *sufficient* condition to win an election, it is usually a *necessary* one.[12]

Political scientists often speak of the "money primary," in which candidates first have to raise certain campaign sums to prove their viability in an election. Media attention to fundraising help solidify elite perceptions about which candidates actually have a chance to win. A candidate's hopes for success in a party primary and in the general election almost always depend on raising sufficient funds, first to convince elites and then to promote the candidate in the media and, as necessary, attack his or her opponent.[13]

Participants in the money primary—those willing to give as much as $2,700 (the current individual federal limit)—skew toward the wealthiest of all Americans. Most Americans do not have an extra $2,700, or even $270, to give to a political candidate. As Larry Lessig explains, only "0.26 percent of us give more than $200 to congressional campaigns, 0.05 percent of us max out to any congressional candidate, and 0.01 percent spend more than $10,000 in a campaign." These figures were from the 2010 election cycle; in the 2012 elections, the number of those giving $200 or more to congressional candidates actually shot up dramatically (to 0.53% of the U.S. adult population). To be a viable candidate in federal elections, one essentially needs to secure the approval—in the form of dollars—of a group that is far more elite even than the top one percent.[14]

And it is not just a random slice of the American population. Professor Nick Stephanopoulos of the University of Chicago describes these donors: "With respect to demographics, surveys . . . all have found that individuals who contribute at least $200 to federal candidates are 'overwhelmingly wealthy, highly educated, male, and white.' In 2004, for example, 58% of these donors were male, 69% were older than fifty, 78% had a family income above $100,000, and 91% had a college degree. In 2012, these donors amounted to just 0.4% of the population, but supplied 64% of the funds received by candidates from individuals." And, of course, there is more to this than mere numbers: "Likewise, with respect to ideology, study after study has concluded that donors hold more extreme views than the public at large."[15]

It is not just Republicans, either. A recent study by Professor Adam Bonica of Stanford and his co-authors found Democrats much more reliant on big donors (and less on organized labor) than one would think from looking at the parties' rhetoric. The authors conclude that "while it is difficult to gauge the effect of the Democrats' reliance on contributions from the wealthy, it does likely preclude a strong focus on redistributive policies."[16]

Wealthy candidates like Meg Whitman can avoid the money primary by dipping into their own funds, although they may emerge as weaker candidates. Those who hope to survive the money primary have to hone their message in front of donors willing and able to give $2,700 (or whatever the applicable state limit) to get the candidate going. Meg Whitman's problem was candidate quality, not money.[17]

What is less clear is whether the unprecedented new level of outside spending by Super PACs and other groups can help candidates who did not do well in the money primary. As we have seen, Newt Gingrich's 2012 presidential campaign was able to hold on as long as it did thanks to support from Winning the Future, the pro-Gingrich Super PAC that relied very heavily on contributions from the Adelsons. But Gingrich did not get the nomination.

Gingrich was already a skilled politician who raised a fair amount of money for his presidential campaign, so we cannot blame his failure on being a flop in the money primary. It will be interesting to see whether big outside spending can make otherwise non-viable candidates viable in non-presidential elections, and whether big outside money can prop up candidates who face competitive elections but lack the funds to stay competitive. In 2014, for example, Tea Party candidate Chris McDaniels came within a hair's breadth of toppling the incumbent Mississippi senator Thad Cochran in the Republican primary. About 83 percent of the spending in support of McDaniel came from outside groups rather than from his own campaign.[18]

The question of how large outside spending will affect election outcomes is particularly important given the explosion of such spending in the post–*Citizens United* era. There is some debate whether outside spending began rising steeply just before or just after *Citizens United*, but there is no doubt that it has climbed in the last few elections, topping $1 billion on federal races alone in the 2012 election cycle. Further, thanks to the rise of 501(c)(4) and related groups, and gaps in our disclosure laws, an ever greater percentage of campaign-related advertising is funded by contributors whose identities are unknown to the public.[19]

We do not know yet how this spending affects campaigns. But we do know how the spenders skew. According to a report by Demos and the U.S. Public Interest Research Group Education Fund, in the 2012 elections "nearly 60% of Super PAC funding came from just 159 donors contributing at least $1 million. More than 93% of the money Super PACs raised came in contributions of at least $10,000—from just 3,318 donors, or the equivalent of 0.0011% of the U.S. population." In the 2016 election season, we now have multimillionaires complaining that they are losing their political clout to billionaires.[20]

In contrast to these points about the role of money in politics, about which political scientists mostly agree, there is sharp disagreement over whether more money spent in campaigns is likely to help challengers win elections. Professor Gary Jacobson has long maintained that in races for the U.S. House, campaign spending is more important for challengers. Given incumbents' name recognition and other advantages, Jacobson argues, additional spending does not help them very much, but challengers need money to get their message out and to secure name recognition. Jacobson has suggested that challenger spending matters the most in af-

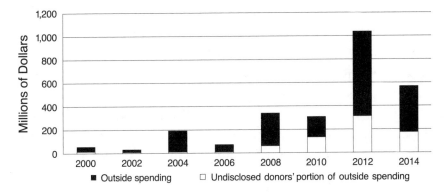

Outside Spending by Two-Year Cycle, 2000–2014
Source: Center for Responsive Politics, Total Outside Spending by Election Cycle,
Excluding Party Committees, www.opensecrets.org/outsidespending/cycle_tots
.php (last visited Feb. 25, 2015); Center for Responsive Politics, Outside Spending by
Disclosure, Excluding Party Committees, www.opensecrets.org/outsidespending/
disclosure.php (last visited Feb. 25, 2015)

fecting election outcomes and that spending limits would help incumbents by protecting them from challengers.[21]

Jacobson's analysis is controversial. Professors Don Green and Jonathan Krasno, for example, found that spending by incumbents could increase their margin of victory, and Professor Alan Gerber found that incumbent spending was just as effective as challenger spending in U.S. Senate elections. The discrepancy between House and Senate results may exist because Senate challengers tend to be better known (and perhaps higher-quality) candidates than House challengers, and challengers and incumbents in Senate races may therefore campaign on more equal footing.[22]

Gerber also reaches the opposite policy prescription from Jacobson, suggesting that campaign spending caps, "even if set lower than some challengers' campaign spending levels, can significantly increase the chances of challenger victory."[23]

☑

"Studies have consistently found little or no connection between campaign contributions and legislative action." That's how Professor Smith seeks to mollify readers worried about the effect of campaign contributions on the actions of elected officials.[24]

Unfortunately, this statement is incorrect. Studies consistently have found little or no connection between campaign contributions by PACs to members of Congress and their *roll-call votes* on particular legislative matters. But that is very different from saying there is no connection between campaign contributions and "legislative action."[25]

To begin with, campaign contributions affect legislative action indirectly by influencing who is elected. As we have seen, although there is no simple connection between money and outcomes, money can matter to election results, especially in close races. And these results affect legislative outcomes because who is elected matters for policy: the bills passed by a Democratic House of Representatives are very different from those passed by a Republican House.

The people giving and spending money on elections support candidates who they think agree with their views. Even before *Citizens United* the wealthy dominated campaign giving. Now, in the *Citizens United* era, the super-wealthy are the ones giving and spending unprecedented amounts of political money.

Politico reporter Ken Vogel, in his book *Big Money,* colorfully describes the new cadre of mega-donors, such as Sheldon Adelson, the Koch brothers, and George Soros and other members of the Democratic-leaning Democracy Alliance, who regularly meet to plot strategy to spend tens of millions of dollars to elect their preferred candidates. "At first blush, they may seem like conniving robber baron archetypes trying to buy government favor, but they remind me more of the wealthy class of sports junkies who plunk down hundreds of millions of dollars to buy a professional team. In fact, there's a good bit of overlap between team owners and political donors."[26]

Even putting aside any motivation they may have to influence the positions of elected officials (bricks-and-mortar casino mogul Sheldon Adelson, for example, has spent a lot of time and money opposing Internet-based gambling), the resources these donors put into play help elect legislators sympathetic to their views. The level and the nature of outside spending make it all the more likely that the wealthiest Americans will have the greatest say over who is elected to office. It would be surprising if the candidates they backed did not favor many of the programs endorsed by these mega-donors. Indeed, recent research by Professor Michael Barber looking at the connection between individual donors and the candidates they support found that candidates tend to reflect the views of those individuals who support them financially.[27]

Mega-donors are not just giving money to Super PACs and secret 501(c)(4) organizations. In Iowa, the Koch-backed Americans for Prosperity has set up its own political network to register voters, get out the vote, and influence political activists—all in a state that has a disproportionately large influence on the presidential nomination process because of its early presidential caucuses. According to the *Des Moines Register,* Americans for Prosperity "now has five field offices, a 27-member staff, a record of orchestrating public events featuring state and national GOP leaders, and a strategy for marketing free-market principles as the best means to improve Iowans' lives."

Not content with the Republican Party, Americans for Prosperity is creating a rival campaign organization that could influence the choice of the Republican presidential nominee in the libertarian direction favored by the Kochs, and it could be a taste of things to come. Perhaps even more astonishingly, in early 2015 the Koch brothers and their network of donors announced plans to spend up to $889 million on the 2016 elections. The amount would make the Koch network rival the political parties themselves in overall spending.[28]

Further, not all donors limit themselves to an "electoral strategy" with their donations, trying to elect candidates sympathetic to the donors' views. Other donors pursue a "legislative strategy," seeking to influence all kinds of legislative action through their spending.

To start, the potential for big spending opened up by *Citizens United* can influence legislative action without anyone spending a dime or saying a word. A recent study by Daniel Tokaji and Renata Strause found that some members of Congress worry that if they take stands opposed by large donors, they may face large outside spending against them at the next election. The threats are mostly implicit, although former senator Ben Nelson recalled being warned on the phone that there would be big money spent against him if he voted in a certain way. Former senator Bob Kerrey explained the tension to the authors.

You're already threatened. . . . You're sitting there saying . . . is Americans for Prosperity going to advertise against me in a primary, yes or no? Is American Crossroads . . . going to spend on me in a primary? . . . If you're sitting there making a decision, well I've looked at the facts and god, it seems to me we are putting more carbon in the atmosphere, and there is a relationship between that and the temperatures rising, and that's going to be very bad for the world. We'd better do something about it, but if I do something about it, I know the Koch brothers are going to run an ad against me. I know they're going to put a lot of money to try to defeat me in a primary.

Kerrey describes similar situations, such as a vote to increase the minimum wage, and anticipating that the Chamber of Commerce would attack him if he supported it. "I know. I don't have to be told. They don't have to threaten me. I just know they're going to do it. If I vote for [a] trade agreement, I know labor is going to advertise against me . . . they don't have to threaten me. I know it." The net result, Kerrey says, is "I'm afraid to do what I think is right. . . . The question you're asking is do they threaten you, and the answer is they don't have to."[29]

We do not know how much this matters: it is hard to quantify how much these threats or fears influence legislative action. None of these threats or fears would show up on a roll-call vote, or appear in campaign spending reports filed with the Federal Election Commission. Yet this is one way campaign contributions can affect legislative action. (By the same token, we do not know how many otherwise excellent candidates are deterred from even running because of the "money primary.")

Those pursuing a legislative strategy have more direct ways to influence legislative action. Both social science evidence and the evidence from elected officials and others submitted in *McConnell v. Federal Election Commission* suggest that money can buy access to elected officials—which only confirms what was already well known.[30]

In the days before McCain-Feingold, the political parties offered menus of access: golfing or coffee with congressional leaders, or even the president, in exchange for six- or seven-figure donations.[31] These days, soft money is banned (though the Roberts court could allow it again within a few years, and recent congressional action to raise party contribution limits is a legislative move back toward soft money), but access continues to be sold. Presidential campaigns offer it to those who bundle large amounts of campaign contributions. ("Bundlers" are people who collect checks from others for the campaign to reach a certain goal, usually in the mid- to high six figures.) The Center for Public Integrity reported that big Obama bundlers "had broad access to the White House for meetings with top administration officials and glitzy social events. In all, campaign bundlers and their family members account for more than 3,000 White House meetings and visits. Half of them raised $200,000 or more." Fredreka Schouten of *USA Today* reported during the 2012 primary campaign: "A widely circulated campaign document shows Romney is offering perks to his biggest fundraisers, including access at the party's convention in Tampa, a weekend retreat . . . in Park City, Utah, weekly campaign briefings and a 'dedicated Romney Victory Headquarters' staff member."[32]

Members of Congress take money given to "Leadership PACs" and use it for campaign events and other activities, where big donors get to wine, dine, and schmooze with congressional leadership. As a *60 Minutes* exposé explained, "Georgia Sen. Saxby Chambliss likes golf, so much so that he spent more than $100,000 the past two years entertaining at some of the finest courses in the world. New York congressman Gregory Meeks prefers football. He spent $35,000 on NFL games. All of this was paid for with political contributions—all in the name of democracy."[33]

What does access get donors? Defenders of the status quo will assure you that all the donors want is a photo of them with the president or the chance to brag about playing golf with the speaker of the House. Across Democratic and Republican administrations, really big donors might secure a cushy ambassadorship. The sale of ambassadorships led to problems for the Obama administration. As the *Washington Post* reported, "The nominee for ambassador to Norway, for example, prompted outrage in Oslo by characterizing one of the nation's ruling parties as extremist. A soap-opera producer slated for Hungary appeared to have little knowledge of the country she would be living in. A prominent Obama bundler nominated to be ambassador to Argentina acknowledged that he had never set foot in the country and isn't fluent in Spanish."[34]

Access also serves larger purposes than ego stroking, however. It can lead to legislative action. Members of Congress do all sorts of things, aside from voting, that counts. They can scuttle legislation (particularly easy for committee chairs and legislative leaders), suggest the omission or inclusion of language in bills that will help or hurt someone's interests, or pressure executive branch agencies to take or not take certain actions. It should come as no surprise that incumbents attract lots of money, that legislative committee members and especially chairs attract contributions from people and entities in the regulated industries, and that large companies and individuals give to both political parties. When members of Congress leave committees, the amount of money they raise goes down and the time they spend working for constituents goes up.[35]

People sometimes use their access to make a direct pitch to an elected official or staffer. This does not mean they are offering bribes. But access does give them a chance to request a certain policy or vote in person, to put an issue on an official's radar, and to make a connection that can later be used to ask for or get a favor. Few people would have such access without making large contributions to those officials.

In a wonderful field experiment, researchers from the University of California at Berkeley sent requests to congressional staffers to meet on a policy issue. Some of the letters, sent to randomly selected congressional offices, just asked for a meeting. Other letters, also sent to randomly selected offices, coupled the request with the information that campaign donors would be attending. The researchers found that when "informed prospective attendees were political donors, senior policymakers made themselves available between three and four times more often."[36]

Sometimes people buy access by hiring lobbyists, who themselves make or bundle campaign contributions. Lobbyists use a variety of tools to gain influence, including mobilizing individual citizens to contact legislators (grassroots lobbying), testifying at hearings, submitting written comments to an agency or committee, or issuing press releases. But their most important tool is personal contact with legislators and staffers. A lobbyist with access to a legislator is in the best position to influence public policy. Once she secures access, the lobbyist influences policy primarily by providing credible information that a legislator or staffer may use to argue for some legislative action.[37]

People often think that lobbyists change legislators' positions through favors or threats, but this appears to be relatively rare. Usually, the lobbyist's role is to provide support and useful information for a position a legislator already holds. At other times, the issue of interest to the lobbyist (and her client) is one the legislator has no firm position or even knowledge about, and which the public is paying little attention to. In such circumstances the legislator is often willing to help a friendly lobbyist achieve her client's interests, especially when the client is a constituent or has business affecting the legislator's district.[38]

Lobbyists can rarely sway resistant legislators on high-profile issues. Even the most highly paid lobbyists, for example, could not derail the large corporate tax increase that became part of the politically popular Tax Reform Act of 1986, a major bill passed during the Reagan administration with bipartisan support. And although the student loan program is an example in which the public interest appeared to have been thwarted by banking industry lobbyists, when the issue of student loan reform became a priority for the Obama administration, industry lobbyists were unable to stop it.[39]

Rather than working to change legislative minds on issues of high public salience, lobbyists work in the shadows. Once it became clear that the 1986 tax bill was going to pass, lobbyists were much more successful in getting favorable treatment for their clients in the details of the bill and its implementation. A similar phenomenon occurred with the Dodd-Frank financial reform bill. The bill's opponents failed to prevent its passage, but once it became law they worked closely with legislative and executive agency staffers to hash out the details of its implementation and accompanying regulations.[40]

Campaign contributions are a key part of a culture of reciprocity in which those who help out the most are likely to get the greatest access. It is a natural instinct to help someone who has helped you. Why *shouldn't* a legislator help a lobbyist supporter by favoring her clients' interests on an issue about which the legislator has no strong preference?[41]

Lobbyists do much more than simply contribute; they have become prolific fundraisers and bundlers of campaign contributions. In 2010, for example, when Republicans appeared poised to retake control of the House of Representatives, the minority leader, John Boehner, provided special access to lobbyists who contributed the maximum of $37,800 to various committees supporting him or who raised at least $100,000 from other contributors.[42]

Another key means of securing legislative access through money is the "revolving door": clients hire former legislators and staffers to work as lobbyists. Many former senators and members of Congress, and dozens of former staffers, are now lobbyists. Half of the senators who left office between 1998 and 2004 became lobbyists. These revolving-door lobbyists have pre-existing relationships with current legislators and staffers, which they can use to help clients. Though it is no longer permissible for a former senator to use the Senate gym for lobbying, and there is now a waiting period after leaving the Senate before one may engage in certain lobbying activities, there is no question that a former senator or major House staffer is likely to get a phone call returned, to say the least.

A recent study found that revolving-door lobbyists tend to follow their former legislative bosses from committee to committee, switching issues as they go. The study's authors saw this as confirmation that the question is not what you know but whom you know. These lobbyists were not being hired because of their expertise on a particular issue; it is their personal contacts that make them valuable. This is in line with a study finding that lobbyists who formerly worked in the office of a U.S. senator suffer on average a 24 percent drop in revenue when that senator leaves office.[43]

A study of health care lobbying before the passage of the Obama health care law by the *Chicago Tribune*, Northwestern University, and the Center for Responsive Politics concluded: "At least 166 former aides from the nine congressional leadership offices and five committees involved in shaping health overhaul legislation—along with at least 13 former lawmakers—registered to represent at least 338 health care clients since the beginning of last year. . . . Their health care clients spent $635 million on lobbying over the past two years. . . . The total of insider lobbyists jumps to 278 when non-health-care firms that reported lobbying on health issues are added in." The *Tribune* article reporting this study describes how a former congressional staffer successfully lobbied to change a proposed $40 billion in taxes on medical devices to $20 billion, saving his industry clients $20 billion.[44]

Once they gain access to elected officials, lobbyists solidify relationships of trust and influence by providing credible information (on both policy and politics) to help the legislative office make informed policy choices and achieve its goals. Access certainly does not guarantee success, and lobbyists often have a difficult time getting elected officials to take action. Moreover, it is easier for lobbyists to react to a changing policy environment than to facilitate major legislative change. Access is best thought of as a necessary but not sufficient condition for a lobbyist to achieve a client's goals.[45]

How do we know that campaign money and campaign-fueled lobbying access can affect legislative action? After all, a legislator's political party is a much better predictor of roll-call votes than campaign contributions. Once again, it is hard to measure the influence of money over legislative actions such as the scuttling of a bill or the addition or deletion of legislative language.

One indirect measure of the power of money is policy outcomes. If the wealthy who have access get their way on federal public policy more than others, it is a good bet that access had something to do with it. In a key paper summarizing years of research, Professors Martin Gilens and Benjamin Page found that in policy area after policy area, U.S. policy favors the interests of the wealthy over those of the rest of the public. "The central point that emerges from our research is that economic elites and organized groups representing business interests have substantial independent impacts on U.S. government policy, while mass-based interest groups and average citizens have little or no independent influence."[46]

The authors quantify the different power of groups, noting that, on most issues, "it makes very little difference what the general public thinks. The probability of policy change is nearly the same (around [30 percent]) whether a tiny minority or a large majority of average citizens favor a proposed policy change." In contrast, "a proposed policy change with low support among economically elite Americans (one out of five in favor) is adopted only about 18 percent of the time, while a proposed change with high support (four out of five in favor) is adopted about 45 percent of the time."[47]

Gilens and Page studied policy preferences and outcomes from 1981 through 2002, and they defined "affluent" Americans as those in the top ten percent of income (about $146,000 or more per year). There is every reason to think that those in the top one percent have even greater sway, and that the loosening of rules on campaign contributions and lobbying since 2008 will increase their influence and that of corporate-aligned interest groups. As Professor Larry Bartels has shown, the problem of economic inequality being translated into political inequality predates *Citizens United*, but it is only likely to increase now that the wealthy have new levers of influence.[48]

In a path-breaking study of the influence of money and lobbying in state legislatures, Professor Lynda W. Powell found great complexity: institutional issues, such as the presence or absence of term limits or a legislator's ambition for higher office, mattered a great deal in a legislator's susceptibility to influence. But she did find strong evidence confirming that contributors try—and often succeed—in gaining access to state legislators through campaign contributions.[49] Other studies show the role of money in specific policy areas. A study of state legislatures' approach to corporate law, for example, found that "when businesses are allowed to engage in unlimited independent expenditures antitakeover laws shift in favor of management."[50]

Thus far we have seen two means by which money can shape legislative outcomes. First, money can influence who is elected to office, which in turn affects legislative outcomes. Second, money often buys access and cooperation, permitting those with wealth, or the lobbyists representing them, to affect legislative policy. The Gilens-Page data show how those with wealth and corporate interests tend to get policy enacted in ways they prefer.

Finally, and most crassly, there is bribery. There is little evidence that campaign contributions are directly buying legislative votes in Congress. Part of the reason undoubtedly is the current contribution limits of $2,700 per election and limits on the transformation of contributions into personal benefits.

If we got rid of campaign contribution limitations tomorrow, and a member of Congress could take $1 million from a single donor, the temptation to accept a bribe would be much greater, especially if some aspects of the $1 million could be converted to the representative's personal use. While today's "Leadership PACs" and other campaign finance vehicles provide some means for transforming political wealth into personal wealth, there is a long way to go.

Bribery is already easy to conceal because people who are bribed tend to keep it secret. It would be even easier if very large campaign contributions were legal. As things stand now, unscrupulous individuals wanting to bribe members of Congress have to hide both the agreement and the payments. If unlimited contributions were allowed, conspirators would have to hide only the agreement: "I will give you $25 million and in exchange you will support a tax break that will save me $1 billion." When individual contributions limits are too low to buy politicians, unscrupulous individuals need to take steps to hide the money they are providing. The same limits also prevent politicians from extorting money from wealthy donors.[51]

Although they are rare on the congressional level, on the state and local level bribery prosecutions appear more common. Elected officials are routinely arrested for taking money in exchange for legislative action. One member of the New York state assembly was recently convicted of accepting a mere $22,000 in exchange for favorable actions related to an adult day care center. Perhaps somewhat less surprising is the millions of dollars in kickbacks that Sheldon Silver, the longtime speaker of the New York state assembly, is accused of receiving in exchange for official acts.[52]

Why do bribery prosecutions appear more frequently on the state and local level? To begin with, state and local officials are better able to affect policy and make decisions than members of Congress. "Pay to play" is a common problem on this level. Further, there may be less media scrutiny of state and local politics, making corrupt politicians more likely to believe they will not get caught.

In a world of unlimited contributions to elected officials, we would have to depend on bribery laws to stop the most corrupt transactions. But this raises big problems, as can easily be seen in the case of former Alabama governor Don Siegelman. Health care executive Richard Scrushy gave a $500,000 contribution to a ballot measure that was the governor's pet project, and Siegelman then appointed Scrushy to a state health care board. Was the contribution a bribe?[53]

Siegelman and Scrushy both went to jail for this transaction, even though it is still not clear whether there was an explicit deal between them exchanging the money for the board appointment. There is also the question of when we should consider campaign contributions to be bribes under federal and state law. Additionally, if prosecutors get to treat some large campaign contributions as bribes, there is the danger of politically motivated prosecutions. Siegelman claimed his trial was driven by politics. Former Democratic presidential candidate John Edwards and former House majority leader Tom DeLay made similar claims about their prosecutions for campaign-related offenses. These difficult questions about the line between proper and improper influence would be far more common if there were no limits on money given directly to legislators.[54]

☑

In the *McCutcheon* case, where the Supreme Court majority struck down federal aggregate contribution limits, Justice Stephen Breyer issued a strident dissent that threw up many arguments against the decision by Chief Justice Roberts. Among the government interests Justice Breyer raised in defending federal contribution limits was an intriguing one: promoting "electoral integrity." Even more intriguing: Breyer cited Yale Law School dean Robert Post's book on electoral integrity, *Citizens Divided*, before it was publicly available.[55]

After the book was published, it became clear that "electoral integrity" is a close cousin to the concern the Supreme Court first raised in *Buckley* about the "appearance of corruption" stemming from big campaign contributions. *Citizens Divided* is a revised version of Post's Tanner Lectures at Harvard, together with commentary from other scholars and a reply from Post. Post writes beautifully and convincingly on the history of campaign regulation in the United States and its relationship to First Amendment doctrine. Among other things, he rejects equality arguments for regulation, a point I will return to later.

When Post finally offers his objection to the unlimited corporate and labor union spending permitted under *Citizens United*, it is that the Supreme Court missed a compelling government interest in promoting "electoral integrity."

> Electoral integrity consists of public confidence that elected officials attend to public opinion. It has rightly been observed that the state's "interest in protecting public confidence 'in the integrity and legitimacy of representative government'" is of the highest order because "public confidence in the integrity of the electoral process . . . encourages citizen participation in

the democratic process." Electoral integrity is in this regard a unique kind of constitutional value, for it depends on what people actually believe. . . . The question of electoral integrity ultimately involves judgment about the contents of public opinion.[56]

He further argues that despite the danger of legislative self-dealing, courts should defer to legislative judgments that limits on campaign money are necessary to preserve this kind of integrity.[57]

Post is not the first to identify "integrity" as a reason to limit money in politics. The late Frank Sorauf, a political scientist who studied money in politics, made similar arguments in the 1990s. "Integrity" can mean different things to different people, but Post's argument is premised on an empirical judgment: that limitations on money in politics are necessary to preserve public confidence in the fairness of the electoral process. This seems like a variation on the "appearance of corruption" argument for campaign limits the Supreme Court first recognized in *Buckley*. There, the Court wrote: "Congress could legitimately conclude that the avoidance of the appearance of improper influence is also critical . . . if confidence in the system of representative Government is not to be eroded to a disastrous extent."[58]

Post, in his lectures, does not explore any evidence connecting campaign finance rules to public confidence, but Stanford professor Pam Karlan, in her response to Post, points to the absence of convincing empirical evidence tying public confidence in the electoral process to campaign finance limits.[59]

Large majorities of the American public support campaign finance limits, and have little confidence in government. But that does not mean the two are causally related. In the most comprehensive examination of public opinion and campaign finance laws, Stanford professor Nate Persily and Kelli Lammie found no such connection. Public confidence in government actually went *down* after enactment of the McCain-Feingold law, perhaps because all the talk of corruption surrounding the bill's passage made the issue more salient. Similarly, University of Missouri professor Jeff Milyo found no important relationship between the presence or absence of campaign finance laws and the extent of public trust.[60]

We do not know how the *Citizens United* era will affect public confidence.

We are seeing not only unprecedented outside spending on elections, much of it going to produce negative advertising that the public says it hates, but we also see a rise in undisclosed donors. It could well be that public confidence will further decline because of the Wild West of campaign financing now coming to American elections. (Confidence could also rise if the country adopted certain reform measures that most voters support.) So far, however, the connection between campaign finance laws and public confidence has yet to be demonstrated.

Even as outside spending has the potential to undermine public confidence in the fairness of elections, it has an upside: all this campaign money educates voters about candidates and issues. Voters hate negative advertising, but these "contrast" ads do let them know where candidates stand on issues. If they can see through the hyperbole, campaign spending may lead to more informed voters. Whether negative advertising also turns off the electorate and demobilizes them remains a hotly disputed topic. Voters also may gain confidence by making donations to campaigns; it is another form of political participation.[61]

So there is a lot we don't actually know. Some of the things we do know: Money does not buy political outcomes, but, along with candidate quality and campaign organization, it is important to winning elections. To be a viable candidate, one usually has to win the money primary. This may skew the selection of candidates toward those supported by the wealthy, because the wealthiest Americans are making almost all of the $2,700 donations and giving more to outside groups. Self-financed candidates may avoid the money primary but still fall short because they do not hone their campaign skills. On the other hand, it is unclear how much outside spending can make up for a candidate's failures in the money primary, and it is unclear whether outside spending can help candidates win in close elections, a question that the explosion of such spending has made exceptionally important. Finally, we do not know if spending limits on candidates help incumbents or challengers more.

The public is disgusted with politicians and with money in politics, but reform efforts have not helped restore confidence in either elections or government. Perhaps a more radical system of campaign rules would make a difference, perhaps not. Much of what people think and say about money and politics is wrong. Despite what those opposed to campaign finance laws say, there is plenty wrong with the role of money in contemporary American politics. Despite what many reformers say, the problem is not one of too many negative ads, or too much money in politics, or of corruption or legalized bribery, though corruption could emerge as a bigger problem if we had a fully deregulated campaign finance system.[62]

As we will see, the main problem with money in U.S. politics is the translation of vastly unequal economic power into unequal political power.

PART TWO

SOLUTIONS

3

The Voting Lottery

IMAGINE A LOTTERY INSTEAD OF ELECTIONS for choosing members of Congress. Everyone who would have been an eligible voter in each congressional district gets a lottery ticket, and the lucky winner gets to choose that district's member of Congress.[1]

This system has much to recommend it: over all, it should produce a Congress filled with members reflecting the preference of the average voter of each district. Every eligible voter has equal political power: they all have the same chance of having their lottery ticket chosen. Campaign costs would go down, as campaigns would no longer need to mobilize voters to get them to the polls. Instead, campaigns would be revved up to appeal to whoever got the equivalent of Charlie Bucket's Golden Ticket.

Now imagine a second lottery for making policy. Instead of having Congress decide what policy to enact, Democrats and Republicans could offer rival proposals, and a voter chosen at random in the United States would choose either the Democratic or the Republican proposal. The voter could not choose a different proposal, or none, or a compromise. The options would be strictly one or the other.

This system also has its advantages. As in the voting lottery, every voter's political power is equal. As in baseball's arbitration system, making the voter choose between the Democratic and Republican options might force the parties to craft proposals likely to appeal to the average voter. Although lobbyists would seek to influence the Democratic and Republican proposals, big special-interest side deals might make a proposal less attractive to the voter who is assigned to pick the policy.[2]

Still, both of these lottery proposals have big drawbacks. Although *on average* the voting lottery would produce a Congress reflecting the views of each district's average voter, the luck of the draw could create wild swings in representation. Voters could grow disillusioned with a process in which they have a better chance of being struck by lightning than deciding the election (although the same goes for their chances of casting the deciding vote in most elections). The policy lottery would limit the choices of measures to those favored by the major political parties. The size of each party's caucus in Congress would be irrelevant. The system would eliminate the potential for deliberation and compromise between the parties. Depending on the details of the policy lottery, change could come too fast, or not fast enough. Not all voters are equally well informed about politics, so the lottery winner could choose a bad member of Congress or a poor public policy. Depending on the time frame, winners might face undue pressure or threats, or illegal financial incentives, to decide one way or another.

In short, there are both benefits and drawbacks to these proposed lottery systems.

Now let's vary the rules of both lotteries in ways that approximate the influence of money on our political processes. In the revised voting lottery, additional lottery tickets are distributed on the basis of wealth. Each eligible resident of the district will get a lottery ticket, but people, corporations, labor unions, and other entities from both inside and outside the district (but not outside the United States) purchase additional lottery tickets via auction. Wealthy candidates may buy extra tickets as well. The number of tickets for sale via auction will be many times the number available to residents. As before, the winner of the lottery will choose the member of Congress.

In the policy lottery, each voter once again will get a ticket, but there will be two additional changes. First, there will be a large number of blank tickets. If one of these tickets gets chosen, then no voter gets to pick either the Democratic or Republican policy. Instead, the law will not change.

If no blank ticket is chosen in the first round, there will be a second lottery in which people, corporations, labor unions and other entities, including foreign people and entities, can bid via auction on "trump or change" tickets. This second lottery will have some blank tickets as well. If the blank ticket is chosen in the second round, the chosen policy of the first-round winner goes into effect. If some other ticket is chosen, the winner of the secondary "trump or change" lottery may either block the measure entirely or make a change that, while preserving the basics of the chosen policy, may modify it in ways that benefit the winner.

These revised lottery proposals raise many of the same objections as the original proposals, such as potential wild swings in representation or policy or the risk that important choices will be trusted to uninformed or irresponsible voters. But they also raise a new objection: wealthy people and entities have a much greater chance of influencing electoral and policy outcomes than ordinary voters. Even when a randomly chosen voter gets a say on policy, the wealthy have a chance to reverse or change it to their advantage.

☑

The revised voting lottery violates modern democratic norms of equal representation and is probably unconstitutional. Since the 1960s, the Supreme Court has recognized that wealth is an inappropriate criterion for the exercise of political power and that voting rules should give equal political power to all voters in a state or other jurisdiction.

In *Harper v. Virginia State Board of Elections*, decided in 1966, the United States Supreme Court struck down under the Equal Protection Clause of the Fourteenth Amendment a $1.50 "poll tax" in Virginia state elections. Voters had to pay this tax (and back taxes) in order to cast a vote in state elections. A few years earlier, the United States had adopted a constitutional amendment that barred poll taxes in federal elections, and Virginia was one of only four states that still used such a tax in its state elections.[3]

In striking down Virginia's poll tax, Justice William O. Douglas wrote for the Court: "Voter qualifications have no relation to wealth nor to paying or not paying this or any other tax. . . . Wealth, like race, creed, or color, is not germane to one's ability to participate intelligently in the electoral process. Lines drawn on the basis of wealth or property, like those of race, are traditionally disfavored. To introduce wealth or payment of a fee as a measure of a voter's qualifications is to introduce a capricious or irrelevant factor."

Justice John Marshall Harlan, in dissent, pushed back against the argument that elimination of the poll tax was constitutionally compelled. He wrote that "it is certainly a rational argument that payment of some minimal poll tax promotes civic responsibility, weeding out those who do not care enough about public affairs to pay $1.50 or thereabouts a year for the exercise of the franchise. It is also arguable, indeed it was probably accepted as sound political theory by a large percentage of Americans through most of our history, that people with some property have a deeper stake in community affairs, and are consequently more responsible, more educated, more knowledgeable, more worthy of confidence, than those without means, and that the community and Nation would be better managed if the franchise were restricted to such citizens." He added: "Nondiscriminatory and fairly applied literacy tests, upheld by this Court . . . find justification on very similar grounds."

Justice Harlan rejected the idea that the poll tax violated the Equal Protection Clause. But he expected the poll tax to fall soon enough in the political process because modern American political thinking rejected the "rational" justifications he offered for it. "These viewpoints, to be sure, ring hollow on most contemporary ears."

The same could be said of literacy tests, which the Court upheld against constitutional challenge in 1959, but which have been illegal under the federal Voting Rights Act since the 1960s. Today, many people view the right to vote as the means by which we divide power among political equals, and most (but not all) are likely to reject "tests" or payments to decide who is worthy to vote.[4]

Although some conservatives think putting up barriers in front of people who wish to vote might winnow out casual voters and help elect the "best candidate" for office, it is hard to find modern examples of serious arguments for a poll tax or literacy test. One of the most recent examples I could find came from the ultra-conservative provocateur Ann Coulter, who (perhaps seriously) advocated both a poll tax and a literacy test on the Fox television show *Hannity and Colmes* in 1999, and reiterated her support for a literacy test in 2015. But this view is well outside the standard range of Republican Party thought. I could find no examples of mainstream Republican politicians taking a similar stance.[5]

As it did with the poll tax, the Supreme Court in the 1960s rejected as unconstitutional district elections (such as for Congress or for a state legislature) using districts with greatly unequal populations. In many parts of the country before the Court's rulings, rural legislative districts had few people in them, while urban districts had many. As J. Douglas Smith writes, "In California, more than 6 million residents of Los Angeles County, nearly 40 percent of the state's total population, elected just one state senator, as did the 14,294 inhabitants of three sparsely populated counties." Because the legislatures were malapportioned, voters in the urban areas could not use their voting power to redraw the maps to create more equal districts.[6]

In rejecting this voting arrangement as unconstitutional, in *Reynolds v. Sims,* the Supreme Court in 1964 specifically compared malapportioned districts to a system giving some people more votes than others:

> It would appear extraordinary to suggest that a State could be constitutionally permitted to enact a law providing that certain of the State's voters could vote two, five, or 10 times for their legislative representatives, while voters living elsewhere could vote only once. And it is inconceivable that a state law to the effect that, in counting votes for legislators, the votes of citizens in one part of the State would be multiplied by two, five, or 10, while the votes of persons in another area would be counted only at face value, could be constitutionally sustainable. Of course, the effect of state legislative districting schemes which give the same number of representatives to unequal numbers of constituents is identical. Overweighting and overvaluation of the votes of those living here has the certain effect of dilution and undervaluation of the votes of those living there. The resulting discrimination against those individual voters living in disfavored areas is easily demonstrable mathematically. Their right to vote is simply not the same right to vote as that of those living in a favored part of the State. Two, five, or 10 of them must vote before the effect of their voting is equivalent to that of their favored neighbor. Weighting the votes of citizens differently, by any method or means, merely because of where they happen to reside, hardly seems justifiable.[7]

Once again Justice Harlan dissented: as a matter of constitutional law, he wrote, it is not up to the courts to force the creation of more equally populated electoral districts. Justice Potter Stewart, also dissenting, acknowledged that vast inequality in districts is unconstitutional, but he believed that states had a choice in whether to move to equally populated districts or to a districting plan that represented a rational division of interests in a state, such as some reasonable division among the interests of cities, rural areas, and suburbs.

Today, the United States retains two voting schemes that violate the one person, one vote rule: the Electoral College and the U.S. Senate, where (thanks to provisions enshrined in the Constitution) each state, regardless of size, is entitled to two U.S. senators. All other normal elections on the federal, state, and local level are conducted under the one person, one vote rule.[8]

It is hard to find modern descendants of Justices Harlan or Stewart calling to eliminate this rule in congressional or state elections. Justice Alito, for example, suggested his disagreement with the one person, one vote cases in 1985, when he applied for a job in Ronald Reagan's Department of Justice, but at his Supreme Court confirmation hearing, he said: "I don't see any reason why it should be reexamined . . . I never was opposed to the one-person one-vote concept."[9]

The revised voting lottery violates the Equal Protection rules of both *Harper* and *Reynolds*. People with wealth have a greater chance to influence election outcomes than those without wealth. Further, by giving non-human entities, including corporations, a chance to buy tickets, the lottery dilutes the voting power of eligible voters. It is like giving those people and entities who can afford to buy extra tickets two, five, or ten extra votes. I have little doubt that if a jurisdiction adopted this lottery the courts would hold it unconstitutional.

It is less certain that courts would find the revised policy lottery unconstitutional. Unlike the right to equal voting power, the Supreme Court has not held that each voter has a constitutional right to equal influence over the creation of public policy.

The lack of precedent means a constitutional argument against such a system could well fail. Yet it would be hard to think of good normative arguments in favor of a system in which those with wealth, including foreign individuals and entities, have a much greater chance than an average voter of having their preferred policies enacted into law, of blocking proposals they do not like, and of altering proposals for their private benefit. Such a system promotes oligarchy or plutocracy and is inconsistent with current thinking about the nature of our democracy.

The most plausible argument in favor of giving the wealthy greater influence over public policy posits that they are more likely than other voters to choose, block, or change policies in ways consistent with the public good. This is a tough argument to prove for two reasons. First, we lack a good measure of the public interest. If one measures the public interest by looking at the preferences of the majority of the voters or of the average voter, any deviation from these preferences by a wealthy person exercising a "trump or change" card by definition goes against the public interest. Nor is there a widely accepted substantive measure that can tell us whether the wealthy would make "better" choices than a voter chosen at random.

Second, when individuals and groups organize to influence the electoral process, there is reason to believe that narrow groups and individuals are more likely to seek legislative changes that provide narrow economic benefits to them—an activity economists call "rent seeking"—than to seek passage of laws in the public interest. Rent seeking hurts economic growth and is harmful to the country. Whatever such rent-seeking activity is, it does not qualify as acting in line with the public interest. The wealthy, like everyone else, would likely pursue legislation consistent with their personal, professional, and ideological goals.[10]

☑

What do these lotteries have to do with campaign finance reform? To this point, I have offered strong reasons to believe that the revised voting lottery is both unconstitutional and out of line with contemporary democratic norms and that the revised policy lottery, although possibly not unconstitutional, is not strongly supported by contemporary democratic norms. In other words, there are strong policy arguments, and perhaps constitutional arguments, against both of the revised proposed lotteries. I want to use the claims against the lotteries to make the equality case for campaign finance reform.

Fortunately, however, I do not need to demonstrate that a court would find either lottery unconstitutional if they were enacted and then challenged. Nor am I making the parallel argument that campaign finance reform to promote political equality is constitutionally *compelled* because the current system violates equal protection guarantees of political equality, although others have made such arguments.[11]

Instead, I plan to demonstrate four things:

First, the public has a compelling interest, backed by decades-old constitutional decisions and contemporary democratic norms, in a certain kind of political equality, which I call "equality of inputs": treating each voter as entitled to equal political power. The revised voting and policy lotteries violate this interest because they favor those with great wealth. If you disagree with me, and believe that political equality is not an acceptable interest that the government or U.S. voters can choose to promote, you are not likely to accept the rest of my analysis. (You would also be likely to reject a ban on poll taxes and to have no problem with some people getting more votes than others.) But if you agree with me on the importance of the equality of inputs, this is only the first step toward allowing equality of inputs to serve as a basis on which the Supreme Court may set limits on campaign money.

Second, the current U.S. system of campaign financing sufficiently resembles the two revised lotteries that the public has a compelling interest in changing the campaign finance system to promote equality of inputs. Again, this is not to argue that the state or federal government *must* reform the system, only that political equality can serve as a compelling interest *if* a state or federal government adopts reform.

Third, it is possible to carefully design a campaign finance reform program that promotes equality of inputs by making wealth less important to both election and policy outcomes without having many bad, or unintended, consequences. I consider this point in the next chapter.

Fourth, a carefully designed campaign finance reform program promoting equality of inputs would not impermissibly violate First Amendment free speech and association rights. I consider this issue briefly the next chapter and in more depth in Part III, "Objections."

How close do the revised lotteries resemble our actual political system? I chose lotteries for my analogies to demonstrate the unpredictable nature of the effect of money on both elections and policy. Money matters in the U.S. political system, but it is not always decisive. As in the lotteries, the wealthy have a much better chance to influence electoral and policy outcomes than those without wealth, but they cannot simply buy the outcomes they want. Sometimes policy goes in directions not supported by anyone, and sometimes those with the most resources can thwart the preferences of the average voter or of even both parties. But despite the probabilistic nature of things, the U.S. political system, like the fictional lotteries, skews heavily toward those who use their economic power to influence politics.

It is hard to be considered a serious candidate in an election without winning the money primary. Self-financed candidates, or those backed by a Tom Steyer or a Sheldon Adelson, a Super PAC, a 501(c)(4), or some other group, immediately get one or more chances to be considered for election. As we have seen, money guarantees these candidates a chance that candidates lacking money usually do not get. It makes candidates competitive, and in close races it can play an important role in determining who wins.

We have seen that money influences policymaking as well. It affects who gets elected, and who gets elected matters greatly for policy. Further, money buys access to elected officials, giving the wealthy greater influence over public policy, especially to block policies and to alter them to include self-interested provisions.

Two key developments are likely to increase the importance of money over elections and policy in coming years. First, as we saw in Chapter 1, the Roberts Supreme Court has eliminated many of the limits on the use of money in elections. Its move to free corporate money and eliminate aggregate contribution limits will likely be followed by reversal of the ban on parties collecting soft money and perhaps even the end of individual contribution limits to candidates.

The Court's rulings also spawned the rise of Super PACs and broke a psychological barrier that had limited how much individuals were willing to spend or contribute to campaigns. In the 2012 elections, a single couple, the Adelsons, spent an unprecedented $98 million or more on federal elections, more than most of country's voters combined will spend on all elections in their entire lifetimes. This record is likely to be broken in 2016 with the Koch brothers' promise that their network will spend nearly nine times that amount ($889 million).

The second key development is the rise of economic inequality. As those at the very top of the income stream continue to amass much more wealth than everyone else—and this inequality becomes an increasingly urgent political issue—the very wealthy are more likely to use their power in the political arena to protect their economic power. The popularity of Thomas Piketty's book on economic inequality demonstrates how the issue has become salient to the general public—even if most readers gave up on his rather dense book after just a few pages.[12]

All the talk of economic inequality has led to a backlash against "class warfare." Tom Perkins, an American multibillionaire, complained in the *Wall Street Journal* in 2014 that progressives are waging "war" on the wealthiest Americans, saying the rich are persecuted like "Jews in Nazi Germany." He subsequently apologized for using the word "Kristallnacht" in his diatribe, but as *The Independent* of London reported, "Perkins was unrepentant about the broader comparison, claiming that the richest one per cent of Americans are being 'demonised' just like Jews were under Nazism."[13] Claims like these suggest a siege mentality among some of the extremely wealthy, which could lead to efforts to secure greater political power to prevent any redistribution of wealth.

Indeed, as federal appeals court judge Guido Calabresi recently observed, the rise of political spending by the super wealthy opened up by the Supreme Court risks a political backlash: "To the extent that campaign contributions cannot be regulated so as to leave them free to reflect intensity of feeling, the pressure for greater economic equality will increase, and this may be detrimental to those efficiencies that flow from an unequal distribution of wealth. Put another way, if campaign finance doctrine fails to recognize the value of a level playing field in the political realm, there may arise stronger pressures to create a more level playing field in the economy as a whole."[14]

These two developments bring the reality of the role of money in U.S. politics closer to my imaginary lotteries. Money and wealth already matter in elections and policy; in the future they are likely to matter much more.

☑

The fundamental problem with the poll tax the Supreme Court struck down in *Harper* and the grossly malapportioned districts struck down in *Reynolds* is that people were not being treated as political equals having a right to equal political power. The (admittedly partially developed) political theory behind these rulings recognizes that, given that we have fundamental disagreements over the meaning of the public interest, the best we can do is to define the public interest procedurally, by ensuring that every voter has a roughly equal chance to influence policies and elections.[15]

This political theory endorses a particular form of equality, which I call an *equality of inputs*. By "equality of inputs," I mean a system in which each voter has roughly equal political power in the electoral or policymaking process. By eliminating the poll tax, the Supreme Court expanded the group of people entitled to exercise political power at the voting booth: it now included poorer voters. By requiring rough equality in the population of legislative districts, the Supreme Court ensured that voters who live in the cities had roughly the same influence over the choice of members of Congress and state representatives as voters living in rural areas and suburbs.

In the campaign finance area too, the Supreme Court until *Citizens United* supported the equality of inputs rationale to limit for-profit corporate spending on candidate elections. As we saw in Chapter 1, the Court first put forward an "antidistortion" argument in the *Massachusetts Citizens for Life* (or *MCFL*) case in 1986, endorsed it in the *Austin* case in 1990, reaffirmed it in the *McConnell* case in 2003 upholding the key provisions of the McCain-Feingold law, and then ultimately rejected it in *Citizens United*.

This antidistortion argument, though misdescribed in *Austin* as a concern about a "different type of corruption," is at bottom an equality of inputs argument. The Court sought to prevent the "corrosive and distorting effects of immense aggregations of wealth that are accumulated with the help of the corporate form and that have little or no correlation to the public's support for the corporation's political ideas."[16]

The *Austin* Court's problem with corporate political spending was that such spending is not calibrated with or proportional to public support. In the earlier *MCFL* case the Court explained that spending on elections could serve as a "rough barometer" of public support for candidates and issues, and that corporate spending can upset this barometer. Its concern with public support, barometers, and proportionality in *MCFL* and *Austin* reflects the same concern with equality of inputs as the Court expressed in the *Harper* and *Reynolds* cases.[17]

But *Austin* did not fully embrace this argument. As Justice Scalia noted in his dissent, spending by a billionaire on campaigns seems to be equally objectionable under the majority's theory because such spending will have little or no correlation to the public's support for the billionaire's ideas. Scalia's intent, of course, was to refute the equality argument, not to argue for its extension to billionaires, but he was right to note the inconsistency in the treatment of corporate wealth compared to other wealth. His position prevailed in *Citizens United*, which rejected *Austin*'s antidistortion argument for corporate spending limits as precluded by the First Amendment.

☑

Equality of inputs is just one of many potential measures of equality. The political scientist Douglas Rae has catalogued dozens of different political equality arguments, each of which would have different implications for designing campaign rules.[18]

Consider two alternative measures that have special relevance to campaign finance. First, one could design a campaign finance system to favor *equality of outputs* instead of inputs, insuring that all candidates (or all major party candidates or all parties) receive equal funding. Second, one could design a campaign finance system to favor *equality of political opportunity* to ensure that all voters have at least minimal means of participating in the campaign funding process. Although some current laws reflect these measures of equality, they are inferior to the equality of inputs measure.

Some methods of public campaign financing, such as the voluntary presidential public financing system during the general election, follow an equality of outputs rationale: both Democratic and Republican candidates, if they opt into the system, receive the same public financing grant from the government and agree not to raise any funds for their campaigns. (That system is now basically defunct, because candidates can—and, partly because of outside spending, must—raise much more than the limits allow.)[19]

Similarly, UCLA professor Dan Lowenstein's proposal to provide major political parties with equal campaign funds to dole out to party-backed candidates may also be justified under the equality of outputs concept. Candidate spending limits also could promote equality of outputs: they could allow candidates to accept up to a set amount from whomever they want, but allow no contributions above that amount. So long as we expect most (serious) candidates to reach the spending limit, and so long as we put aside potentially unequal outside spending, such spending limits assure an equality of outputs. But with today's explosion in outside spending, candidate spending limits alone would not do much to assure equality of outputs.[20]

The equality of outputs rationale does not seek to ensure that campaign money reflects the candidates' support among voters. Instead, it assumes voters are equally divided between the major parties or candidates and gives each candidate a chance to duke it out with equal resources. The assumption of an equal party divide might make sense for the presidential public financing system, where we have seen close contests for president over the past few decades. But it does not reflect reality in many noncompetitive congressional districts, for Senate campaigns in some states, or for many state and local offices. As political theorist Charles Beitz puts it, "equality for candidates would follow only on the hypothesis that opposing candidates were likely to be supported by roughly equal portions of the electorate, and there is no reason to believe this in the general case."[21]

Equality of outputs then is inconsistent with equality of voter inputs. Under an equality of outputs model, one candidate with a great deal of voter support receives the same funding as a candidate with very little support. Equality of outputs is also inconsistent with the commitment to equal voting power in the one person, one vote cases such as *Reynolds,* and more consistent with the idea, expressed by Justice Stewart in his *Reynolds* dissent, for allowing the state to decide on representation of areas based on common interests. These cases are both premised on equal *voter* power, not equal *candidate* or *party* power.

For these reasons, equality of outputs is not as compelling a model for promoting political equality as equality of inputs. After noting the argument that an equality of outputs plan might promote candidate competitiveness, Professor Beitz points out that it is unclear how competitiveness and equality are related: "Equality for candidates requires a different kind of argument, but no such argument presents itself that could plausibly be described as deriving from a conception of political equality."[22]

The second alternative to equality of inputs is *equality of political oppor-*

tunity. Here, voters each get some baseline influence without upper limits on how much they or others can spend. This approach is sometimes called "floors without ceilings." It is a call to level up without any leveling down.[23]

For example, the voluntary public financing system for presidential primaries, also largely defunct, provides matching funds for up to the first $250 that each presidential candidate raises from an individual. But individuals may give up to $2,600 to candidates, and parties and outside groups such as Super PACs can raise and spend as much as they like supporting a candidate. But while this primary system nods in the direction of equality of political opportunity, it does not fully embrace it because many voters do not have the $250 to give to any candidate. A program that gave a grant to each voter of $250 to spend on presidential campaigns would be closer to the equality of political opportunity ideal.

Equality of political opportunity is similar to equality of inputs in that it gives each voter *some baseline amount* of political funding power. But the two approaches are not the same. Assuring that every voter can contribute $250 while allowing those who can to contribute $100 million or more preserves equality of political opportunity but fails miserably under the equality of inputs measure. In the current era of unlimited contributions to Super PACs and other outside groups, equality of political opportunity would provide no meaningful level of political equality.

Equality of inputs is thus more desirable than equality of outputs or equality of political opportunity as a basis for designing a campaign finance system. A key follow-up question, which I address in the next chapter, is whether it is fair to equate equality of inputs with equality of *campaign money* rather than, as Professor Beitz suggests, a broader measure of *campaign resources.*[24]

Political and legal theorists who have addressed the issue focus on equality of campaign money. The political philosopher John Rawls, after citing the Supreme Court's one person, one vote cases, said when it rejects political equality as a compelling interest, the Supreme Court "fails to recognize the essential point that the fair value of the political liberties is required for a just political procedure, and that to insure their fair value it is necessary to prevent those with greater property and wealth, and the greater skills of organization which accompany them, from controlling the electoral process to their advantage."[25]

The legal theorist Cass Sunstein, who likewise thinks the Supreme Court was wrong to reject political equality as a rationale for campaign finance laws, frames his objection in these terms: "The goal of political equality is time-honored in the American constitutional tradition, as the goal of economic equality is not. Efforts to redress economic inequalities, or to ensure that they are not turned into political inequalities, should not be seen as impermissible redistribution, or as the introduction of government regulation into a place where it did not exist before. A system of unlimited campaign expenditures should be seen as a regulatory decision to allow disparities in resources to be turned into disparities in political influence."[26]

Judge Calabresi makes two related equality arguments for campaign limits, both of which are consistent with an equality of inputs argument. First, "if an external factor, such as wealth, allows some individuals to communicate their political views too powerfully, then persons who lack wealth may, for all intents and purposes, be excluded from the democratic dialogue. . . . Without restrictions on the size of campaign contributions, the wealthy could flood the campaign coffers of their preferred political candidates, rendering all other contributions negligible by comparison." Second, unlimited campaign money interferes with the ability of individuals to express their intensity of preference in campaigns. "The wider the economic disparities in a democratic society, the more difficult it becomes to convey, with financial donations, the intensity of one's political beliefs. People who care a little will, if they are rich, still give a lot. People who care a lot must, if they are poor, give only a little. . . . Today, the amount of an individual's campaign contribution reflects the strength of that individual's preferences far less than it does the size of his wallet. In this sense, all political donations—by rich and poor alike—lose a crucially important aspect of their communicative value when campaign funds are unrestricted."[27]

Finally, Justice Stephen Breyer has embraced what appears to be an equality of inputs rationale for campaign finance limits. Breyer explained in his concurring opinion in the Supreme Court case *Nixon v. Shrink Missouri Government PAC* in 2000 that *Buckley*'s rejection of equality rationale as being "wholly foreign to the First Amendment" "cannot be taken literally." He wrote that "restrictions upon the amount any one individual can contribute to a particular candidate seek to protect the integrity of the electoral process—the means through which a free society democratically translates political speech into concrete governmental action. Moreover, by limiting the size of the largest contributions, such restrictions aim to democratize the influence that money itself may bring to bear upon the electoral process. In doing so, they seek to build public confidence in that process and broaden the base of a candidate's meaningful financial support, encouraging the public participation and open discussion that the First Amendment itself presupposes."[28]

Breyer took a similar line in his book *Active Liberty*, in 2005, that "the upshot is a concern, reflected in campaign finance laws, that the few who give in large amounts may have special access to, and therefore influence over, their elected representatives or, at least create the appearance of undue influence."[29]

In both his *Shrink Missouri* concurrence and his book, Justice Breyer tempered his support for campaign finance laws by noting the potential costs to the competitiveness of campaigns and the dangers that such laws might help incumbents, issues I return to in Part III. But there was no question of his defense of equality arguments for limiting campaign money.

But if he was clear in 2000 and 2005 in his support for political equality to justify carefully constructed campaign finance laws, Breyer muddled his message considerably in *McCutcheon v. Federal Election Commission*.

As I mentioned in Chapter 1, *McCutcheon* considered the constitutionality of federal "aggregate" contribution limits, which restricted the total amount a person could contribute during a two-year period to all federal candidates, party committees, and PACs. A 5–4 majority rejected the aggregate limits as unjustified by the government's interest in preventing corruption, describing this interest and the related appearance-of-corruption interest in very narrow terms akin to bribery. Breyer wrote the dissenting opinion. But rather than raise equality concerns as he had in the past, he couched his objections in anticorruption terms.

> Accordingly, the First Amendment advances not only the individual's right to engage in political speech, but also the public's interest in preserving a democratic order in which collective speech *matters*.
>
> What has this to do with corruption? It has everything to do with corruption. Corruption breaks the constitutionally necessary "chain of communi-

cation" between the people and their representatives. It derails the essential speech-to-government-action tie. Where enough money calls the tune, the general public will not be heard. Insofar as corruption cuts the link between political thought and political action, a free marketplace of political ideas loses its point. That is one reason why the Court has stressed the constitutional importance of Congress' concern that a few large donations not drown out the voices of the many. See, *e.g.*, Buckley.[30]

The passage is odd in many ways. First, Breyer does not explain what he means by "collective speech" or why such speech "preserv[es] the democratic order." The concern with collective speech appears not to be an argument about corruption (despite his claim that it has "everything to do with corruption"), and to the extent that the concern suggests some kind of political equality issue, the point is undeveloped. Whose collective speech is at issue and how do aggregate limits affect such speech? The term "collective speech" does not appear in his *Shrink Missouri* concurring opinion or in *Active Liberty,* nor in any other of his writings I could find.

Further, at the end of this passage Breyer mysteriously says, citing *Buckley,* that "the Court has stressed the constitutional importance of Congress' concern that a few large donations not drown out the voices of the many." Yet the Court has not done so; quite the contrary. In the part of *Buckley* that Breyer cited in *McCutcheon,* the Court noted that the government indeed had defended contribution limits in the 1974 federal campaign finance law on equality grounds—"the limits serve to mute the voices of affluent persons and groups in the election process and thereby to equalize the relative ability of all citizens to affect the outcome of elections"—but it then declined to decide whether this interest was strong enough in relation to the constitutional challenge to candidate contribution limits, holding contribution limits justified on anticorruption grounds. Later in *Buckley,* the Court rejected this same equality interest as "wholly foreign to the First Amendment."[31]

Nowhere in *Buckley* did the Court "stress the constitutional importance" of preventing the voice of the wealthy drowning out the voice of the many. It did the opposite. That rationale got packaged up as "a different type of corruption" in *Austin,* but those who have studied *Austin* closely view it as an equality argument. Justice Marshall's clerk who worked on the *Austin* case eventually admitted that the case put forward an equality argument dressed in anticorruption clothing, and the Supreme Court recognized and rejected *Austin* as an equality argument in *Citizens United*. The Court has now rejected this equality interest several times as inconsistent with the First Amendment.[32]

Why does Breyer so mangle things in his explanation of the interests at stake in *McCutcheon*? For the same reason, I believe, that he also latched on to Robert Post's arguments about "electoral integrity" and public confidence supporting campaign limits: in the forty years since *Buckley* the Court has always framed the campaign finance debate as about "corruption" or the "appearance of corruption" and never about political equality. Breyer was trying to rebut the *McCutcheon* majority on its own terms. With the Supreme Court having narrowed the definition of corruption to something close to bribery and the appearance of corruption to something close to an appearance of bribery, Breyer appears to be fighting back by trying to recast his equality arguments as anticorruption arguments.

This lack of clarity is not surprising. Major legal scholars such as Post seem to be looking for ways to reverse *Citizens United* without overtly relying on equality interests and without overturning longstanding First Amendment doctrine.

Consider the arguments for campaign finance reform offered by Larry Lessig. Like Post, Lessig has one of the sharpest constitutional minds in the country. Like Post, he has offered what he claims is a novel constitutional theory to justify campaign finance limits: "dependence corruption." And like Post, Lessig appears to have repackaged an old interest under a new label.[33]

The problem with our current political system, as Lessig describes it, is that elected officials are dependent on the funders in the money primary rather than "dependent on the people alone," a phrase he borrows (rather inaptly) from the *Federalist*. He sees elections as a two-stage event—a money primary and then a general election—and believes the wealthy have too much influence over who is elected. He has even compared this two-stage election to the old white primary in the South. Dependence corruption is a classic equality of inputs argument, even if until recently Lessig denied it.[34]

The term "corruption," like the term "integrity," has such allure because it is not only pejorative but malleable. At one extreme—the extreme chosen by the Supreme Court in *McCutcheon*—corruption occurs only when a politician exchanges a political favor for a personal benefit, as in a bribe. At the other extreme, it includes anything that deviates from or distorts a pure system. It is this broader reading of corruption that allowed the Court in *Austin* to describe its equality concern as a "different kind of corruption."

Neither definition of corruption is more correct than the other. As Professor Deborah Hellman of Virginia and Professor Yasmin Dawood of Toronto demonstrate, broad anticorruption arguments meld into concerns about political equality. Professor Zephyr Teachout's recent book, *Corruption in America*, illustrates the point. We can call both personal graft and the unequal effect of money on elections and policy "corruption," but we have then made the meaning of the word so broad that it becomes imprecise and essentially contested as a judicial construct.[35]

Is it corruption, for instance, when political parties or candidates auction off political access to the highest bidder or best fundraiser? The soft money system that existed before McCain-Feingold (and which the Roberts court could bring back) was one form of this auction; the current treatment of presidential campaign finance "bundlers" is another. A candidate or party promises access, but not results, to whoever brings the most cash.

Under the definitions put forward by Hellman and Dawood, we might call such a system corrupt. Teachout in her book suggests we should. But the Supreme Court in *Citizens United,* and even more emphatically in *McCutcheon,* rejected the idea that the sale of access is corruption. Politicians granting access to big donors, the Court opined, is an example of appropriate candidate "responsiveness" to contributors. As Chief Justice Roberts put it in *McCutcheon:*

> We have said that government regulation may not target the general gratitude a candidate may feel toward those who support him or his allies, or the political access such support may afford. "Ingratiation and access . . . are not corruption." *Citizens United.* They embody a central feature of democracy—that constituents support candidates who share their beliefs and interests, and candidates who are elected can be expected to be responsive to those concerns.[36]

These constituents include wealthy outside donors and artificial entities who have no right to vote in the candidate's jurisdiction but who nonetheless give money to the candidate and to supportive outside groups. Roberts begins his *McCutcheon* opinion by including these big donor "constituents" in an ode to democracy: "There is no right more basic in our democracy than the right to participate in electing our political leaders."

The sale of access to the highest bidder cannot be "corrupt" to a Court that celebrates it as a paradigm of democracy. More interestingly, the sale of access might not always be "corrupt" even under broader definitions of corruption. Consider a puzzle that confounded Professors Bruce Cain, Daniel Lowenstein, and David Strauss two decades ago: if we gave all voters equal amounts of dollars to use on political campaigns, and politicians then sold access or promised to do whatever the voters supporting them with their dollars wanted, would we consider such a system corrupt? Or does this "responsiveness" lose its corrupt nature because every voter has equal political power? The professors could not agree on the answer, and given the varying definitions of corruption, there will be no consensus on this question. Teachout, for her part, suggests that even a voucher-based system of political equality might be corrupt if politicians sold access to those who collect voucher dollars.[37]

The constitutionality of campaign finance laws should not turn on whether we can fit an argument about influence into the anticorruption box. It is cleaner to stop shoehorning equality concerns into broad definitions of corruption and to defend political equality as an interest in its own right. It also avoids unfairly tarring members of Congress and other elected officials with the label of being "corrupt." Equality but not corruption recognizes the problems with large independent spending where there is no contact or even understanding between spender and elected official. A focus on equality allows us to ignore questions such as whether an eight-figure spender expects something in return for her spending. Whether or not she does, this is not the central problem with such an obscenely large amount.

Limits on large contributions going directly to candidates are fully justified under even the narrowest definitions of corruption. But as the Supreme Court continues to define corruption narrowly, fewer and fewer campaign finance laws will satisfy it. Advocates and scholars have made no judicial headway by arguing for expansive definitions of corruption. It is time to move beyond the semantic battle and to defend political equality head-on.

That defense begins (but does not end) by recognizing political equality, and especially equality of inputs, as a compelling justification for campaign finance laws. The people and its government have a vital interest in preventing disparities in economic power from being further transformed into disparities in political power. We need to stop this transformation especially in our age of rising inequality and when the Roberts court insists on blowing up most of the limits on political money. Otherwise American elections and policy battles are no better than lotteries in which the rich get to purchase many extra tickets and most voters will consistently lose.

4

Level Up, Level Down

IN *ARIZONA FREE ENTERPRISE CLUB'S FREEDOM CLUB PAC V. BENNETT*, Chief Justice John Roberts thought he had found the constitutional smoking gun that doomed a key aspect of Arizona's public financing law. But his analysis said more about his own disturbing view of democracy than about whether the law should survive judicial review.[1]

In 1998, Arizona voters passed a "Clean Money" voluntary public financing plan for state offices. Candidates who collected a small number of $5 contributions and signatures could opt into the program. In exchange for agreeing to spending limits, engaging in at least one debate, and a few other conditions, participating candidates got a grant of public money to run their campaigns. Further, to make the program attractive and viable, the state provided that participating candidates could get additional money (up to double the amount of the original grant) if they faced either a big outside spending campaign against them or an opponent spending large amounts of her own personal funds on the race. It was these extra matching funds that opponents challenged as a First Amendment violation.[2]

The First Amendment claim was odd. The extra matching did not stop anyone from speaking or from spending money to support any candidates. It was not a spending limit. When the case came before the United States Court of Appeals for the Ninth Circuit, Judge Andrew Kleinfeld, one of the most conservative judges on that court, rejected the First Amendment claim out of hand. "That is not a restriction on speech. Intelligent, ambitious people seeking political office, or any other goal, are likely to study the rules and develop strategies taking maximum advantage of the rules. The kinds of strategic choices generated by the Arizona rules do not differ in kind from the choices presented to candidates by other election laws. For example, candidates will run their campaigns differently according to whether there is a fixed election day or an extended period for mail-in ballots, at large elections of multiple candidates in one district or single winner elections in multiple smaller districts, or partisan or nonpartisan elections. That different laws generate different strategies does not make them restrictions on speech."[3]

But a five-justice Supreme Court majority (the same five who were in the majority in *Citizens United* and *McCutcheon*) believed that candidates and outside groups faced a penalty under the law. "Once a privately financed candidate has raised or spent more than the State's initial grant to a publicly financed candidate, each personal dollar spent by the privately financed candidate results in an award of almost one additional dollar to his opponent. That plainly forces the privately financed candidate to shoulder a special and potentially significant burden when choosing to exercise his First Amendment right to spend funds on behalf of his candidacy."[4]

Recognizing that a law raises First Amendment concerns is only the first step in deciding whether or not it is unconstitutional. As we saw in Chapter 1, courts next determine whether a law imposes a large burden on protected First Amendment rights, in which case they apply the "strict scrutiny" standard against the government, or whether it imposes a lesser burden, in which case "exacting scrutiny" or another lower standard may apply. Having determined the weight of the thumb on the scale, the court then balances government interest against these infringements on First Amendment rights.

In *Arizona*, the Supreme Court decided that the law imposed a big enough burden on speech that it was subject to strict scrutiny, the first time it had ever subjected a public financing law to that very tough standard. It then unsurprisingly held that the law failed under that level of scrutiny.

The smoking gun Chief Justice Roberts thought he found was evidence on the Arizona elections commission website that the Arizona law had been passed to further political equality, a forbidden government interest.

At oral argument in the case Roberts remarked: "Well, I checked the Citizens' Clean Elections commission website this morning and it says that this act was passed to, quote, 'level the playing field' when it comes to running for office. Why isn't that clear evidence that it's unconstitutional?"[5]

In the *Arizona* opinion he eventually drafted, Roberts wrote: "Prior to oral argument in this case, the Citizens Clean Elections Commission's Web site stated that 'The Citizens Clean Elections Act was passed by the people of Arizona in 1998 to level the playing field when it comes to running for office.' The Web site now says that 'The Citizens Clean Elections Act was passed by the people of Arizona in 1998 to restore citizen participation and confidence in our political system.'"[6]

Justice Elena Kagan, in a dissent dripping with sarcasm, minimized the relevance of the website statement. "The majority makes a much stranger claim: that a statement appearing on a government website in 2011 (written by who-knows-whom?) reveals what hundreds of thousands of Arizona's voters sought to do in 1998 when they enacted the Clean Elections Act by referendum. Just to state that proposition is to know it is wrong." More broadly, she rejected all of the evidence the *Arizona* majority offered to show the voters' intent: "The majority claims to have found three smoking guns that reveal the State's true (and nefarious) intention to level the playing field. But the only smoke here is the majority's, and it is the kind that goes with mirrors."[7]

Justice Kagan argued that the law did not infringe the challengers' rights at all, that it was justified as an anticorruption measure to make candidates less beholden to private contributors, and that even if equality was *one* of the reasons for passing the law, the law was still constitutional if it was also justified on anticorruption grounds: "This Court, after all, has never said that a law restricting speech (or any other constitutional right) demands two compelling interests. One is enough. And this statute has one: preventing corruption. So it does not matter that equalizing campaign speech is an insufficient interest. . . . That proposition disposes of this case, even if Arizona had an adjunct interest here in equalizing electoral opportunities. No special rule of automatic invalidation applies to statutes having some connection to equality; like any other laws, they pass muster when supported by an important enough government interest. Here, Arizona has demonstrated in detail how the matching funds provision is necessary to serve a compelling interest in combating corruption. So the hunt for evidence of 'leveling' is a waste of time; Arizona's law survives constitutional scrutiny no matter what that search would uncover."[8]

Justice Kagan made many arguments in *Arizona,* but she notably did not argue that equality or "leveling the playing field" could serve as the sole interest to justify Arizona's extra matching provision. This omission was disappointing but not surprising. To begin with, the Court had already rejected the equality interest in *Buckley, Citizens United,* and other cases: why bother defending equality? Further, Kagan had no appetite to defend the antidistortion version of *Austin* as solicitor general, and she was seeking to preserve what she could of the requirement that corporations pay for their election activity with funds from a political action committee. As a law professor, Kagan had written an article casting serious doubt on *Austin* antidistortion theory, warning that politicians could hide behind the rationale to pass laws intended to benefit incumbents.[9]

But Kagan gave up the equality argument too easily. There was a big difference between the equality argument at issue in the *Arizona* case and the one at issue in *Buckley* and *Citizens United,* and it should have led to a different result in the *Arizona* case. The equality arguments in *Buckley* and *Citizens United* involved "leveling down": equalizing the ability to influence elections or policy by putting a ceiling on how much an individual or entity could spend. But in *Arizona,* the people's interest in leveling the playing field was accomplished by "leveling up": giving money to bring the amount spent by one side closer to large spending on the other side.

Recall the reasoning the Supreme Court used in *Buckley* to reject the equality rationale for spending limits:

> The concept that government may restrict the speech of some elements of our society in order to enhance the relative voice of others is wholly foreign to the First Amendment which was designed to secure the widest possible dissemination of information from diverse and antagonistic sources, and to assure unfettered interchange of ideas for the bringing about of political and social changes desired by the people.[10]

The extra matching funds at issue in *Arizona* did not "restrict the speech" of anyone: instead, they *added* to the amount of campaign spending and

speech. The big spenders challenging the Arizona law were not just asking for a right to speak; they were asking for a right to speak without a
response. Further, the extra matching funds provision seemed, to use *Buckley*'s terms, "designed to secure the widest possible dissemination of information from diverse and antagonistic sources, and to assure unfettered
interchange of ideas for the bringing about of political and social changes
desired by the people."

There was little evidence to support the challengers' assertion that the
extra matching funds deterred outside spenders and candidates from spending money. As Justice Kagan noted, outside spending had risen 243 percent
since the law was passed. Further, she argued, all campaign finance rules, including those the Court had repeatedly upheld as constitutional, could have
such an effect. And Arizona's public financing plan could not have been
intended to protect incumbents from political competition: the measure
was passed by voters via Arizona's initiative process, not by the legislature,
which in fact has been trying to hobble the measure for years.[11]

For a Supreme Court that favors as much campaign spending as possible
to promote rigorous debate, the extra matching funds that Arizona made
available should have been viewed as a win for First Amendment values.
Instead, the Court shut down one of the few tools that reformers favoring
public financing had available. Without that extra funding, it would be too
risky for candidates to enter competitive races in which they could be mas-
sively outspent by nonparticipating opponents or outside groups. It is hard
not to see the Court's ruling as intended to shut down a viable path for
public financing of elections.

More generally, the Court's analysis in *Arizona* failed to recognize that
campaign finance laws that promote equality by "leveling up" should survive First Amendment challenges under the *Buckley* rationale, because
these laws increase the amount of campaign speech and spending, and do
not restrict the speech of anyone.

Consider, for instance, New York City's public funding law and legislation proposed by Representative John Sarbanes for federal elections, both
of which provide extra matching funds for small donations. These measures promote equality of inputs by multiplying the effect of small donations. Making a $100 contribution from an individual worth $400 or $600

to a campaign through extra matching funds is a great way to amplify the voice of those who have relatively little to give to campaigns. It does not stop anyone else from spending as much as they want.[12]

Under the reasoning of *Arizona*, however, it is not clear that extra matches for small donations would survive constitutional review. These multiple matches, whatever their effect in preventing corruption, arguably serve the purpose of leveling the playing field by making candidates less dependent upon large contributions. But if a state already has contribution limits in place for nonparticipating candidates, a court could hold that multiple matches for small contributions do not serve a serious anticorruption purpose. As the chief justice explained in *McCutcheon*, contribution limits are already "prophylactic" in that most contributions do not lead to corruption (as the Supreme Court majority narrowly defines it). Contribution limits would make the multiple-match public financing unnecessary to prevent corruption, and leave only the vulnerable equality interest to balance against any First Amendment infringements.[13]

Or consider other, more ambitious level-up proposals. Since the 1960s, reformers have suggested funding elections by providing all voters with campaign finance vouchers. I proposed such a system in the 1990s, Professor Bruce Ackerman of Yale has long championed them, and Professor Lessig now advocates them too.[14]

Vouchers level up by giving each voter some amount of money (say $100) to be used in federal elections. In my plan, voters could give voucher money to candidates, to political parties, or to outside groups, which could in turn use it for campaign advertising and other activities. Entrepreneurs would arise to collect voucher dollars, and public support for candidates, parties, and groups should more closely match the support for such groups in society as a whole. (Of course, antifraud measures would be needed to ensure that entrepreneurs and others do not take the money for personal uses, as seems to happen these days with some super PACs and other outside groups.)[15]

Vouchers are a nice way to implement the kind of barometer equality or equality of inputs idea that the Supreme Court praised in *Austin* and *MCFL*. Placing public financing directly in the hands of voters should increase the robustness of political speech in campaigns by giving more people a chance to participate and to direct money to the campaigns they favor. Voucher systems are better at leveling up than multiple matching fund programs are because vouchers reach the millions of voters who cannot spare even $100 to use on political campaigns. They also allow parties, candidates, and interest groups to compete in providing the best results for voters.

Yale professor Heather Gerken and Alex Tausanovitch have also proposed using publicly funded advocates to deal with disparities in lobbying ability. As we saw in Chapter 2, lobbying skews heavily toward the wealthy, business interests, and the best organized. Gerken and Tausanovitch explain: "The crux of our proposal is to provide legislators with 'policy research consultants' who could help them develop and pass legislation without depending on the assistance of private lobbyists." They propose to do on the policy side what multiple matches for small donations or campaign finance vouchers could do on the election side: level up through government subsidies for political activity.[16]

These types of measures—multiple matching funds for small donations, campaign finance vouchers, and lobbying subsidies to help lobbying in the public interest—would level the playing field without squelching or limiting any political speech or any spending. Further, unlike the law at issue in *Arizona*, none of these programs are tied to the spending of others, meaning no one is "penalized" for someone else's campaign- or policy-related activity. Even if the extra matching funds in *Arizona* deterred wealthy persons' speech (a weak argument to be sure), one cannot make that claim against these other measures. The worst one can say is that taxpayer money would go to fund speech a taxpayer may not like—an everyday occurrence when you consider all of the speech the federal government directly or indirectly funds.

Still, each of these level-up measures could be motivated by a desire to "level the playing field" separate from any possible anticorruption purpose. Certainly one of the chief benefits of my voucher proposal is that it gives each voter not only a vote but also a significant amount of money to use in campaigns.

This egalitarian purpose should not lead courts to hold such measures unconstitutional. To the contrary, courts should recognize political equality, especially equality of inputs, as a compelling interest that can justify campaign finance laws if the First Amendment costs are not too great. Level-up laws are constitutional because they carry virtually no First Amendment costs associated with them: they *increase,* rather than *decrease,* the amount of money spent on political campaigns. These measures do not censor anyone, privilege the media, or protect incumbents—the three charges often raised against campaign finance limits.

In sum, once one accepts that political equality is a societal interest that is a legitimate—indeed compelling—concern for the public or the government to pursue, campaign finance and lobbying rules that have a leveling-up effect and do not restrict anyone's speech should easily succeed in court if challenged as a violation of someone's First Amendment rights. The motive to level the playing field is neither "nefarious" nor "clear evidence that [a law] is unconstitutional." It is a worthwhile goal if the First Amendment costs are not too high—and when it comes to leveling up, they never are.

Not all level-up measures are a good idea. Some claim that empowering small donors leads to more polarized campaigns and legislatures, for example, because small donors tend to be the most ideological and to support highly ideological candidates. That is not a constitutional objection, but it is an important policy objection that I consider in Chapter 7.

Further, even those who accept the goal of political equality might reject equal subsidies to voters as a means of achieving political equality. Professor Beitz, for example, argues that it may be more appropriate to equalize all resources in campaigns rather than simply to equalize money. Opponents of limits such as Professor Smith argue that equalizing money in elections simply makes other attributes, such as celebrity, more important. Smith gives the example of a small-business owner who does not have the charisma of a celebrity but wants to influence elections with the only tool he has: money.[17]

Given these objections, advocates of level-up plans that equalize political money must demonstrate that "money is different" from other attributes, as NYU professor Burt Neuborne has put it. There are two reasons to believe this is so, and that one can justify taking modest steps to equalize campaign money but not other campaign resources.[18]

First, most other campaign resources are either randomly distributed or are themselves good proxies for equal popular support. Beitz mentions incumbency as an example of a highly beneficial campaign resource, and Smith gives the example of celebrity. Both attributes tend to be randomly distributed. Once elected, Democrats and Republicans, conservatives and liberals, each have the advantage of incumbency. Any attempt to randomly distribute the benefits of incumbency would approximate what already exists in the world.

The same is true of celebrity. Even if Hollywood stars tend to be liberals, when we think about who counts as a "celebrity" the list includes people of every political stripe: former professional athletes like Jim Bunning and Steve Largent, radio and television commentators like Sean Hannity and Ann Coulter, and academics like Elizabeth Warren. A little Googling reveals that Kim Kardashian is a Democrat who also expressed support for the social conservative Rick Santorum for president. We cannot of course randomly distribute celebrity, but we can be confident that for everyone listening to Oprah or Jon Stewart there is someone else listening to Rush Limbaugh or Chuck Norris. Whether we should be taking our political cues from Kim Kardashian is another question entirely.[19]

Other campaign resources are good proxies for public support. Think of a church leader or a union boss, whose endorsements and calls for campaigning go heeded by the faithful. These people have clout precisely because they have followers: their power, unlike the spending of a wealthy individual or corporation, is a rough barometer of popular support. Far from seeking to minimize such leaders' importance in order to assure political equality, we should celebrate them. In a system in which political power is divided among equals, the National Rifle Association's ability to motivate voters through its scoring of congressional votes is not something to be condemned, but celebrated. Campaign reformers who want to shut down the NRA because they think it has too much power need to consider that the NRA is powerful largely because millions of people support its agenda. That some of its power derives from large contributions from gun manufacturers raises more troubling questions.[20]

Perhaps the largest source of influence outside of candidates, parties, and campaigns is the news media. Some critics argue that the media, which are generally exempt from campaign finance restrictions, would have great and unjustified power in a system with otherwise strict limits. This is an important argument, and I devote all of Chapter 6 to the media's role in a campaign finance system.

As Professor Neuborne notes, money's other great advantage compared with other campaign resources is its fungibility—unlike celebrity or incumbency, it can actually be parceled out among candidates—who can use it to buy anything that is for sale. Money is uniquely capable of being transformed into what a campaign needs most: advertising, outreach, staffers, and more. Aside from candidate quality and incumbency, both of which are randomly distributed, nothing comes close for a campaign to the benefits of money, even if it usually cannot turn a candidate lacking quality into a winner. There is great truth to the nineteenth-century political strategist Mark Hanna's old adage: "There are two things that are important in politics. The first is money, and I can't remember the second."[21]

In short, the best way to level up is to do more to equalize campaign money across voters. It would be impossible to equalize all campaign resources, which cannot be equally distributed and are not restricted to any particular class of candidates or interests, or to any political party. Random distribution of non-monetary attributes, such as celebrity, works to promote a vibrant pluralist system. It is only money that is fungible, and it can overwhelm other, randomly distributed attributes. Leveling up with money is a practical and fair way to achieve greater political equality.[22]

No state or federal government is required to level up as a matter of constitutional law. But when government chooses to do so, the Supreme Court should stand out of the way. Proof of a leveling purpose is less a smoking gun than a sign of genuine public concern about vast inequalities of wealth being transformed into vast inequalities of political power.

✔

Leveling up is the easy constitutional case—or at least it would be easy if not for the Supreme Court's allergic reaction to anything meant to level the playing field.

Leveling down is harder, and I devote not just the rest of this chapter, but also the next three chapters, to arguing for the constitutionality and desirability of reasonable campaign finance limits in order to promote political equality. I propose (to keep things concrete) the following limitation on campaign contributions and spending in federal elections, coupled with either a voucher program, a multiple small match program, or another level-up program.

> An individual or entity may contribute, spend from one's own personal or general treasury funds, or both, no more than $25,000 in each federal election on election-related express advocacy or electioneering communications supporting or opposing candidates for that election. Such limits shall not apply to the press, to political committees that solely spend contributions received from others, or to money contributed or spent in a voluntary government-created public finance program. An individual also cannot contribute and/or spend more than $500,000 total on all federal election activity in a two-year election cycle.

This brief formula leaves a lot of unanswered questions: Why $25,000? Why a $500,000 aggregate limit? What is "express advocacy or electioneering communications relative to a clearly identified candidate for federal office"? Who counts as "the press," especially in this era of new media and social media? Why exempt "the press" at all? What about the potential that individuals would create new "entities" to evade these limits?[23]

I will answer all of these questions, but I do not want to start with the details, partly because I am not wedded to some of them (such as the $25,000 figure), and partly because they distract from the larger question of desirability and constitutionality of limits. Instead, I begin with the big-picture question: Can campaign finance limits ever be consistent with the First Amendment?

Admittedly, in addition to serving anticorruption goals, a $25,000 individual limit on contributions and spending *per federal election* can promote equality by (to use *Buckley*'s terminology) "restrict[ing] the speech of some elements of our society in order to enhance the relative voice of others." Not all reformers concede the point. Some claim that money is not speech and limits on money in politics therefore do not infringe on First Amendment rights. Justice Stevens, for example, has made the unhelpful claim that money is not speech but property. Yet money facilitates speech, or at the very least implicates political speech, and a $25,000 limit would prevent super-wealthy individuals and entities who want to spend millions of dollars on election-related advertising for a federal candidate from doing so. It would also stop an "angel" from single-handedly bankrolling a long-shot candidate.[24]

To concede the point is not to end the discussion but to begin it. *Buckley* is a precedent that may be overturned by a vote of five justices, who could change the meaning of the First Amendment as quickly as the Roberts court did in *Citizens United*. Indeed, I will argue that changing the Court is the most promising path to reform.

Consider *why* the Court in *Buckley* wrote that limiting some political spending is "wholly foreign to the First Amendment." In the Court's view, the purpose of the First Amendment is "to secure the widest possible dissemination of information from diverse and antagonistic sources, and to assure unfettered interchange of ideas for the bringing about of political and social changes desired by the people." This statement suggests that a different Supreme Court majority could find constitutional a set of campaign finance rules that supports these goals—that recognizes the need to balance society's right to promote political equality with ensuring robust political speech and competitive elections. This is what Justice Breyer may have had in mind in the *Shrink Missouri* case in 2000 when he wrote that *Buckley*'s statement rejecting political equality as an interest "cannot be taken literally."[25]

It is not hard to imagine how a system of campaign limits could be consistent with robust American democracy. We have had such limits for decades. As we saw in Chapter 1, federal election law limited corporate and labor union spending on elections from the 1940s until *Citizens United*, yet our elections have been fiercely contested. Even today, contribution limits are imposed on individuals and parties, and there is a total ban on corporate and labor union contributions to candidates. Neither Benjamin Bluman, Brazilian corporations, nor the government of Russia can spend a penny on our election campaigns, but we would not say we are subject to meaningful censorship of our elections. To the contrary, most people view limits on foreign interference in our elections as a legitimate, even compelling, interest.

Rules against vote buying and bribery also count as limitations on the use of money and speech to influence elections. We do not allow candidates to buy voters' votes, and we do not allow voters or others to buy legislative votes by members of Congress. It is no answer to say that a prohibition on legalized bribery is not a First Amendment violation because it is justified on anticorruption grounds. It is still a limitation on money used for political speech—justified, but a limitation nonetheless.

And as we will see in the next part of this book, countries like Great Britain and Canada run their elections under strict rules that impose draconian limits on outside advertising in elections, much tighter than the limits we have in the United States. Yet we would consider both Great Britain and Canada successful democracies able to hold hotly contested elections.

I begin, then, with the premise that modern U.S. law has always limited the role of money in elections: bribery, foreign money, and vote buying are all prohibited; we have individual and party contribution limits and a ban on direct corporate and labor union contributions to candidates; and from the 1940s until *Citizens United,* we have had no direct corporate or union spending on elections. Yet during those decades we have had a vibrant democracy with tremendous social change and upheaval as well as great progress toward civil rights, the fighting of some wars, and intense partisan competition for Congress and the presidency. Few would think of the United States in those years as a country of censorship, and few would think of mature democracies such as Canada and Great Britain, which have much more severe spending limits, as undemocratic.

That is not to say that a vibrant American democracy could thrive under any limits at all or that the United States should emulate the limits of some other democracies. The question is one of balance.

☑

"The record indicates that, as of January 1, 1975, one full-page advertisement in a daily edition of a certain metropolitan newspaper cost $6,971.04 —almost seven times the annual [$1,000] limit on expenditures 'relative to' a particular candidate imposed on the vast majority of individual citizens and associations" under the 1974 amendments to federal campaign rules. The Supreme Court in *Buckley* noted this fact (without saying that the "certain metropolitan newspaper" was the *Washington Post*) in explaining why it found the individual $1,000 limit on spending in support of or opposition to a candidate to be a large infringement on speech: the limit "would appear to exclude all citizens and groups except candidates, political parties, and the institutional press from any significant use of the most effective modes of communication."[26]

My proposed $25,000 limit could be subject to the same criticism: a full-page advertisement in the *New York Times* in 2015 cost $100,000 or more. A full-page advertisement in the *New Hampshire Union Leader,* an important newspaper in a key presidential primary state, cost just under $5,000 in 2012. Under the limits I propose, a person acting alone and subject to these limits could run only a handful of ads in a relatively small paper, and not one full-page advertisement in a national newspaper.[27]

One response to these statistics, especially from younger readers, might be: What's a newspaper?

Campaigning has changed a lot in the four decades since the Supreme Court decided *Buckley.* Newspaper advertisements are not the main way congressional candidates, political parties, and outside groups reach voters. Today it is all about social media, YouTube videos, websites and advertisements on websites, phone calls, email lists, and direct mail. Television ads are rare in congressional races. One can set up a meaningful website or social media campaign for a congressional district, and do many targeted web ads, on a $25,000 budget. More to the point, many of today's "most effective modes of communication" do not involve massive spending of money, although statewide campaigns still rely greatly on television and radio advertising as well as direct mail.[28]

The $25,000 limit is not much of a burden for almost all U.S. voters. Very few Americans have that much to spend on a campaign—we saw in Chapter 2 that only 0.0011 percent of the U.S. population contributed $10,000 or more to a Super PAC in the 2012 elections. For most of us, the upper limit is no restriction at all. Sure, we 99.9989 percent get to participate in politics by voting, and more Americans, thanks to the Internet, are participating in elections by making small donations as well. But only a tiny sliver of Americans are playing at the $10,000 level, much less the $25,000 level. And indeed, as Aaron Blake of the *Washington Post* reported, the rate of small-donor participation has gone down in the *Citizens United* era even though it is technologically easier than ever to make a donation. We have more money going to federal election activity, but from fewer donors.[29]

For the small minority of people who have this kind of money and wish to spend it on a presidential campaign, there is an easy path to do so in a meaningful way: give that $25,000 to a candidate, the candidate's party, or an outside group to pool with others' money to spend on election-related activities. In today's multifaceted and socially connected world, no donor should find it hard to connect with a candidate, party, or group whose ideology and strategy matches his own. The pooled money could be spent on an effective advertising campaign, including full-page newspaper advertisements and television and radio advertisements. And campaigns and groups can collect more money from artificial entities, such as corporations, labor unions, and other groups. Plenty of money would flow into elections under a $25,000 cap.

The greatest impairment falls on the tiny number of people who both can and want to spend more than $25,000 and want to spend it alone. Such an amount can go far in an Internet-based campaign for a candidate. There is no question that someone can make his or her political views known to many people and try to convince them how to vote for much less than $25,000. (I would index my proposal to campaign costs, so this would always be true.) Under my proposal, no one (aside from foreign individuals, entities, and governments) would be stopped from spending a generous sum on political campaigning or pooling money with like-minded others for this purpose. Even corporations could get in on the act from their general treasury funds, without having to use a PAC.

But what about the multimillionaire who feels an urgent need to spend or contribute more money? Or the rich person who wants to run television advertisements in a presidential or U.S. Senate race? Or the wealthy person who wants to contribute or spend over and over and over in the same election, maybe for her own election to office?

Think of Shaun McCutcheon, the Alabama businessman whose suit challenging the federal aggregate limits is helping to bring down what remains of federal campaign finance law. Ronald Collins and David Skover, in their chronicle of the *McCutcheon* litigation, report that McCutcheon spent almost $384,000 on federal election campaigns in the 2011–12 season alone. Yet he sued to be freed from the strictures of current campaign finance law that prevented him from spending much more.

"Though rich," Collins and Skover tell us, "McCutcheon cannot be counted among the super-rich." They quote McCutcheon as saying, "I do not come from a rich family."[30]

Not "super-rich"? Anyone who can spend $384,000 in campaign contributions and have enough left over to finance a lawsuit is plenty rich, even if not at Sheldon Adelson's or George Soros's levels. In 2011 the amount McCutcheon spent on federal elections was more than seven times the annual median U.S. household income. It was just shy of the amount of annual income it took to fall in the top one percent of wage earners. But $384,000 was not McCutcheon's *income;* it was the amount he could spare that year for political activities (and only those that were related to federal elections and were reported).[31]

Shaun McCutcheon asserts a right to maximize his influence over elections and policy by spending as much as he can afford on political activities. Millions of other Americans feel just as passionately about politics and policy but lack McCutcheon's means. As Professor John Shockley wrote of the *Buckley* decision, "In thus striking down limits on expenditures the Court freed the wealthy to engage in significant use of the most effective modes of communication. But what are the Justices saying about the great majority of the American people who cannot spend more than $1,000 on candidates they support? By the Court's own words, a majority of the American people are excluded from effective communication."[32]

Spending limits stop wealthy people such as McCutcheon from spending unlimited sums in political campaigns, but their purpose is to promote political equality and deter corruption. A $25,000 contribution limit per election per candidate (actually $50,000 for a primary and a general election) is quite generous for a system also committed to political equality. The same can be said of an upper limit of $500,000 on all federal elections in a two-year period, aimed at stopping the richest of the rich from having totally outsized influence over federal elections, but generous to be sure.

Many readers may find these limits too generous. Many poor voters cannot afford to spend anything at all—over forty-six million people lived below the poverty line in the United States in 2012—and would be able to spend only $100 in vouchers I am proposing to give them for *all* federal races together. Someone such as McCutcheon could spend 500 *times that amount* (in primary and general elections) in each of *as many* congressional races and federal elections as he wants until he reaches a half a million dollars in a two-year period. The wealthy would still have disproportionate influence under my proposal, but that compromise is necessary to assure both robust political speech and some measure of political equality.

Finding the appropriate balance between political equality and First Amendment rights of speech and association is the nub of the issue. Can we create a system that assures robust political debate and gives everyone a meaningful opportunity to participate in elections, without allowing the wealthy to have so much influence over electoral and policy outcomes that they dominate everyone else?

To opponents of limits, the government can impose virtually no limits on election spending because elections involve core political speech protected by the First Amendment. The argument assumes that the First Amendment has both a fixed and absolute meaning that prohibits any limitation on spending for political activities.

But as Professors Fred Schauer and Rick Pildes note, there is no single set of First Amendment rules. There are, rather, different First Amendment rules that the Supreme Court has crafted for different contexts. Pildes and Schauer argue for "electoral exceptionalism," seeing a space for the Supreme Court to define elections as not just about discussion of political issues, but as means by which we choose our representatives during a defined time period. It is appropriate, they argue, for courts to craft special rules for judging the constitutionality of campaign finance rules under the First Amendment.

It is hardly clear that the values underlying the First Amendment would be more supportive of speaker (or candidate) immunity than they are of speaker (or candidate) participation. As numerous debates about public access to the press and press access to government have made clear, it is not self-evident that the values of democratic deliberation, collective self-determination, guarding against the abuse of power, searching for truth, and even self-expression are better served by treating government intervention as the unqualified enemy than by allowing the state a limited role in fostering the proliferation of voices in the public sphere or of increasing the importance of message and effort by decreasing the importance of wealth.[33]

Further, it is wrong to think of a system in which individuals can spend unlimited sums on elections as "unregulated." As Cass Sunstein has noted, a Supreme Court decision that unlimited spending on elections is permissible is just another means by which the federal government sets election rules. There is no neutral means of deciding how to regulate election speech and spending.[34]

Robert Post has argued that the state can set rules for elections in its "managerial" capacity, to ensure electoral integrity by assuring public confidence in the fairness of the government and electoral processes. Although he rejects campaign finance limits passed in the name of political equality as inconsistent with earlier First Amendment traditions, he advocates imposing similar limits (on, for instance, corporate spending) under his theory of electoral integrity. He views his theory as offering "the liberal wing of the Court a way to translate its commitment to representative integrity into terms that are compatible with the discursive democracy established by the First Amendment. The value of electoral integrity captures much of what attracts liberal Justices to the importance of maintaining the integrity of our electoral system."[35]

These scholars view elections as a different sphere of First Amendment activity, and believe it is wrong to suggest that the only legitimate interpretation of the First Amendment is as a prohibition on any and all campaign finance limits.

An analogy is useful, even if it only takes us so far. When two parties have a trial, or two parties have lawyers argue a case before the Supreme Court, we let them both spend as much as they want in hiring their lawyers and legal teams. But we do not afford the wealthier party an opportunity to purchase extra time for making its arguments to the jury or the justices. We do not want wealth to have excessive influence over legal decision making. We exclude evidence, and judges sometimes bar lawyers from making certain arguments that can prejudice a jury. We do not demand complete equality, but we do impose certain rules meant to make litigation a fairer fight.[36]

The analogy is not perfect because lawsuits are about judges or juries making decisions under conditions of deliberation. Elections are about the division of power by political equals, these days usually without much reasoned deliberation, and there is always a danger when the state decides the rules for political competition. This danger is at the core of First Amendment fears about regulation of political money.

Yet in both litigation and elections the concept of a fair fight makes sense: we do not believe someone should get more justice just because she has much more money than her opponent. Similarly, society may reasonably decide that one person should not get more influence over elections or policy just because she has much more money than everyone else. Whether that argument succeeds depends on how the Supreme Court understands the First Amendment's interaction with other legitimate social needs.

☑

To this point I have sketched the reasons to believe that generous contribution and spending limits, coupled with level-up programs such as campaign finance vouchers, strike the right balance between these inevitably conflicting goals. I propose the $25,000/$500,000 limit as a deliberate compromise between the two competing positions, aimed at both promoting robust electoral speech and competition but not allowing those with wealth to have overwhelming influence over our elections and politics. I would add some ancillary rules to limit the power of lobbyists—most important, I would bar lobbyists from being involved in the fundraising business, barring them from bundling or even asking nonrelatives to make a voucher donation or other contribution to candidates, parties, and outside groups engaged in election-related activity. I would also impose a five-year anti-revolving-door provision, which would bar senators, members of Congress, and their staffers from working as lobbyists or in assisting lobbyist efforts.

To some strict egalitarians, my proposal no doubt errs too much on the free speech side, giving too much power to the tiny sliver of Americans who can spend up to $25,000 in each race or $500,000 over a two-year period. But I suspect most objections will come from the other side: those who believe the $25,000 limit is an impermissible restriction on political activity.

In the next chapters I delve deeper into the three main arguments critics have raised against limits: (1) that limits are a form of impermissible censorship; (2) that limits favor the media in a way that is both unjustifiable and nonsensical in today's new media environment; and (3) that limits have bad (unintended) consequences, ranging from favoring incumbents to hurting political parties to increasing polarization.

Unlike the constitutional case for leveling up, the case for leveling down is hard. The relentless criticism of campaign finance limits that opponents have unleashed in scholarship and legal attacks over the past few decades has some merit. Rather than ignore these arguments or give them cursory consideration, as many in the reform camp tend to do, I take them on their own terms.

Importantly, the arguments against limits are the same whether the limits are intended to promote political equality or to serve some other purpose, such as Post's "electoral integrity" or Lessig's "dependence corruption." If the state bars corporate spending, or imposes a $25,000 limit on contributions or spending on elections, that restriction imposes the same free speech costs regardless of the governmental interest behind the law. Unless we want to say that an identical law may be constitutional or not depending on the motivation of those who pass it (something Chief Justice Roberts implicitly suggested in *Arizona*), limits are either constitutional or not depending on their effects on First Amendment rights. The responses to criticisms of limits that I will outline therefore apply whether one accepts political equality as the reason for limits or prefers some other justification.

Making the case for campaign finance limits is tough but not impossible: a campaign finance program that levels up and levels down, subsidizing speech and imposing generous limits on contributions and spending, is fully consistent with a reasonable interpretation of the First Amendment's rights of speech and association.

PART THREE

OBJECTIONS

5

Censorship

MALCOLM STEWART PROBABLY KNEW HE was in trouble before oral arguments began. As a deputy solicitor general of the United States, Stewart had the unenviable task of trying to persuade a skeptical Supreme Court to uphold a lower court ruling denying the right of an incorporated ideological group, Citizens United, to pay $1 million to Comcast to broadcast a ninety-minute documentary called *Hillary: The Movie*. The movie's subject, Hillary Rodham Clinton, was seeking the 2008 Democratic nomination for president, and Citizens United wanted to convince people she was "not fit to be commander-in-chief." Stewart's argument in *Citizens United* came shortly after the Court had issued a decision in the *Wisconsin Right to Life* case, hobbling key parts of the McCain-Feingold campaign finance law.[1]

Although no one in *Hillary: The Movie* expressly said "Vote against Clinton," the Federal Election Commission determined that the McCain-Feingold law's "electioneering communications" provision barred Citizens United from using its general treasury funds (which included money it had collected as donations from for-profit corporations) to pay to have Comcast offer the movie as a free on-demand download. Citizens United would have to pay Comcast out of its political action committee, funded from donations from individuals. Or it could have paid Comcast from its own general treasury funds so long as it did not take any money from for-profit corporations for this purpose. Citizens United challenged the commission's position on how it had to fund its Comcast payment as a First Amendment violation.[2]

The Court's skepticism toward campaign finance rules came about because Justice Samuel Alito had replaced Justice Sandra Day O'Connor, shifting the balance of power on this question in the Supreme Court from 5–4 extremely sympathetic to campaign finance laws to 5–4 extremely dubious of them. Just a few years earlier, O'Connor had cast the deciding vote to uphold this key "electioneering communications" part of the McCain-Feingold law.

Now that deciding vote belonged to Justice Alito, and at the *Citizens United* oral argument he asked Stewart a question that may have changed the trajectory of the case: Would Congress have the power to ban books paid for with a corporation's general treasury funds? Stewart gave a technical and rather unsatisfying answer:

> MR. STEWART: I think the . . . Constitution would have permitted Congress to apply the electioneering communication restrictions to the extent that they were otherwise constitutional under *Wisconsin Right to Life*. Those could have been applied to additional media as well. And it's worth remembering that the preexisting Federal Election Campaign Act restrictions on corporate electioneering which have been limited by this Court's decisions to express advocacy.
>
> JUSTICE ALITO: That's pretty incredible. You think that if . . . a book was published, a campaign biography that was the functional equivalent of express advocacy, that could be banned?
>
> MR. STEWART: I'm not saying it could be banned. I'm saying that Congress could prohibit the use of corporate treasury funds and could require a corporation to publish it using its—
>
> JUSTICE ALITO: Well, most publishers are corporations. And a publisher that is a corporation could be prohibited from selling a book?
>
> MR. STEWART: Well, of course the statute contains its own media exemption or media—
>
> JUSTICE ALITO: I'm not asking what the statute says. The government's position is that the First Amendment allows the banning of a book if it's published by a corporation?
>
> MR. STEWART: Because the First Amendment refers both to freedom of speech and of the press, there would be a potential argument that media corporations, the institutional press, would have a greater First Amendment right. That question is obviously not presented here. . . .

The argument went downhill from there, with other justices, even the liberal Justice Breyer, piling on to the book-banning line of questioning.

Stewart's response was not incorrect. First, the statute did not prohibit a corporation from paying to print a book mentioning a federal candidate in the period close to the election. Second, even if the statute covered this activity, it might fall under a special exemption for the media (more about that in the next chapter). Third, the law did not *ban* a corporation from paying for express advocacy of a federal candidate's election or defeat in a book; instead, it required that the corporation pay for that advocacy with funds collected by its PAC from corporate executives, shareholders of the corporation, and others, rather than from the money the corporation made selling soap or software. Fourth, the Court had already held in cases such as *Austin* and *MCFL* that the government could make corporations go through a PAC for all spending expressly advocating the election or defeat of a federal candidate.

Stewart might have added, but did not, that when Congress passed the McCain-Feingold law, it made extensive findings based on empirical evidence that individuals, corporations, and labor unions were using "issue ads" on radio and television to get around disclosure requirements and the limits on corporate and union express advocacy for federal candidates. Congress made no such finding about the use of books, and therefore the constitutionality of a PAC requirement for corporate-funded books containing the book equivalent of "electioneering communications" was deeply questionable.[3]

Stewart's response, although legally reasonable, was politically unreasonable. Because he did not start his answer with "No," the specter of banned books and un-American censorship loomed heavily over the case. Afterward, Adam Liptak of the *New York Times* described the argument's heavy focus on the book-banning question: "Several of the court's more conservative justices reacted with incredulity to a series of answers from a government lawyer about the scope of Congressional authority to limit political speech. The lawyer, Malcolm L. Stewart, said Congress has the power to ban political books, signs and Internet videos, if they are paid for by corporations and distributed not long before an election."[4]

Citizens United had been seen as a small case in which the Court could have sided with the ideological group without making major changes in U.S. campaign finance law. It could simply have said, for example, that

McCain-Feingold did not cover video-on-demand. The Court also could have said that because Citizens United, an ideological group, took relatively little money from for-profit corporations, it could get the exemption the Court created in the *MCFL* case allowing it to fund *Hillary: The Movie* out of its general treasury funds. But the book-banning questions raised the stakes.

After oral argument, the Supreme Court majority apparently drafted a broad opinion that would have overturned *Austin* and the other cases upholding corporate spending limits. Justice Souter wrote an angry draft dissent accusing the majority of overreaching by deciding an issue not even briefed by the parties before the Court. At the end of its term in June 2010, the Court did not decide the case as expected, but instead scheduled it for reargument on the question of whether those cases upholding the corporate limits should be overturned. Souter's draft dissent has never been released. As Justice Stevens explained to Liptak, "The draft dissent caused the majority to pause . . . thanks to 'the strong expression of the feeling among the dissenters that procedurally the case was not in the proper posture to reach the issue that they ultimately decided.'"[5]

At a special oral argument session in September 2010, weeks before its customary start date on the first Monday in October, the Court reheard argument in *Citizens United*. Unsurprisingly, the newly appointed solicitor general, Elena Kagan, chose to argue the high-profile case herself. It was not only her first oral argument before the Supreme Court; it was her first appellate oral argument ever. But she came prepared to take on the difficult task of again defending the federal limit on corporate spending in elections. She later told legal writing guru Bryan Garner in an interview that "it was nerve racking to do an argument of that importance for my first one. But every time I got too nervous about it, I would say it's okay because we know which way this is going to come out. You're going to lose."[6]

At the oral argument, Justice Ruth Bader Ginsburg gave Kagan a chance to address the book-banning question. Kagan explained that the government's answer had "changed," and it now believed it would be unconstitutional to apply the corporate PAC requirement to books, something the Federal Election Commission had never tried to do anyway.[7]

Chief Justice Roberts then pushed Kagan on the point:

CHIEF JUSTICE ROBERTS: But we don't put our . . . First Amendment rights in the hands of FEC bureaucrats; and if you say that you are not going to apply it to a book, what about a pamphlet?

KAGAN: I think a . . . pamphlet would be different. A pamphlet is pretty classic electioneering, so there is no attempt to say that [the federal limit on corporate spending] only applies to video and not to print. . . .

That answer too did not sit well with the Court's conservatives—when does a pamphlet end and a book begin?—and Kagan was right that she knew how the case was going to end. On a 5–4 vote, the Supreme Court went big in *Citizens United,* overturning *Austin* and other cases and holding that corporate spending limits violated the First Amendment. Justice Stevens ended up incorporating pieces of Souter's draft dissent into his own. Journalist Marcia Coyle reports that Stevens's draft "owed so much to Souter's own draft dissent that Stevens had included a footnote thanking him. He was later persuaded by colleagues to delete the footnote."[8]

In his majority opinion, Kennedy used the book-ban issue to make the claim that the federal law amounted to censorship.

The law before us is an outright ban, backed by criminal sanctions. Section 441b makes it a felony for all corporations—including nonprofit advocacy corporations—either to expressly advocate the election or defeat of candidates or to broadcast electioneering communications within 30 days of a primary election and 60 days of a general election. Thus, the following acts would all be felonies under § 441b: The Sierra Club runs an ad, within the crucial phase of 60 days before the general election, that exhorts the public to disapprove of a Congressman who favors logging in national forests; the National Rifle Association publishes a book urging the public to vote for the challenger because the incumbent U. S. Senator supports a handgun ban; and the American Civil Liberties Union creates a Web site telling the public to vote for a Presidential candidate in light of that candidate's defense of free speech. These prohibitions are classic examples of censorship.[9]

Kennedy's statement that federal law imposed "censorship" was unfair. Bryan Garner, who not only interviewed Kagan about writing and oral argument but is a renowned expert on legal writing and co-author with Justice Scalia of a book on legal meaning and interpretation, defines censorship in his legal dictionary as "governmental suppression of material thought to be unsuitable for distribution or viewing on grounds of morality, religion, politics or national security." A classic example of a censorship law was the Sedition Act portion of the short-lived Alien and Sedition Acts, which Congress enacted in 1798. Among other things, the Sedition Act made it a felony to "write, print, utter, or publish . . . any false, scandalous and malicious writing or writings against the government of the United States, or either house of the said Congress, or the said President, or bring them, or either of them, into contempt or disrepute; or to excite against them . . . the hatred of the good people of the United States."[10]

Unlike the Sedition Act, the federal system for regulating corporate and labor union campaign spending before *Citizens United* is not fairly described as "governmental suppression" of political material. It did not stop corporations from uttering or speaking. Justice Kennedy did not mention that thanks to *MCFL*, incorporated nonprofit advocacy groups, including the Sierra Club and the National Rifle Association, could already engage in as much electioneering as they wanted—in print, online, and on television and radio—so long as they did not take money from any for-profit corporations or labor unions for election purposes. That rule was meant to ensure that people did not set up corporate nonprofits as conduits to funnel for-profit corporate money into federal elections.

Nor was it fair for Justice Kennedy to call the law a "ban" or censorship of political speech even for for-profit corporations: these corporations could set up PACs and spend their PAC money on all of these activities and more. True, the message would have to come from something called General Motors PAC rather than General Motors Incorporated, but so what? General Motors could fully control General Motors PAC, decide which candidates it would support, and pay its administrative expenses. If the public wanted to know what General Motors thought of a candidate, the position of General Motors PAC would no doubt reflect it. But a "ban" sounded much more censorious, and Kennedy wrapped himself in the First Amendment to free for-profit corporate treasuries to be used in campaigns.

What for-profit corporations could not do until *Citizens United* was take the money they made selling cars or other goods and use it to run advertising for the election or defeat of a candidate for federal office. That limitation is neither a ban on speech nor censorship: it is a limit on political activity imposed for compelling reasons. As we shall see, some of the biggest opponents of campaign finance laws seem to support even tougher limits in other circumstances.

☑

Floyd Abrams does not seem like someone who believes in censorship. Indeed he has devoted his professional career to a very strong reading of the First Amendment and has been an admirable defender of unpopular speakers and causes.[11] Given his smarts and experience, I confess I was a little nervous when a student group at the University of Michigan Law School invited me to debate Abrams in March 2012 about campaign finance and *Citizens United*. The debate went about as you would expect. Abrams argued that limits on the ability of corporations to spend unlimited sums from their general treasury accounts is a form of censorship, and I took the view that such limits are reasonable and necessary given society's strong interest in not letting money have too much influence on the outcomes of elections and policy.[12]

I had one argument that I knew would be hard for Abrams to answer: what about Benjamin Bluman and the ban on foreign money in elections? After all, if the Supreme Court is right in *Citizens United* that the identity of the speaker does not matter, and that there can be no corruption, distortion, or loss of public confidence when corporations, labor unions, and individuals contribute or spend unlimited sums on elections, how can the government bar Bluman, a Canadian lawyer working in the United States, from distributing a "Vote for Obama" flyer he paid fifty cents to print at the Kinko's copy store? And this, unlike the corporate PAC limit, is a real ban—foreign individuals, corporations, or governments cannot set up a PAC or do anything else to get around an outright prohibition on Bluman or other foreign individuals or entities spending or contributing a single penny to support or oppose a candidate for any office in the United States.

HASEN: . . . I guess my biggest question, what I'd like to hear is: if more speech is always better, I would like to hear Floyd's response to the idea that there is nothing objectionable if foreign governments want to spend money to try to influence the outcome of our Congressional elections. Let's say the control of the Senate or control of the House comes down to a few seats, how about $30 million, $50 million, $100 million spent on a Congressional race to do that?

ABRAMS: First, I do think foreign influence is different than American influence. Maybe it's question-begging to say it, but I think that different considerations come into play when you're talking about whether we choose as a nation to allow foreign nations to play a role in our elections. I think that's a different question than the one of whether we should distinguish within this country and our people about who can do what. One thing that I find unacceptable is the notion that if this documentary had been made by a media company, that they should be exempt—Congress has exempted them—and if it were made by some other American company, that it should not be exempt. If NewsCorp, Mr. Murdoch's company, had made this—and they would have been very pleased with this documentary—if they had made it, that it should be protected speech under the First Amendment, but if Mr. Murdoch sold his newspapers then it becomes unprotected speech. That cannot be the law. And I think it is very clear from the opinion of the five-person majority that they don't think that can be the law either, that it should not be dependent upon the nature of the American speaker, whether it's an American person, or people, or company, or union, that the rules—whatever the rules are—should be the same.

Abrams effortlessly pivoted from the most difficult issue for those who say they oppose all campaign finance limits—the foreign influence question —to the most difficult issue for the reform side—media influence. But in our entire debate, he never expressed any concern about the absolute censorship of people like Benjamin Bluman. He phrased his concern about "foreign nations" rather than individuals like Bluman. And he was right that his answer was "question begging." Saying that foreign influence is different does not explain why it is unobjectionable to shut up people like Benjamin Bluman when it is not all right to shut up General Motors.

Bradley Smith is also a strident free speech supporter whose *Unfree Speech* is perhaps the most influential book-length argument against campaign finance regulation. A professor at Capital University Law School in Ohio who formerly chaired the Federal Election Commission, he is the brains behind the Center for Competitive Politics, a public interest group in Washington, D.C., that litigates, advocates, and lobbies against campaign finance laws.[13]

Despite his agitation for campaign finance deregulation, Smith was not at all bothered by the total and absolute ban on Benjamin Bluman passing out his cheap flyers in Central Park. After the Supreme Court upheld the ban without even issuing an opinion, Smith wrote on his center's website:

> We doubt that political contributions by Ben Bluman, a Canadian law-yer working in New York, or A[sena]th Steiman, a Canadian-I[s]raeli dual citizen doing a medical residency in New York, would terribly corrupt U.S. elections, and we doubt that either the District Court o[r] the Supreme Court thought so, either. But as we noted in our earlier commentary on the case:
>
>> [T]here are reasonable constitutional distinctions that can be made between non-resident aliens and foreign corporations, on the one hand, and resident aliens, citizens, and domestic corporations on the other.
>>
>> Beyond that, the Court's opinion is carefully reasoned and takes pains not to allow itself to be misinterpreted, noting that it does not discuss the question of resident aliens, or speech about politics and issues that does not expressly advocate the election or defeat of a candi-date, or the barriers to criminal prosecutions.
>
> . . .
>
> The core of the Court's *Citizens United* doctrine is that U.S. citizens have a right to participate in political life, even if they have adopted the corporate form to undertake their activities. Well known, Lockean principles about the nature of political communities suggest that different rules might apply to persons who are not members of that political community—persons who are mere temporary residents.[14]

The last comment is the most interesting. Smith supports the govern-ment's ability to strip a human being, Benjamin Bluman, of the right to spend a penny to support a federal candidate, based on a judgment, made by self-interested legislators, that Bluman is not sufficiently a member of the "political community" to have the right to speak about American elections.

Yet Smith derides as censorship and incumbency protection a federal law that limits, but does not fully deny, the ability of non-human corporations to spend money in federal elections. Corporations, legal fictions that exist only by the grace of the state, are entitled to infinitely more political speech (as defined by spending) in Smith's world than an actual human being living in New York. Self-interested legislators can decide that "different rules might apply" to foreign individuals, but in Smith's view, they cannot make the same judgment about artificial entities such as corporations, endowed by their creator with nothing like a human spirit.

The Indiana attorney Jim Bopp has probably filed more suits against campaign finance laws than anyone else in the United States. He was the brains behind *Citizens United* and many other challenges to campaign finance limits and disclosure laws. A strong opponent of abortion and same-sex marriage, Bopp is one of those "no law means no law" First Amendment absolutists when it comes to campaign finance. With one big exception.

When the Supreme Court summarily affirmed the *Bluman* case, deciding not even to explain why it is constitutional to prevent Bluman from passing out his flyers, I argued on the Election Law listserv that the Court's treatment of *Bluman* after *Citizens United* created an incoherent jurisprudence. Bopp fired back, defending the Court's decision to fully deny foreign individuals any constitutional rights to spend money on elections:

> There is no "doctrinal incoherence"[;] it is perfectly consistent for the Supreme Court to hold that there is no compelling interest in prohibiting corporate and labor union speech but that there is a compelling interest in prohibiting foreign interests from contributing to candidates in U.S. elections. I for one agree that the Red Chinese Army, the Iranian government and Hamas can be prohibited from contributing.[15]

Bopp agreed that the law is a severe burden on foreigners' First Amendment rights, but he said it is justified by a compelling interest: "it is perfectly consistent to reject the *Austin* distortion ruling that justified bans on corporate and labor union speech, but say that foreign governments, foreign terrorist [organizations] and armies, etc. are different than you[r] everyday American corporation such that the foreign interests can be ban[ned]."[16]

Just as he had picked the most sympathetic corporation as his plaintiff in the *Citizens United* lawsuit—a grassroots nonprofit political outfit rather than a multibillion-dollar for-profit corporation—Bopp picked the most unsympathetic foreigners to justify a foreign spending ban. Who wants to put our elections in the hands of the Red Chinese Army (does anyone still call it that?), the Iranian government, and Hamas? They sure look a lot more menacing than the Canadian lawyer Benjamin Bluman.

What is most ironic about Bopp's comments is that they support the foreign-money ban even though the ban arguably is not, to use some First Amendment phrases, "content neutral" or "viewpoint neutral." Bopp wants to shut up Hamas, the Chinese army, and the Iranian government presumably because of what they might say and where they might spend their money. He is even more interested in shutting up foreigners than some reformers are in shutting up the wealthy.

☑

Abrams, Smith, and Bopp are among the most prominent critics of campaign finance laws, and among the most ardent defenders of the First Amendment. But even they do not go all the way on campaign deregulation. They support the ban on foreign spending in elections—but not corporate and labor union PAC limits—because it is "different" or "reasonable" or "compelling" to do so. Presumably they also, on anticorruption grounds, support laws against bribing candidates or buying votes.

Where to draw the line between permissible regulation of campaign money and impermissible regulation is a judgment call. Consider the views of the noted First Amendment scholar Eugene Volokh. Volokh, unlike First Amendment absolutists, believes that limits on contributions to candidates are constitutionally permissible but spending limits applied to anyone are not. I debated him once about campaign finance many years ago at a Federalist Society luncheon, and all the harsh questions were directed to him, not me, because he did not take a fully deregulationist position. (I suspect the audience wrote me off as a lost cause.)[17]

As to foreign spending in *Bluman,* Volokh argues that "a total ban on all paid-for speech about candidates made by non-permanent-residents—regardless of the amount of the payment or of any other circumstances—[does not seem] narrowly tailored to any potentially compelling government interest in national security or freedom from foreign influence."[18]

If Volokh believes Benjamin Bluman should have the right to pay for and distribute his campaign flyers does it mean that Abrams, Smith, and Bopp support censorship? Or is Volokh the supporter of censorship because he

believes in the constitutionality of limits on individual contributions to candidates?

In truth, none of these eminent people support censorship. Each recognizes that while the First Amendment guarantees important rights of
speech and association, and ensures robust political speech and political
competition, there are "different" "compelling" reasons to support certain
"reasonable" limitations on campaign contributions and spending. They,
like me, believe it is sometimes permissible to burden speech for a compelling enough reason. We just differ on those reasons. I can imagine in an
alternative universe deputy solicitor general Malcolm Stewart getting to ask
Justice Alito if he would be all right with the banning of books about U.S.
presidential candidates paid for by foreign corporations, individuals, and
nations in the period before the election.

This is no different from the idea that American society can support a
broad right to artistic and cultural expression, some of it even lewd and
unpleasant, while barring child pornography. It is simply an incorrect reading of First Amendment doctrine and practice to say that "no law" means
literally no regulation ever of speech, expression, or the spending of money
on speech or expression. The law should stand on the side of expression,
but when there is a compelling interest on the other side, then reasonable
limitations do not count as an unconstitutional "abridgement" of freedom
of speech.

The question, then, is what reasons should be sufficient and when it is
reasonable to impose limitations consistent with a commitment to robust
speech and political competition. Of course one can draw a principled distinction between limiting foreign influence and limiting domestic (corporate) influence. That's not the point, though, when it comes to questions of
what counts as "censorship." That reformers draw the lines differently than
Abrams, Smith, and Bopp does not mean reformers support censorship.
The test of censorship is whether, to use Garner's terms, a set of campaign
finance rules constitutes an improper "suppression" of political material.
So long as a system respects robust political debate, gives everyone the
right to speak and to support or oppose a candidate, and does not prevent
the opportunity for meaningful campaigning, it should not count as censorship.

As we saw in the previous chapter, it is not fair to say that before *Citizens United* campaigns labored under the threat of censorship. There was robust political competition in which candidates and parties fought hard, hundreds of millions of dollars were spent on elections every two years, and many voices were heard. The laws stopped no person (aside from foreign individuals) from expressing an opinion or spending money on elections. Corporations and labor unions had to use PACs to spend money on elections and did so routinely. To describe this period as a time of censorship is to mangle the English language and disregard the actual workings of public policy. As Garner notes in his dictionary, censorship, "whose mention immediately implicates the First Amendment, is one of those politically charged vogue words that people use irresponsibly."[19]

The key question about my proposal to limit contributions and spending to $25,000 per individual or entity per candidate per election is whether such a system would amount to censorship. To Abrams, Smith, and Bopp, it surely would: I would be one of the "speech police" stopping people such as Shaun McCutcheon from spending $384,000 on the 2011–12 election season (though actually I would allow him to spend up to $500,000, with no more than $25,000 on any one election), the Adelsons from contributing and spending $100 million on the 2012 election season, or environmentalist Tom Steyer from contributing and spending nearly $74 million to support Democrats in 2014. A $25,000 limit would not be a "content neutral" or "viewpoint neutral" law, in their view, because someone with an intent to ensure that great disparities in wealth are not translated into great disparities in political power would have the intent to "shut up the wealthy."[20]

Never mind that Abrams and the others support a law that stops someone from spending fifty cents on "Vote for Obama" flyers while my proposed $25,000 individual contribution and spending limit would be infinitely more generous to those who want to spend. It is relatively easy to support the foreign-money ban because Hamas and the Chinese Army are not popular in America. But First Amendment advocates usually argue for extra protection for unpopular political speech.

Still, my proposal, like the foreign spending ban, is nonetheless an infringement on liberty; there is no way around that. It tells the Adelsons and Steyers that they can spend only so much to influence the outcomes of elections and public policy: when you hit $25,000 for a candidate, or $500,000 total in a two-year period on federal elections, you have to stop.

The previous chapter explained that this infringement may be justified for a compelling reason: the promotion of political equality. To make that call, there is no alternative to courts carefully balancing rights and interests.

If Congress ever adopted the $25,000 limit, how should courts conduct this balancing? Ideally, it would be good to run a few elections with these limits in place, and see whether campaigns remain robust; whether (as I expect) people would pool their resources with others through government-provided voucher dollars and contributions to candidates, parties, and interest groups; and whether we still have rigorous campaigns in which everyone who wishes to express a view about the election can do so. We could also examine incumbency rates and see whether the limits affect the already astronomically high retention rates for members of Congress. Without such an experiment, we will have to rely on second-best evidence.

☑

Albuquerque, New Mexico, had candidate spending limits in place from 1974 to the mid-1990s, and its experience provides some clues as to how an American jurisdiction might handle such limits. How could Albuquerque have kept its law for more than two decades after the *Buckley* case in 1976 held such limits unconstitutional? Surprisingly, it appears that no one bothered to challenge them for twenty years.[21]

In 2001, a city mayoral candidate, Rick Homans, tried to get a federal court to bar enforcement of the spending limits, which were set at just under $175,000 in that election. The trial court denied the request, a decision later reversed on appeal.

The court made a number of factual findings suggesting robust campaigning and widespread satisfaction with the system of candidate spending limits. In contrast to the nationwide incumbency rate of 88 percent for mayors, Albuquerque had a zero percent incumbency rate in city mayoral elections held under spending limits. Many successful Albuquerque mayoral candidates spent less than the spending limit, and the 1997 winner spent less than $44,000 on his campaign. Only 27 percent of donors in the city gave the maximum $1,000 contribution to mayoral candidates in

1995; in Cincinnati, which had no limits, the figure was 53 percent. The limits also may have encouraged voter turnout: in 1997, when a court temporarily enjoined the spending limits, turnout went down. Spending limits appeared to allow poorer and middle-class candidates to run for office and were strongly supported by the voters. A federal district court considering a challenge to the law later explained: "Fifty-seven percent (57%) of surveyed Albuquerque voters think that federal elections are overly influenced by special interest money. In contrast, only twenty-three percent (23%) think that Albuquerque elections are overly influenced by special interest money."[22]

The United States Court of Appeals for the Tenth Circuit reversed the district court's decision not to preliminarily enjoin Albuquerque's spending limits, holding they were unconstitutional under *Buckley*. Around the same time, in a case out of Vermont, the United States Court of Appeals for the Second Circuit reached a contrary conclusion and appeared ready to let Vermont candidate spending limits go into effect. The Supreme Court in an appeal from the Vermont case held that candidate spending limits were barred under the *Buckley* precedent.[23]

Albuquerque's long experiment sheds only a little light on how a $25,000 individual contribution and spending limit would work, especially in federal elections. But the Albuquerque system does illuminate whether spending limits necessarily lead to censorship, and the trial court's findings do not show significant government suppression of speech. Candidate campaigns were vigorous and contested; incumbents did not benefit and perhaps may have been hurt by spending limits; voter turnout was higher than in other cities; and the public approved of the program. It does not sound like Albuquerque from the mid-1970s to the mid-1990s suffered much from the "speech police" and government censors.

Further afield, Great Britain and Canada have campaign finance systems with spending limits that are significantly stricter than anything I propose. In Great Britain, these limits apply to campaigns. Outside groups also have faced limits on their spending since 1999. Further, there are no regular campaign commercials. Parties are allocated a certain amount of television time to use to persuade voters during a defined and short election period.[24]

Canada too has strict limits on election-related spending. In 2004, in

Harper v. Canada the Supreme Court of Canada upheld limits on spending by outside groups of $3,000 Canadian dollars per electoral district and $150,000 total. The Court held that limits were justified as a means to "seek to create a level playing field for those who wish to engage in the electoral discourse. This, in turn, enables voters to be better informed; no one voice is overwhelmed by another."[25]

Both the British and Canadian systems are much stricter in some senses than my proposal (although disclosure laws in Britain are in some ways more lax), which would not impose spending limits on candidates or parties. Candidates, parties, and outside groups could still advertise and engage in other campaign activity. I expect politics would remain fierce and robust under these generous limits, especially because they would be accompanied by campaign finance vouchers that would inject billions of dollars into the campaign finance system.

Even Great Britain and Canada's much stricter campaign finance systems are not fairly characterized as systems of censorship. In Freedom House's ratings of Freedom in the World, Great Britain, Canada, and the United States all have perfect "scores in the categories of "Freedom," "Political Rights," and "Civil Liberties." The British and Canadian campaign finance systems are not as wide open as in the United States, but that does not mean these countries do not have free and open elections, with robust political competition.[26]

Courts have a crucial role to play in assuring that any set of campaign finance rules does not infringe too much on robust campaigns, speech, and associational freedom. Without courts taking an independent and careful look at campaign laws, the danger to speech and associational freedoms is just too high.

Balancing is difficult business. As Ohio State University professor Dan Tokaji points out, the Supreme Court of Canada has tried to play just such a role in examining constitutional challenges to Canada's campaign finance rules. In the *Harper* case, it accepted political equality and leveling the playing field to justify the country's campaign finance laws against constitutional challenge, finding that the law only minimally impaired rights to free expression. But Professor Yasmin Dawood wonders whether the Canadian court may have erred too much against the rights of free expression of outside groups, much like U.S. courts have erred too much against the social interest in political equality: "Too great an emphasis on equality can lead to an impairment of free speech liberties of citizens, while too great an emphasis on liberty can lead to vast spending by powerful groups on electoral advertising."[27]

✔️

The U.S. Constitution, some rightly say, is not a suicide pact. A reading of the First Amendment that mandates a fully deregulated campaign finance system in which a small minority can transform their vast wealth into vastly superior political power threatens our democracy itself. It is not a reading that the Constitution mandates.

Still, campaign limits present real dangers. The greatest of these is that overly strict limits can lead to censorship, which a serious democracy cannot tolerate.

But in a system of reasonable and generous campaign finance limits, this danger is small. We know this from our long experience with corporate and labor union spending limits; from the foreign spending ban, which even the most ardent campaign finance opponents support; from the experience of Albuquerque, New Mexico; and from the much stricter systems used in Canada and Great Britain.

Justice Alito's question about book banning in the *Citizens United* case misleadingly raised the specter of government control of information, the end of vibrant American democracy, and a return to the Alien and Sedition Acts. In fact, reasonable limits on contributions and spending coupled with government subsidies of campaigns through vouchers are fully compatible with robust elections featuring a variety of voices. More speech from more people, with reasonable limits on the ability of the wealthiest Americans to spend endlessly, is not censorship but rather a recipe to promote both political equality and the First Amendment.

6

The (New) Media

IN 1990, JUSTICE SCALIA DELIVERED A powerful dissent in *Austin v. Michigan Chamber of Commerce*, and his words should give pause even to people who strongly support campaign finance limitations.

> "Attention all citizens. To assure the fairness of elections by preventing disproportionate expression of the views of any single powerful group, your Government has decided that the following associations of persons shall be prohibited from speaking or writing in support of any candidate: _____."
> In permitting Michigan to make private corporations the first object of this Orwellian announcement, the Court today endorses the principle that too much speech is an evil that the democratic majority can proscribe. I dissent because that principle is contrary to our case law and incompatible with the absolutely central truth of the First Amendment: that government cannot be trusted to assure, through censorship, the "fairness" of political debate.[1]

The previous chapter explained why a system of reasonable limits, with close court supervision to ensure robust campaign speech, does not fairly count as "censorship." Limits on political spending, coupled with generous market-driven campaign subsidies through vouchers, can enhance the ability of all persons (and entities) to get their views out without letting those with wealth wield disproportionate influence over the electoral and political processes. But Scalia's admonition regarding the danger of government speech regulation, the principal justification for close judicial scrutiny of all campaign finance limits, cannot be dismissed lightly.

Scalia went beyond calling the corporate PAC requirement "censorship." He pointed to the biggest conceptual problem with any argument for campaign finance limitations enacted to further political equality: how to treat the media. The problem has only gotten thornier since Scalia wrote this dissent, thanks to the emergence of the Internet and social media. Any argument for reform must grapple with how to treat both the old and new "press."

Michigan's law in 1990, like federal law at the time, barred corporations from spending their general treasury funds in elections, requiring them to use a PAC instead. But the law exempted media corporations, such as incorporated broadcasters and newspapers: without such a media exemption, a corporate-owned newspaper, for example, could not use its general treasury funds to print an editorial endorsing a candidate for federal office —or, depending on the definition of election-related activity, even report on campaigns right before the election.

Justice Scalia thought Michigan's media exemption was hypocritical and out-of-sync with *Austin*'s antidistortion rationale, which he dubbed "the New Corruption."

> Amassed corporate wealth that regularly sits astride the ordinary channels of information is much more likely to produce the New Corruption (too much of one point of view) than amassed corporate wealth that is generally busy making money elsewhere. Such media corporations not only have vastly greater power to perpetrate the evil of overinforming, they also have vastly greater opportunity. General Motors, after all, will risk a stockholder suit if it makes a political endorsement that is not plausibly tied to its ability to make money for its shareholders. But media corporations make money *by* making political commentary, including endorsements. For them, unlike any other corporations, the whole world of politics and ideology is fair game. Yet the Court tells us that it is reasonable to *exclude* media corporations, rather than target them specially.[2]

Scalia concluded by noting that the Supreme Court, in upholding the ability of Michigan to bar corporate spending but exempt corporate media, did not *mandate* a media exemption: "The theory of New Corruption it espouses is a dagger at their throats. The Court today holds merely that media corporations *may* be excluded from the Michigan law, not that they *must* be."[3]

The question of how to treat the media is, for the reform community, what the foreign-money question is for the deregulationist community. Say that there should be an exception, and you run the risk of inconsistency or outright hypocrisy; say there should not be an exception and you are considered too extreme.

I learned this lesson firsthand when I wrote an article for the *Texas Law Review* in 1999 called "Campaign Finance Laws and the Rupert Murdoch Problem" (for short, I sometimes call this article "The reason I will never get a federal judgeship"), which argued that if we ever moved to a system of accepting political equality as a rationale for campaign finance regulation, then any newspaper wanting to endorse a candidate on its editorial page would have to form a PAC and pay for the space the way other corporations have to pay for ad space. (I would have continued applying the exemption to *reporting* on campaigns and issues. Since then, I have changed my position and now believe an exemption is justified, for reasons I will soon explain.)[4]

The article was not well received. First Amendment scholar Scot Powe wrote a law review response titled "Boiling Blood." When I presented the paper at a meeting of the American Political Science Association, my mentor and colleague Daniel Lowenstein of UCLA half-jokingly described it as "Stalinist." In March 2001, when the Senate was debating the McCain-Feingold campaign finance law, Senator McConnell placed into the record a *National Journal* column by Stuart Taylor, Jr., criticizing my article. McConnell introduced it by stating that Taylor "cautions the media to reconsider its hypocrisy in so zealously attacking the first amendment freedom of every other participant in the political process." Even an eminent First Amendment scholar who privately told me I was right to reject the media exemption for endorsements of candidates as a matter of principle would not say so publicly.[5]

The media question is difficult, and most reformers simply ignore it or quickly gloss over it. After retiring from active service on the Supreme Court, Justice Stevens wrote a book calling for six amendments to the Constitution, including one that would allow for greater campaign finance regulations. He did not address the media exemption question.[6] When pressed in an interview by Adam Liptak of the *New York Times* on the treatment of the media under his proposed amendment, Stevens equivocated.

[Liptak] asked him whether the amendment would allow the government to prohibit newspapers from spending money to publish editorials endorsing candidates. [Stevens] stared at the text of his proposed amendment for a little while. "The 'reasonable' [limitation on campaign finances in his amendment] would apply there," he said, "or might well be construed to apply there."

Or perhaps not. His tentative answer called to mind an exchange at the first Citizens United argument, when [deputy solicitor general Malcolm Stewart] told the court that Congress could in theory ban books urging the election of political candidates.

Justice Stevens said he would not go that far.

"Perhaps you could put a limit on the times of publication or something," he said. "You certainly couldn't totally prohibit writing a book."[7]

☑

The media exemption is the third rail of the campaign finance debate for good reason. Everyone from ardent reformers to strict deregulationists values a free press. On the other hand, the media are very powerful—how can a campaign finance system rein in the spending of most powerful individuals and groups but leave Rupert Murdoch's media empire, the *New York Times,* and Comcast-NBC-Universal untouched? This was the point Floyd Abrams pivoted to when I pressed him on how to treat foreign campaign money during our debate in 2012. He said: "One thing that I find unacceptable is the notion that if this [Citizens United] documentary had been made by a media company, that they should be exempt." In the United Kingdom, where every entity but newspapers faces campaign finance limits, Oxford University professor Jacob Rowbottom questioned whether the exemption made newspapers too powerful: "it is time to think about how newspapers can better reflect a wide range of opinions and not give so much power to the proprietor."[8]

Further, if you believe (as many conservatives do) that there is a liberal media bias, then stopping everyone but the press from unlimited spending for or against candidates for public office skews the debate toward left-leaning candidates.

Finally, exempting old, institutional media (sometimes derisively referred to as the "mainstream media") but not new media could unfairly benefit certain established groups. It also raises the difficult problems of determining what should count as "media" in the modern age.

In the end though, press exceptionalism makes sense. It is a cliché (but still correct) to refer to the press as the "fourth branch of government," providing an important check on the actual government. Two *Washington Post* writers broke the story of Watergate, and newspapers have delved perceptively and carefully into many scandals involving government officials. "Freedom of the press" remains sacrosanct in both elite and popular American culture.

When Congress passed the media exemption, it did so without much debate. Legislative history materials from Congress explain that "it is not the intent of the Congress . . . to limit or burden in any way the first amendment freedoms of the press and of association. Thus, [the media exception] assures the unfettered right of newspapers, TV networks, and other media to cover and comment on political campaigns." There is some evidence Congress included the exemption in part to help unions.[9]

The Supreme Court recognized the benefits of the institutional press in the *Austin* case. The challengers argued that Michigan's PAC requirement for corporations violated the Equal Protection Clause because the law contained a media exemption very similar to the federal media exemption. Although Justice Scalia and the other *Austin* dissenters believed this preferential treatment for press corporations rendered Michigan's law unconstitutional, the majority recognized a special role for the institutional press that justified the exemption.

> Although all corporations enjoy the same state-conferred benefits inherent in the corporate form, media corporations differ significantly from other corporations in that their resources are devoted to the collection of information and its dissemination to the public. We have consistently recognized the unique role that the press plays in "informing and educating the public, offering criticism, and providing a forum for discussion and debate." [Michigan's media exception] conceivably could be interpreted to encompass election-related news stories and editorials. The Act's restrictions on independent expenditures therefore might discourage incorporated news broadcasters or publishers from serving their crucial societal role. The media exception ensures that the Act does not hinder or prevent the institutional press from reporting on, and publishing editorials about, newsworthy

events. A valid distinction thus exists between corporations that are part of the media industry and other corporations that are not involved in the regular business of imparting news to the public. Although the press' unique societal role may not entitle the press to greater protection under the Constitution, it does provide a compelling reason for the State to exempt media corporations from the scope of political expenditure limitations.[10]

In his *Citizens United* dissent, Justice Stevens made much the same point about special press treatment, saying it was justified "in recognition of the unique role played by the institutional press in sustaining public debate." Robert Post, who supports corporate spending limits with a press exemption to further a government interest in "electoral integrity," agrees: "Corporations that serve the checking function should receive constitutional protections appropriate to that value. Corporations that do not serve the checking value should not receive these constitutional protections."[11]

The media exemption also is justified as a way of overcoming a collective action problem in elections, whereby individuals "free ride" on the press's efforts in identifying the best candidates. Rational voters have little incentive to gather information about candidates for political office, and what they do gather they acquire fortuitously and from competing campaigns, which cannot always be counted on to provide valuable information. Still, people do not like to vote when they think they know too little. Media coverage and endorsements help them make decisions about voting for candidates, particularly candidates for less prominent offices. A recent economics study focused on the muckraking era found that, in order to sell content, the profit-maximizing press spurs the enactment of public-regarding regulation by combining reporting of newsworthy events with entertainment (such as the reporting of scandal).[12]

The press's checking function and other democracy-enhancing functions now convince me that press exceptionalism is justified. In the same way that a $25,000 limit on individual contributions and spending deviates from strict principles of political equality in order to further an important competing value—ensuring robust political speech and competitive campaigns—press exceptionalism deviates from strict principles of political equality to further the press's key role in informing voters, fostering debate, and keeping politicians honest and competent.

My earlier skepticism about the press exemption for media endorsements (I wanted to keep the exemption for reporting on candidates and campaigns) was based on a few factors. First, back in 1999 when I first researched the question, it appeared that newspaper editorials and endorsements tended to be biased in particular ways. Contrary to claims of liberal media bias, their endorsements tended to support Republicans and incumbents.[13]

More recent research, however, shows the partisan effect may be overstated, and that voters are judicious in relying on endorsements. They appear to understand that newspapers have political leanings, and they pay attention mainly when the papers cut against their own grain: when liberal-leaning papers endorse Republicans or conservative-leaning ones endorse Democrats. Moderates are most influenced by these counterintuitive endorsements. Further, newspaper endorsements tend to line up with the position of the median voter in the newspaper's coverage area and to take more moderate positions than those of the area's interest groups.[14]

The evidence on whether media reporting is biased toward liberal outcomes is mixed and hotly disputed, but such bias, if it exists, will likely continue to decrease with disruptions in traditional media and the emergence of the partisan press. Today, the danger is less that people will be swayed unduly by a liberal media elite than that they will be attracted to news media that reinforce their existing views and encourage greater partisanship. I think of Justice Scalia, who told *New York* magazine that he gave up reading the *Washington Post* because it became "so shrilly, *shrilly* liberal." Instead he gets his news and commentary from the *Wall Street Journal* (with its very conservative editorial section), the *Washington Times,* and talk radio.[15]

Second, and somewhat in tension with the first point, it did not appear that endorsements are all that important to voters, at least in presidential races. A PAC requirement for endorsements thus seemed unlikely to deprive voters of much valuable information. But the more recent research described above shows that media endorsements can help voters, especially when they appear credible.

Finally, the media are not alone in serving a checking function: parties, non-media corporations, and others can also provide voters with valuable information. Giving an exemption only to the media could limit other individuals' and entities' abilities to serve the checking function. Further, the Speech Clause gives the non-press great protection for expression and political activity.

My opposition to press exceptionalism dissipated as I watched what was happening to state and local politics with the decline of local newspapers. One of the greatest dangers to democracy, especially on the local level, is that the economics of the Internet and social media may drive the remaining local newspapers, already decimated by steep declines in advertising revenue, out of business. Laws that discourage the press's checking function would undermine this crucial role at the very time that the press is so vulnerable and its democracy-enhancing functions are more important than ever.[16]

Lifting the exemption just for press endorsements but not reporting also would create the problem of deciding when reporting and analysis crosses the line into endorsement. In any case, if newspaper endorsements do not matter that much, then making people's blood boil by trying to regulate them makes no sense.

In addition, if the worry is that the media become too powerful thanks to industry concentration and have too much influence over electoral politics, the solution is to use antitrust law to ensure a continued diversity of opinion through diffuse ownership. This is not a call to reinstitute the Fairness Doctrine to regulate media content (something that raises deep First Amendment concerns). Instead, it is a recognition that a multiplicity of voices and viewpoints in a competitive marketplace reinforces the checking function of the press. We can assure greater political equality *within* the news media by ensuring a competitive press industry.[17]

Even today, media corporations serve the checking and democracy-enhancing functions of the government much better than other entities do. Ted Turner's CNN, Rupert Murdoch's Fox News, and Comcast's MSNBC educate, engage, and sometimes infuriate viewers on issues relevant to candidates, policies, ideologies, and campaigns. That's not true of the core activities of other corporations, unions, or entities that ordinarily sell soap, provide services, or organize workers. Non-press corporations, consistent with their fiduciary duty to shareholders to maximize share value, engage in election-related activities to further their bottom lines. The checking function is incidental to the commercial enterprise.

Subsidiaries of the Comcast Corporation, such as the unit that sells Internet access to consumers, do not perform the same checking and democracy-enhancing functions as Comcast's press portions. The press exemption applies only to the portion of a corporation that is in the business of reporting news, discussing ideas, and making arguments.[18]

To be sure, a corporate-owned press entity could push candidates whose votes would help its own or its party's bottom line. There is a danger that the press portions of Comcast will be pressured to shape their coverage and viewpoint to further Comcast's corporate interests. As A. J. Liebling remarked, "Freedom of the press is guaranteed only to those who own one." These are serious concerns that make the argument on press exceptionalism the most difficult one on the reform side. But on average the press is much more likely to serve a checking and democracy-enhancing function than non-press entities, and so long as we do enough to fight media overconcentration it is reasonable to craft campaign finance laws that exempt the press even if doing so undercuts the goal of furthering political equality.[19]

Reasonable, but perhaps unconstitutional.

☑

"We have consistently rejected the proposition that the institutional press has any constitutional privilege beyond that of other speakers." So declared the Supreme Court in *Citizens United* (quoting Justice Scalia's *Austin* dissent), in a statement Robert Post called "manifestly incorrect" and Iowa professor Randall Bezanson called "stunningly incorrect." Much turns on whose judgment about the meaning of the Press Clause is right.[20]

Post pointed to the Supreme Court's decision in *Minneapolis Star v. Minneapolis Commissioner,* a 1983 case, which held unconstitutional under the First Amendment a tax applied uniquely against the institutional press. As he explained, "States can impose unique taxes on virtually every kind of business, including non-press communicative businesses like film distributors, but they are constitutionally prohibited from imposing a singular tax on the press." Here, the Court recognized that the press serves as an "important restraint on government." Professor Bezanson wrote that Kennedy's opinion "does not address numerous earlier cases that arguably support the opposite conclusion, albeit often in dicta."[21]

Other Supreme Court cases also have protected the editorial function of the press, but have not necessarily limited these protections to the press as an institution. In *Mills v. Alabama,* the Court struck down an Alabama law that made it a crime to publish newspaper editorials on election day urging people to vote in a certain way on issues submitted to them. Alabama had argued that the law was a reasonable restriction to protect the public from last-minute charges that could not be responded to by those attacked. Assuming without deciding that Alabama's interest was legitimate, the Court noted a lack of narrow tailoring: "The state statute leaves people free to hurl their campaign charges up to the last minute of the day before the election. The law . . . then goes on to make it a crime to answer those 'last-minute' charges on election day, the only time they can be effectively answered."[22]

The Court in *Mills* also stated that the "Constitution specifically selected the press . . . to play an important role in the discussion of public affairs." It recognized the role of the press "as a powerful antidote to any abuses of power by governmental officials and as a constitutionally chosen means for keeping officials elected by the people responsible to all the people whom they were selected to serve."[23]

Similarly, in *Miami Herald Publishing Co. v. Tornillo,* in 1974, the Court struck down a Florida law that granted a political candidate a right to equal space to answer criticism and attacks on his record in a newspaper. Advocates of this law argued that it was intended to "ensure that a wide variety of views reach the public." Although the Court noted the rise of monopoly power in the newspaper industry, Chief Justice Warren Burger's majority opinion rejected the argument: "A responsible press is an undoubtedly desirable goal, but press responsibility is not mandated by the Constitution and like many other virtues it cannot be legislated." He concluded that "it has yet to be demonstrated how governmental regulation [over editorial content] can be exercised consistent with First Amendment guarantees of a free press as they have evolved to this time."[24]

No one disputes that the First Amendment specifically protects freedom of the press in addition to freedom of speech. The main constitutional dispute is whether it protects "the press" as an institution and the work of journalists and editorialists or whether the guarantee of "freedom . . . of the press" protects *anyone's* dissemination of information. Under the former definition, Congress may single out the institutional press for extra constitutional protection. *Citizens United* embraces the latter definition: "the press" is an activity or technology, and an exemption for the institutional press runs afoul of the First Amendment by protecting some speakers over others.

The debate over the meaning of the Press Clause has divided First Amendment scholars. Eugene Volokh argues that the original understanding of the clause was that it protected the technology (the printing press) and not an industry. Running with this argument, Professor (and former federal appellate judge) Michael McConnell contends that *Citizens United* itself is properly understood as a press case: he argued that the Supreme Court should have ruled that the Citizens United group, whether incorporated or not, had a constitutional right to spend whatever it wanted in putting its documentary on the air, because creating and airing a documentary is a press function.[25]

McConnell and others point to additional Supreme Court precedents that seem to reject press exceptionalism, such as *First National Bank of Boston v. Bellotti*, a 1978 case in which Chief Justice Burger wrote in a concurring opinion that he did not think it possible "either as a matter of fact or constitutional law" to separate media corporations from other corporations. University of Alabama professor Paul Horwitz believes Justice Burger's arguments seem "to have carried the day" as official Supreme Court doctrine, but that the Court still gives the institutional press extra constitutional protections through such legal doctrines as the rule on defamation, requiring proof that statements on matters of public concern be subject to suit only if made with knowledge of falsity or in reckless disregard of the truth, in which "courts have woven the notion of the professional judgment of journalists into the fabric of the law itself."[26]

There are reasons to question the originalist argument. Professor Sonja West, for example, argues that Volokh's historical understanding of the press as technology is too simplistic. West argues that the "evidence reveals that members of the framing generation experienced the press as a tool of limited capability and reach, which was accessible only to certain speakers and used primarily to publish certain kinds of messages." More important, the press-as-technology reading would have disturbing legal consequences. As Bezanson explained, the approach would render the Press Clause a nullity, whether or not it is correct as an originalist interpretation (a methodology which—for reasons well beyond the scope of this book—should not be decisive when it comes to interpreting the First Amendment or the rest of the Constitution).[27]

If everyone gets freedom of the press because we all use the same technology to disseminate words and pictures, and this freedom coexists with freedom of speech, then the Press Clause does no work. As Horwitz put it, for McConnell, the Press Clause is in part about the right to publish but is "in even larger measure, a non-discrimination provision." Everyone gets its protections. Further, "speech" is a technology too.[28]

Without special constitutional protection for those engaged in regular journalism, it is not clear what happens to press access to government events, to a press "shield" for anonymous sources, or to press protection from ordinary claims of "fraud" when reporters do undercover investigations. Not only would such activity lose special constitutional protections; as Bezanson explained, if the Press Clause duplicates the Speech Clause, then any special laws protecting the press, such as shield laws, could be unconstitutional because they favor one class of speakers (the institutional press) over others. Yet this is exactly the argument the Supreme Court appeared to endorse in *Citizens United*.[29]

McConnell's article in the *Yale Law Journal* on treating *Citizens United* as a Press Clause case demonstrates what it means when everyone gets treated the same under that clause. Under his interpretation, all money spent by anyone on advertising for or against a candidate counts as Press Clause activity. Presumably these advertisers would also include the "Red Chinese Army, the Iranian government and Hamas," although McConnell does not say anything about whether the Press Clause would protect ads paid for by foreign individuals or entities who have the right in this country to print newspapers.

McConnell presented his Press Clause interpretation as a narrower and more reasonable way to resolve the dispute in *Citizens United,* but his analysis leads essentially to the same result the Court reached: full constitutional protection for independent corporate spending. The only minor difference between the professor and the Court is that McConnell's Press Clause path would not apply to campaign spending not directly tied to advertising, such as money spent on voter registration or get-out-the-vote activities. (McConnell questions whether these activities, if paid for by Democratic supporter George Soros, should get constitutional protection.) But courts may still protect spending on these activities under the Speech Clause of the First Amendment.[30]

Fortunately, it is not necessary to read protection for the press out of the Constitution. The earlier Supreme Court cases mentioned above, although inconsistent with *Citizens United,* affirm a path toward special constitutional protection for the institutional press because of its checking function. Work by Professors Bezanson, Horwitz, and Georgia Tech's Sonja West offers principled arguments for continuing special protections for the press as an institution or protection of those who regularly engage in journalistic endeavors, as well as tools for deciding who should count as the press.[31]

These scholars argue that journalists even in the new media age consistently serve a checking function that is not served by non-press entities. The emergence of journalistic norms of fact checking and the function of holding government accountable differentiate the press from everyone else. As Horwitz put it, "News stories are the product of a complex process that includes finding and refining stories, amassing the information that goes into a story, and deciding what should get into print and what should be left out. As anyone who has worked with the institutional press knows, that process calls on a significant set of skills and traditions. . . . Before a story is published, every line, every quote, every judgment call is subjected to checking and rechecking, debate and counter-debate, and institutional second-guessing."[32]

The Supreme Court's reading of the Press Clause in *Citizens United* is no more convincing or inevitable or correct than its reading of the Speech Clause. Assuming we can figure out who counts as "the press" in the era of the Internet and social media, there remain compelling constitutional reasons to single it out for special treatment.

☑

"NRA News" arose out of the fight over the constitutionality of the McCain-Feingold law. The National Rifle Association, like Citizens United, is an ideological non-profit corporation that takes money from some for-profit corporations. Under the federal law in place until *Citizens United,* those donations meant that the NRA could not spend its general treasury funds to support or oppose federal candidates, either through "Vote for Bush"-type express advocacy or television or radio ads featuring federal candidates in the period just before the election. Instead, just as if it were a for-profit corporation, all of its campaign-related spending had to come through a PAC.

The NRA challenged the McCain-Feingold law as quickly as it could. In fact, it filed its challenge before anyone else (having apparently been tipped off by the Bush White House that the president was going to sign the bill quietly, with no public ceremony for Senators McCain and Feingold), and it got into a battle with Senator Mitch McConnell over whether his suit or theirs would have bragging rights to the consolidated case name: instead of *McConnell v. Federal Election Commission* we could have had *National Rifle Association v. Federal Election Commission.* McConnell won that fight, although both he and the NRA lost the lawsuit.[33]

The NRA argued that the McCain-Feingold law gave media corporations an unfair advantage, an argument the Supreme Court rejected in this case but later accepted in *Citizens United.* When the NRA lost in *McConnell,* it set up its own "NRA News" network to provide programming and commentary on the Internet, television, and radio.[34]

Some initially derided NRA News as a "loophole" intended to attract "soft money contributions" from for-profit corporations through the guise of the media exemption. At first, it was not clear if NRA News would ever be more than a gimmick to get around the limits on corporate spending in federal elections.[35]

But over time, NRA News proved itself to be a genuine source of news and commentary—with, needless to say, a pro–gun rights slant—and much more than a convenient workaround for corporate-funded campaign ads. Even now, after the *Citizens United* decision freed the NRA to finance political ads directly from its corporate treasury, NRA News continues to produce all kinds of content for its website, radio programs, and other outlets. It is a bona fide outlet for news and commentary, and fully part of the institutional press (much of which these days is partisan).

Someday, perhaps soon, we may have the Koch Brothers Network competing with the Tom Steyer Network offering twenty-four hours of news, commentary, and election-related stories preaching to the faithful on television and the Internet. (Some may say current cable news organizations such as Fox News or MSNBC serve as their proxies already.) But if these organizations build themselves into genuine journalistic endeavors, they would be entitled to the same journalistic protections as other, more established voices. The question we should ask about entities that request the press exemption is whether they function regularly as journalists, and not who backs them.

The NRA News story illustrates the importance of having a good definition of "the press" that is not ideologically driven and that can account for changes in technology. As West explained, "it is neither elitist nor discriminatory to separate the press from other types of speakers. Our equality principles are satisfied as long as we ensure that all speakers have a fair opportunity to attain this status."[36] West would protect not only the institutionalized press but also regularly updated journalistic blogs and other individuals and entities engaging in regular journalistic functions.

In *Citizens United,* the Court assumed that the rise of new media obliterated any coherent concept of the press: "Soon . . . it may be that Internet sources, such as blogs and social networking Web sites, will provide citizens with significant information about political candidates and issues. Yet [the federal corporate spending ban] would seem to ban a blog post expressly advocating the election or defeat of a candidate if that blog were created with corporate funds."[37]

That is certainly wrong. Put aside the fact that Internet sources before the decision in *Citizens United* already were providing citizens with significant information about political candidates and issues. The legal analysis is wrong: Corporations used corporate funds to create Twitter, Facebook, and

Blogger, but tweets, Facebook posts, and occasional blog posts by individuals were not subject to any limitations under the law banning corporate expenditures on federal campaigns.

Perhaps the Court meant to make the narrower point that *a corporation's* election-related content on a corporate-funded blog, such as a message to "Vote for Romney" on the website of General Motors, would be banned under the old law. If that is what it meant, it is not much different than where things stood under the law for old media: a corporation's election content could not appear in corporate-funded television advertising either. Such advertising would have had to be paid for through corporate PAC funds under the old rules. The Internet changed nothing in this regard. This is a variation on the "book banning" canard we saw in the previous chapter.

But the Court's mention of blogs and social media does raise the more important question of who counts as the media. One could say we are all "the press," since anyone can gather and report news on Twitter, or provide commentary about a candidate or campaign on Facebook, or post a campaign-oriented video on a blog. If this view is correct, that lends credence to McConnell's call that all independent expenditures should be protected by the First Amendment's Press Clause.

Many of us today, in West's words, are "occasional public commentators," but we are not all press. As Horwitz noted, personal blogs are not press, and whether we should recognize all blogs (or whatever eventually replaces them) as an institution worthy of special First Amendment treatment is a separate question from whether we treat blogs as the press.[38]

In drawing the line between "the press" and everyone else, we might start with the Federal Election Commission's own regulation on the subject, which provides in key part that "any cost incurred in covering or carrying a news story, commentary, or editorial by any broadcasting station (including a cable television operator, programmer or producer), Web site, newspaper, magazine, or other periodical publication, including any Internet or electronic publication, is not a [campaign] expenditure unless the facility is owned or controlled by any political party, political committee, or candidate."[39]

Of course, this definition leaves room for argument and uncertainty.

What else besides a regular newspaper or magazine counts as a "periodical publication"? How often must a blog be published to meet this definition? Can those engaged in pure electoral advertising argue they are engaged in providing "commentary" or an "editorial"? The line-drawing problem suggests we may need finer-tuned approaches than what the commission has used in the past.

Following the Supreme Court's test to determine whether someone counts as a "minister" for purposes of the Free Exercise Clause of the First Amendment, Professor West pointed to four factors that should be of the greatest importance in identifying "the press": "(1) recognition by others as the press; (2) holding oneself out as the press; (3) training, education, or experience in journalism; and (4) regularity of publication and established audience."[40]

Under these standards, what most people who publish on the Internet and social media create is not press content even if these posters occasionally perform press-like functions. Only those bloggers and posters who regularly serve journalistic functions would be entitled to the press exemption. As Professor West put it, "In theory all citizens armed with laptops and Internet connections might be able to gather and convey news and check powerful government and private interests. But the reality is that there are some speakers who do this work more consistently and effectively than others. And common sense suggests that repeat-player specialists with proven track records will do the most valuable work."[41]

Professor David Anderson emphasized that it is not necessary, as West suggested, to see the press as *unique* in fulfilling its essential democratic functions: "Democracy requires dialogue, and dialogue requires some agreement about the subjects to be discussed. What the press does, usefully though not uniquely, is organize public dialogue. News outfits sift, select, and package the news, and in so doing create a community among people who share the outlet's conception of news sufficiently to subscribe, tune in, or click. . . . The case for enforcing the press clause is not dependent on any belief that the press is unique. . . . It is enough that the press is one of the entities that usefully serves these functions and is the one the Framers saw fit to recognize. Protecting them all would be impossible and protecting none would be intolerable."[42]

Professor West's test is controversial. Some see the first prong as circular (people are the press who are recognized as the press), and some excellent journalists who have no formal journalism training (such as Adam Liptak, the Supreme Court reporter for the *New York Times*) might have trouble under West's second prong. But West's is a flexible test; there is little doubt that Liptak would count as the press under this test: the key question is whether the person or entity is regularly fulfilling the checking and educational functions of the press, and the Supreme Court reporter for the *Times* undoubtedly fulfills those functions.

A final possible source for defining "the press" comes from "press shield" laws, which protect members of the institutional press from revealing their confidential sources at court hearings. A recent study counted thirty-eight states plus the District of Columbia as having some form of press shield law: "Each statute or rule is different from the rest, but all of them attempt to define who is protected. Some do so by occupation (who does the covered person work for?), others by function (what does the covered person do?), and most combine the two. The statutes also vary widely in how specifically they define the persons and occupations that qualify for protection." A proposed federal shield law also includes a useful definition of "journalism" that could provide the basis for crafting the right line between those entitled to the press exemption and those who are not.[43]

The press shield approach too is not perfect, and there is sometimes litigation over whether bloggers and others get the benefit of a state's press shield. As the study notes, "Determining whether someone who does not fit the profile of a traditional journalist could be protected by existing statutes is largely guesswork without more appellate-level case law." But for purposes of the media exemption we could settle on one of the clearer state approaches (or the proposed federal approach) to the question of who counts as the press; states' experimentation provides an excellent source to examine how to craft the best line between the institutional press entitled to the media exemption and everyone else.[44]

In short, whether or not the Federal Election Commission test, the West test, or a state or (proposed) federal reporter shield definition is the best way to define the press, the task of determining who gets the benefit of the press clause for campaign finance purposes is difficult but doable. There will no doubt be borderline cases. But that is par for the course in constitutional adjudication. If we cannot define the press for purposes of the campaign finance exemption, we would not be able to define it for other purposes either, such as a shield law. And if we cannot define the press, perhaps we cannot define "a minister" or a "religion" either for purposes of applying constitutional and statutory protections for ministers and religious institutions. We might not be able to regulate "obscenity" consistent with the First Amendment either, even if we know it when we see it. Line drawing is an inevitable, difficult part of constitutional adjudication extending far beyond the Press Clause. The key to line drawing is making the rules as clear as possible, so that courts can ferret out an impermissible government motive.

I could not resist a chuckle when the Supreme Court recently set forth new standards for determining who counts as "the press" for purposes of getting a coveted Supreme Court press pass. The issue became urgent because of a question over credentialing the popular website SCOTUSblog, which provides indispensable information about the Supreme Court but is owned by a prominent Supreme Court practitioner, Tom Goldstein. The Court's new guidelines made ownership by a practitioner a bar to obtaining a press credential (although SCOTUSblog apparently found a workaround by having its main reporter, Lyle Denniston, create his own website to cover the Court).[45]

The Court, which held in *Citizens United* that defining the press for campaign finance purposes is impossible, had no difficulty defining who could get a Court press pass and limiting the pass to full-time "journalists" working for "media organizations":

> A "media organization" is an entity that has as its principal business the regular gathering and reporting of original news for the public, that disseminates its reporting through publicly accessible media, and that has operated continuously for the two years preceding the application for credentials. A media organization can distribute information in any medium (print, television, radio, electronic, or otherwise) and can exist as any form of business or other entity. We require the applicant to operate or to be employed by a media organization because individuals so engaged are more likely to regularly and broadly disseminate information about the Court to the public. . . . We require that an applicant or the applicant's media organization have a

record of "substantial and original news coverage of the work of the Court" to ensure that hard passes are allocated to those who have greatest need for the privileges they confer. . . . Journalists and organizations with records of substantial and original coverage of the Court are more likely to disseminate information about the Court's work to the public.[46]

If the Court can draw lines for its own press passes, it can draw lines for constitutional campaign finance purposes as well.

More important, even those who fall on the non-press side of the line—however it is drawn—in the campaign finance area still may engage in robust political activities. Withholding the media exemption from occasional bloggers, tweeters, snapchatters, and Facebook posters does not mean that the campaign finance laws unduly infringe on this type of individual political speech. One of the great benefits of social media is that it creates an era, in Volokh's words, of "cheap speech." Access to Twitter, Facebook, and similar sites is free (at least if you ignore the hidden costs of sacrificing your data privacy), and access is open to anyone with an Internet connection. In this way, political speech on the Internet and social media—including the use of social media to organize like-minded people for political purposes—furthers a "level-up" egalitarianism that works like the voucher system in empowering voters. None of this activity under my proposed campaign finance rules would count toward the $25,000 individual limit when a voter pays nothing out of pocket to engage in this speech.[47]

Some have predicted that the era of cheap speech will affect elections profoundly. Campaigning will become significantly cheaper as voters no longer get their news and information from television or radio advertisements. I doubt campaign costs will go down significantly; the emergence of the Internet and social media has certainly not made it happen so far. Campaigns simply find new ways to spend money on voters, such as through targeted advertising on social media websites. But if costs ever do go down, and money becomes less important, we still need to think about how to treat the press and everyone else under our campaign finance laws.[48]

☑

The parallel between the deregulationists who give way on the question of foreign spending in elections and the reformers who give way on the question of the media exemption can be overstated. The inconsistency on the deregulatory side exposes the truth that the identity of the speaker really does matter, and there can be compelling reasons to limit political advertising in ways that balance the need to preserve robust political speech. It shows that too much money in politics, at least if coming from the "wrong" people or entities, can be socially harmful. That is a point that deregulationists never straightforwardly admit.

The lack of consistency in the reform side's treatment of media corporations demonstrates that political equality, while important, is not the only value of a campaign finance system. Sometimes equality must give way to free speech concerns. In the case of the Press Clause, political equality must give way to protection for the institutional press and regular journalists. The press's checking function is important enough, and the dangers to political equality small enough, that the media exemption is justified.

Justice Scalia's *Austin* dissent warned that "media corporations not only have vastly greater power to perpetrate the evil of overinforming, they also have vastly greater opportunity." But the problem of large spending on election campaigns is not "overinformation" provided to voters. The problem is the collateral benefits that accrue to the wealthiest who spend on and contribute very large sums to campaigns and election-oriented groups.[49]

Media campaign coverage and endorsements raise this danger too. Media coverage provides the collateral benefit of influence to those in the institutional press who write about candidates and campaigns. But two factors counterbalance the danger. First, media influence tends to be spread across the political spectrum. The wide range of political views creates an equivalent range of markets for news and commentary. For every *New York Times* on the left, there is a *Wall Street Journal* on the right. We have Fox News and MSNBC. We have liberal and conservative bloggers and talk radio hosts, Rush Limbaugh and Jon Stewart. There is good reason to think we have a more balanced distribution of opinions in the media than among those who fund campaign ads.

Second, the institutional press, unlike General Motors or the SEIU, has as its core mission the idea of keeping the government and those in power in check, and abides by journalistic norms that are foreign to most of those who contribute and spend on elections.

On balance, giving the media freedom from campaign finance rules that others must follow raises troubling questions for those of us committed to political equality. But compromise on this question is not only necessary to protect press freedoms; the checking function served by media corporations enhances rather than detracts from American democracy.

7

(Un)Intended Consequences

IN SEPTEMBER 2014, TED OLSON TOOK to the op-ed page of the *Wall Street Journal* to complain about Senate Democrats' attempt to overturn *Citizens United* via a constitutional amendment. Olson, who had successfully argued in the Supreme Court both *Bush v. Gore,* which ended the Florida presidential recount on behalf of George W. Bush in 2000, and *Citizens United,* said that the Democrats' real purpose in putting forward the amendment was not to prevent corruption or restore the integrity of elections but to protect incumbents from political competition: "When politicians seek to restrict political speech, it is invariably to protect their own incumbency and avoid having to defend their policies in the marketplace of ideas."[1]

Opponents of campaign finance laws regularly suggest that incumbents pass these laws with self-interested motivations. Senator James Buckley credited his unlikely win as a U.S. senator from New York running on the Conservative Party line in 1970 to support from a few wealthy donors. Eugene McCarthy, who ran an insurgent campaign against President Lyndon Johnson in 1968 thanks to the support of one large donor, J. Stewart Mott, made a similar point. Although McCarthy did not win the Democratic nomination for president, the success of his campaign convinced Johnson that he should withdraw from the race.[2]

Buckley feared that the limits Congress enacted in the 1974 amendments to the Federal Election Campaign Act would prevent insurgent candidates like himself and McCarthy from breaking through against incumbents, who had name recognition and other advantages of office. This fear motivated him not only to oppose the amendments in Congress, and to amend the bill to fast-track constitutional challenges to the Supreme Court, but also to become the lead plaintiff in *Buckley v. Valeo*.[3]

On the Court, opponents of campaign finance limits have picked up the theme that these laws are little more than a protection racket. Justice Kennedy called the McCain-Feingold law of 2002 an "incumbency protection plan." Justice Scalia saw it the same way: "To be sure, the legislation is evenhanded: It similarly prohibits criticism of the candidates who oppose Members of Congress in their reelection bids. But as everyone knows, this is an area in which evenhandedness is not fairness. If *all* electioneering were evenhandedly prohibited, incumbents would have an enormous advantage. Likewise, if incumbents and challengers are limited to the same quantity of electioneering, incumbents are favored. In other words, *any* restriction upon a type of campaign speech that is equally available to challengers and incumbents tends to favor incumbents."[4]

It is not earth-shattering news that politicians might support campaign finance legislation—or any other legislation—at least partly from self-interested motives. When campaign reformers from Common Cause and other groups pushed Congress in the wake of Watergate to pass the sweeping campaign finance law in 1974, they appealed to the legislators in two ways. First, they packaged the measure as a means of reining in the "skyrocketing costs of campaigns," which members of Congress saw as an increasingly time-consuming problem. Second, the Watergate hearings and other corruption scandals made the issue salient to the public, which clamored for change. Reformers urged politicians to give the people what they wanted: real limits on money in elections. President Gerald Ford, who took over for President Nixon after Nixon resigned, did not support the Federal Election Campaign Act amendments of 1974 but felt he had no choice but to sign the bill.[5]

Self-interest was also behind the passage in 2002 of the Bipartisan Campaign Reform Act, the "McCain-Feingold" campaign finance law, which limited party "soft money" and corporate and labor union "issue advocacy." Republican senator John McCain had become a champion of campaign finance reform years earlier, after he was caught up in the "Keating Five" affair. As the *Arizona Republic* explained, McCain and four other senators "were accused of trying to pressure federal thrift regulators to back off their political benefactor [Charles] Keating, whose Lincoln Savings & Loan would collapse during the savings-and-loan crisis of the late 1980s at a cost of $3.4 billion to taxpayers. At the time, Keating was an influential and larger-than-life business figure in Arizona and he generously contributed campaign cash to his favorite politicians."[6]

For years afterward, McCain railed against the corruption he saw as endemic in the system of soft money, issue ads, and rising campaign costs. He wrote in 2002 that the Keating scandal "still made him 'wince' even years later," according to the *Arizona Republic* article on him published in 2014, "and that the memory provoked 'a vague but real feeling that I had lost something very important' in pursuit of 'gratifying ambitions, my own and others.'"[7]

McCain and others tried to pass versions of their reform plan for seven years. They succeeded only after the Enron scandal of the early 2000s made enough members of Congress feel they had to do something about the problem of money in politics. Enron, a Texas-based company, manipulated energy prices, especially in California, wreaking havoc not just in the electric-power market but causing shortages in Western states. It succeeded thanks to lax regulation, and many thought that contributions to members of Congress and to related PACs protected Enron from the kind of regulation that would have prevented all the problems.[8]

Was McCain acting out of self-interest in supporting campaign finance reform? In one sense, he certainly was. Being a reformer or a "maverick" was a part of his branding, and he initially may have taken up the cause to help dissipate the stench of the Keating Five scandal. But there is no good evidence that the specifics of McCain-Feingold, such as its ban on party soft money and treating corporate and labor union "issue ads" as election ads, were designed to make it harder for an opponent to run against him for Senate in Arizona. In that sense, he was likely not acting in his narrow self-interest.

Even Justice Scalia admitted that self-interested motivations to support campaign finance regulation could be subconscious: "I cannot say for certain that many, or some, or even any, of the Members of Congress who voted for this legislation did so not to produce 'fairer' campaigns, but to mute criticism of their records and facilitate reelection. Indeed, I will stipulate that all those who voted for [the Act] believed they were acting for the good of the country. There remains the problem of the Charlie Wilson Phenomenon, named after Charles Wilson, former president of General Motors, who is supposed to have said during the Senate hearing on his nomination as Secretary of Defense that 'what's good for General Motors is good for the country.' Those in power, even giving them the benefit of the greatest good will, are inclined to believe that what is good for them is good for the country."[9]

Whatever was in the hearts of senators and members of Congress, they drafted McCain-Feingold with the cooperation of a group of reformers, including Fred Wertheimer, who had been instrumental in getting the 1974 reforms passed. To judge from the rest of their agenda, reform groups like Common Cause certainly had no love of incumbents. Independent outside people supported campaign finance without having anything to gain from incumbency protection.[10]

The idea that politicians favor campaign reform simply to avoid tough elections lacks substance. If these laws really helped incumbents across the board, why isn't reform supported equally by both parties? Why did the McCain-Feingold law pass the U.S. Senate by a vote of only 60–40, compared with the 2006 renewal of the Voting Rights Act, which passed the Senate 98–0?[11]

It cannot be that those incumbents who vote for the law do so to only to protect themselves, and that only opponents of these laws are acting from principle. These days, with mostly Democrats supporting campaign finance regulation and mostly Republicans opposing it, that would make Democrats the party of self-interest and Republicans the party of principle, which is exactly how Republicans want to portray things.

The legislative motivation is a lot more complicated. Following *Citizens United,* the Democratic Party itself, much like Senator McCain in the early 2000s, uses campaign finance reform as a way of exciting the base and (ironically) for fundraising. Republicans rail against campaign finance laws as Orwellian censorship, playing to their own base with claims that Democrats want to pass a constitutional amendment to restrict speech and to suppress their competition. The few Republicans who supported reform in the past, like Senator McCain, are mostly silent.

Republicans have not always been the party of First Amendment purity. In the 1940s, they strongly favored campaign finance laws that reined in the ability of labor unions to spend on political campaigns. In the 2000s, they supported increased disclosure for "527 organizations" which were spending money in the 2004 presidential election mostly to help Democratic presidential candidate John Kerry and other Democrats. But since *Citizens United*, Republicans have opposed improved disclosure laws. At the same time, Republican-oriented groups have been more aggressive than Democratic ones in taking advantage of the disclosure loopholes.[12]

The history of the Republican position on campaign regulation raises a more plausible theory of legislative motivation than simple incumbency protection: elected officials support these laws not because they benefit incumbents generally, but because they may help their own party. In the past, this idea had little support, as one could find Democrats and Republicans on both sides of the campaign issue. Today, however, both Democrats and Republicans seem to believe that the new *Citizens United* campaign finance regime makes it easier for Republicans and harder for Democrats to raise money and win elections. In turn, we have seen increased partisanship on the issue of campaign reform, with Democrats generally stating a preference favoring reform and Republicans opposing it.

Now it may be that Democrats are just giving lip service to reform, proposing a constitutional amendment (which I discuss more in the next chapter) to please their base, safe in the knowledge that it would never pass. But they appear to genuinely want to pass some legislation, such as better disclosure laws (including the "DISCLOSE Act"), and Republicans genuinely have opposed any such legislation. More broadly, if the wealthy are likely to support Republicans over Democrats, we should not be surprised if the latter are the ones supporting rules to rein in spending by the wealthy.

Still, politicians' taking self-interest and their parties' chances into account is hardly unique to the issue of campaign finance. They do the same on immigration, defense, and same-sex marriage. It is no more an indictment of campaign finance law to say that elected officials support or oppose it to gain favor with voters than it is to say they support or oppose

Obamacare to gain favor with their voters. Campaign reform, like health care reform, should be judged on its own merits, not on the motivation for passing it.

Once we remove legislative motivation from our consideration of the merits of campaign finance laws, we can focus on two more relevant questions: does the public support campaign reforms, and do reforms actually bias outcomes toward incumbents?

On the question of public support, polls consistently show two things: the public favors campaign finance reform by wide margins, but the issue is not a priority. A Gallup poll conducted in June 2014, for example, showed 80 percent of Americans supporting campaign finance limits. As the *New York Times* explained, unlike Congress, voters were united across party lines. "The poll found that broad majorities of all Americans, regardless of their political philosophy, party identification, age, education, sex or income level, preferred limits on campaign donations." Support is broad but shallow. Professor David Primo of the University of Rochester, looking at the evidence on public support for campaign limits in the early 2000s, found "in poll after poll, campaign finance is near the bottom of the list of important issues, trailing behind homelessness."[13]

The wide if hardly fervent support for campaign finance laws is good evidence that the public does not see such reforms as protecting incumbents. The public supports term limits by wide margins even though politicians hate them, and voters have passed term limit initiatives in many states. Further, voters on the state and local levels consistently vote for campaign finance ballot measures, including those imposing limits (which courts generally strike down). Voters seem to have made the judgment that limiting money in politics is worth the risk of incumbency protection.

Perhaps incumbency-protecting politicians have duped the public and good government groups into believing campaign finance laws are in the public interest. More likely, the public recognizes the equality costs of allowing the wealthiest individuals and entities to give hundreds of millions of dollars promote the election or defeat of candidates.

Further, the evidence from social science suggests that laws such as contribution limits do little to enhance the large advantages incumbents already possess. As we saw in Chapter 2, political scientists have hotly debated whether spending limits, if allowed by the Supreme Court, might help incumbents. Professor Gary Jacobson, who has consistently argued that spending limits help incumbents, believes that challenger spending is what chiefly determines the competitiveness of elections, and that limiting spending would benefit incumbents by making it harder for challengers to make themselves known to voters. Other political scientists have disputed Jacobson's arguments, believing spending limits, if anything, might help challengers. Of course, we cannot test these propositions while the Supreme Court prohibits spending limits as unconstitutional.[14]

Ultimately, the question whether a package of campaign finance laws helps incumbents is an empirical one that requires seeing the laws in action for a few election cycles. Further, it cannot be answered for any and all such laws, but depends upon the specifics of the laws. A law that imposes strict spending limits on candidate campaigns but allows unlimited outside money, for example, could have a very different effect from a law imposing spending limits across the board. The fact that Canada and Great Britain have had competitive elections with stricter spending limits does not mean we would have competitive elections under the U.S. system, which is not parliamentary and has much longer campaign seasons.

There are strong reasons to think the particular campaign finance reform I have proposed—$100 campaign vouchers for each voter in federal elections, plus $25,000 hybrid individual contribution and spending limits per election with a $500,000 two-year aggregate cap—would not add to the advantage incumbents possess or inhibit political competition. To begin with, there is some evidence that even modest public financing laws, such as Arizona's, can increase competition, or at least not help incumbents.[15]

Vouchers are likely to have a more profound effect. Much of the billions of dollars in voucher money will likely flow to political parties and political interest groups (such as an NRA or Planned Parenthood group). These groups would have tens of millions of dollars to direct to the most competitive races and the highest quality candidates. This kind of market-based subsidy should spur political competition, which private money collected in up to $25,000 chunks for each election period could further spur. Given the tremendous advantage incumbents already have, there is a decent chance that vouchers plus limits would actually decrease incumbency ree-lection rates. It would create a political marketplace that is both more plu-ralist and more egalitarian.

Ideally, if Congress enacted a plan like mine, the Supreme Court should wait a few election cycles to examine not only the effect of such laws on free speech and association rights but also to see that the laws do not lock incumbents in office. If the Court will not defer, it should look at political scientists' projections of the law's likely effect on political competition. If the Court approves the constitutionality of the law under the political equal-ity rationale, it should make its approval conditional, and open to a renewed challenge after a few election cycles when the law's effects on the political system, free speech, political equality, and incumbency have become ap-parent. If adjustments are necessary to keep political speech robust and elections competitive, then the Court should require them.

☑

Fear of unintended consequences fills discussions of campaign finance reform and provides a strong reason for caution on any and all regulation. The debate over incumbency invokes the potential that reformers and the public, pushing ill-considered programs with the best intentions, could in-advertently stifle political competition. The risk that my voucher + limits proposal would benefit incumbents seems minor, but the broader concern about unintended consequences merits its own examination.[16]

There is no question that campaign finance laws—and judicial rewrit-ing or vacating of such laws—have the potential to change politics in ways not intended by anyone. The Supreme Court's *Citizens United* opinion and later the D.C. circuit court's *SpeechNow.org* opinion, for example, freed up outside spending but did nothing to change the rules limiting politi-cal parties' ability to raise large soft money contributions (the part of the McCain-Feingold law that for now remains standing). The result has been a growth of "shadow party" Super PACs and 501(c)(4) groups.[17]

These outside groups seem much more amenable to negative advertis-ing because they can afford to gamble on ruining their brand. So what if "Priorities USA" or "Crossroads GPS" has to reboot under a new name?

The Democratic and Republican parties and their candidates cannot take the same chances with scorched-earth advertising, even if such advertising does educate voters about the differences between candidates.[18]

Political scientists and others have debated whether the growth of outside groups after *Citizens United* and *SpeechNow.org* has weakened political parties. Some claim the parties remain strong. Others say that McCain-Feingold weakened parties and the court decisions made things worse. Disagreement over how to measure the "strength" of political parties, who counts as the "party," and the effects of other political factors such as gerrymandering and party infighting make it hard to judge who is right. No one doubts that parties are more ideologically divided and pure than they have been in decades; the question is what role, if any, campaign finance rules play in that polarization.[19]

Of course, with power over campaign rules divided between courts and legislatures, not to mention a role for the Federal Election Commission, there is no single decision maker setting the campaign finance rules. The 1974 FECA amendments never went into full effect because of court orders. We had only a handful of elections under the new McCain-Feingold rules (which were designed not to provide an ideal campaign finance system but to survive Supreme Court review), and then came *Citizens United*. We have very little idea how, if at all, our politics would change if Congress had the full ability to choose a set of campaign finance rules.

The key insight of those who worry about unintended consequences is what Professors Sam Issacharoff and Pam Karlan have dubbed the "hydraulic" critique of campaign finance. As the Supreme Court put it in the *McConnell* case, "Money, like water, will always find an outlet." Plug up one route (such as political parties) and the money will flow elsewhere (such as to Super PACs).[20]

It is true that people often look for loopholes to get around campaign finance limits, but the idea that the amount of money the system generates stays constant regardless of the rules is belied by the brief period when the McCain-Feingold law was fully in effect. During that period, corporate money going into elections declined. Perhaps corporate interests would have found a way around the rules eventually, but for a time the law seemed to limit corporate money. One plausible reason is that many corporations did not *want* to give money to political parties or to influence elections, but corporate leaders felt pressured (even extorted) by campaigns to give large soft-money donations. The Committee for Economic Development and some eminent business leaders, including Warren Buffett and Paul Volcker, filed a brief supporting the constitutionality of the McCain-Feingold law and complaining about extortion of corporations by politicians seeking soft money.[21]

Nonetheless, some people will want to get around the rules—election lawyers exist for a reason, and there is every reason to believe they would look for loopholes in any voucher + limits program. If the program adopts a definition of election-related advertising akin to that of McCain-Feingold (counting only television and radio advertising broadcast in the sixty days before a general election or thirty days before a primary, and targeted at the relevant audience), then advertising could shift to earlier periods. Legislative drafting cannot be perfect or anticipate the creativity of lawyers.

Further, if the voucher + limits program drove too much money into outside groups and there was not enough private money flowing to political parties, the voucher program itself could be tweaked, perhaps by giving voters a separate $10 voucher that must be given to a political party or be forfeited, leaving $90 to go to any federal candidate, political committee, or a political party. Professor Dan Lowenstein long ago proposed routing public financing for elections through parties in part to strengthen parties, an idea that has gained renewed attention, and the voucher program could be altered to do that.[22]

More generally, the voucher + limits law must be written with the flexibility to respond to the reactions of political actors and its own unintended effects. No system of regulation is perfect, and the best campaign laws must leave room for dynamic response.

Perhaps the greatest potential unintended consequence of a voucher program is the possibility that voucher dollars could be misused for personal gain. Voters could be offered kickbacks or prizes for sending voucher dollars to unscrupulous fraudsters; campaign consultants could set up important-sounding interest groups and use most of the funds on consulting fees to themselves; and a black market in voucher dollars could arise.

Strict enforcement will be necessary to stop the fraud and bribery that would inevitably arise with a system that so empowers voters. No doubt, some people will try to take advantage of the system for personal gain, just as our current campaign finance system already enables plenty of unscrupulous activity. Consider the case of campaign treasurer Kinde Durkee, who embezzled $7 million from various Democratic campaign accounts over a decade. Many of the new Super PACs and other outside groups seem to be aimed mainly at enriching the people running them. The People's Majority PAC, for example, promised to spend "every penny" on political activities but instead spent nearly $10,000 on meals at fancy restaurants and not a penny on election ads in 2013. An analysis by the Center for Public Integrity found that less than one-sixth of the money spent by Super PACs and similar entities in 2013 actually went to campaign ads. Where does the rest of it go? Reporter Eliza Newlin Carney (who coined the term "Super PAC") sees "consultant fees" as a big area for potential abuse.[23]

There can also be technical snafus in implementing a voucher system. Remember Healthcare.gov, the awful rollout of the new federal health insurance program commonly known as "Obamacare"? It probably makes sense to roll out vouchers in a piecemeal way with a pilot program, so that the kinks can be worked out. No system is perfect, and we should judge the voucher + limits program a success if it brings significant improvement in political equality while maintaining robust election speech and competitive elections.

☑

The cost of a voucher program, while not an "unintended consequence" of my proposal for reform, is unfortunately unavoidable. Giving every voter $100 worth of vouchers to use in federal elections every two years will not be cheap: the costs will run into the billions of dollars.

The cost alone could make the program politically unsellable, but there's a persuasive pitch to make that the money would be well spent. In our current, mostly unregulated system of political spending, the wealthiest people and the companies and entities with the greatest influence secure benefits for themselves in the billions from Congress all the time. Economists call this activity rent seeking. The ability of these wealthy individuals and entities to do so following the enactment of a voucher program should decline significantly, as voters gain more relative power. By making our elections publicly financed, capping the spending of the wealthiest on political spending, and limiting the fundraising activities of lobbyists, the total amount of this inefficient rent seeking should decrease. The billions spent on vouchers would be a bargain.[24]

The most serious unintended consequence that might emerge from my vouchers + limits program is a rise in political polarization. Polarization in Congress has led to legislative gridlock. With all congressional Democrats to the left of all congressional Republicans, and with the parties moving further apart with each election, it is difficult to find common ground to pass legislation.

Whether gridlock is a serious concern is beyond the scope of this book. Elsewhere I have argued that it is a problem, and that most of the easy proposals for fixing it, such as redistricting reform or campaign finance reform, are unlikely to work. Instead, more fundamental change is needed, such as moving to a parliamentary democracy in which one party has full control of the government until the voters turn it out of office.[25]

Those who do not worry about polarization can ignore the concern that vouchers + limits could make it worse. For the rest of us, the nub of the problem is that in today's elections, donors giving small amounts of money are often the most ideological donors, so any system giving more power to small donors risks exacerbating polarization.[26]

That small donors are intensely partisan is no surprise. If you are not wealthy, it is going to take a lot to get you to part with your money, and political passion will do it. A passionate voter will more likely be motivated to contribute by a Sarah Palin or an Elizabeth Warren than a moderate in either party. Fundraising appeals sent via email and social media often use anger and fear to get voters to click on the link and donate money.

Whether these partisan donors drive further partisanship in Congress is less certain. The battle matters especially for those campaign reformers who push for public financing plans providing multiple matches for small donations. If small donors produce polarization, multiple matches could then supersize the effect.

Further, it is not just small donors who can be polarized. As Thomas Mann and Anthony Corrado note: "It is hard to believe that small donors could possibly exceed mega-donors to Super PACs and politically active nonprofits in their ideological zeal or distaste for compromising with the other party. The industrialist billionaire Koch brothers are the most prominent donors and funders on the right, with an announced budget target of $290 million in 2014, a network of political organizations and funding partners, and an agenda perhaps best characterized as libertarian and protective of the fossil fuel energy industry. The Democrats have their own billionaires who are active on the independent spending front, including those who are financing a network of progressive organizations called the Democracy Alliance, which has steered a reported $500 million to liberal groups since its inception in 2005, and has announced plans to spend $374 million to boost liberal candidates and causes in 2014 and beyond. Both are closely associated with and avidly courted by their respective parties."[27]

Regardless of whether current large donors or current small donors present a greater risk of exacerbating polarization, the voucher + limits plan is much less likely to fuel polarization. Under the plan, every voter, not just the most ideologically polarized voters, can contribute to campaigns. Because the voucher dollars are free, and (assuming adequate enforcement) cannot be converted to cash or personal use, many more people who have an interest in politics will "vote" their voucher dollars. These will include the more moderate voters who are too poor or not motivated enough to contribute their own funds. To be sure, the most partisan people will be most likely to vote their vouchers. But many people in the middle, if given the chance, are likely to do so as well. And limiting the amount people can give could decrease legislative polarization, perhaps especially if we filter some vouchers through broad-based political parties.[28]

In fact, voucher dollars, if widely used, could have a moderating effect. The voters in the middle of the ideological spectrum who support candidates, or broad-based political parties, could counteract forces of division and polarization, which will be more likely to come from various interest groups collecting vouchers.

Once again, if practice shows vouchers end up supporting polarizing independent groups, and this leads to a more polarized Congress or legislatures, then the voucher plan could be tweaked to require that a certain high percentage of one's voucher dollars go directly to broad-based parties rather than to polarizing groups. Periodic review of the law, or voter approval, could get around any polarizing Congress blocking further reform.

The bottom line is that no campaign finance program can be designed to perfectly accomplish its goals and be impenetrable to attempts at evading its rules. The hydraulic effect of money in elections is just about as certain as the hydraulic effect of gravity on water. The key to a workable campaign finance plan, and the way to beat unintended consequences, is to design flexibility and change within the plan itself.

PART FOUR

CHANGING THE SYSTEM

8

Wrong Paths

IN SEPTEMBER 2014, IN THE MIDST OF A Senate debate over a constitutional amendment to overturn *Citizens United,* Senator Ted Cruz took to the floor and expressed his deep concern about the fate of *Saturday Night Live* creator and producer Lorne Michaels should the amendment pass. After waxing poetic about growing up with the NBC television show and describing his favorite sketches and characters, Cruz went in for the kill: "Lorne Michaels could be put in jail under this amendment for making fun of any politician. That is extraordinary. It is breathtaking, and it is dangerous."[1]

It was typical bombast from a Tea Party darling. Cruz's reasoning went like this: under the Democrats' proposed amendment, the federal government could pass laws barring corporate spending on elections. NBC (now owned by the cable giant Comcast) is a corporation. If the amendment passed, Congress could pass a spending ban that government officials could apply to *Saturday Night Live*'s political satire. Michaels could then go to jail for broadcasting political satire close to the election.

Democratic senator Tom Udall of New Mexico, the driving force behind the push for a constitutional amendment, bristled at Cruz's suggestion. "We heard some scary things in the last couple of days. Lorne Michaels is going to jail. And he is sharing a cell with a little old lady who put up a $5 political yard sign. Books and movies are banned. The NAACP, Sierra Club, and moveon.org have been prohibited from speaking about politics—scary stuff but none of it is true."[2]

The fact-checkers at "Politifact" consulted with a number of lawyers and law professors and concluded that Cruz's statement was "Half-True" and his *Saturday Night Live* scenario "far-fetched." "Most experts we talked to agreed that the proposed amendment's language left open the door to that possibility. But many of those same experts emphasized that prosecuting, much less imprisoning, a comedian for purely political speech would run counter to centuries of American tradition, and would face many obstacles at a variety of government levels and run headlong into popular sentiment."[3]

Senator Cruz was not the only one engaging in hyperbole: if you listened to Democrats on the Senate floor, the United States was essentially doomed if the amendment didn't pass. Senate majority leader Harry Reid, a Democrat from Nevada, declared that after *Citizens United*, the United States had become a society in "in which radical billionaires are attempting to buy our democracy."[4]

Each side offered plenty of red meat to feed its base. For every Cruz reference to Democrats as book banners and censors, there was a Reid attack on the Koch brothers and their diabolical plans to recreate America in their libertarian image. Orrin Hatch, a Republican from Utah, invoked the late Senator Edward Kennedy, a liberal stalwart who had opposed earlier efforts to change the First Amendment. Hatch did not mention that he was the chief sponsor of a 2006 amendment Kennedy opposed, which would amend the Constitution specifically to ban flag burning. Cruz, a few weeks after his floor speech about Lorne Michaels, announced plans to introduce an amendment to bar federal courts from overturning same-sex marriage bans passed by the states.[5]

The Democrats' amendment proposal got the support of all the Senate Democrats voting that day and none of the Senate Republicans. Cruz missed the final Senate vote, perhaps because he was doing media appearances after a controversial event the night before in which he was booed off stage for telling a group of Middle Eastern Christians to stand with Israel.[6]

The exercise by Democrats revealed the tensions between rights of free speech and political equality. As initially drafted, the amendment would have allowed Congress and the states to regulate money in elections, but it did not stipulate that the regulations be "reasonable." Senator Cruz and others railed against the proposed amendment at a Senate Judiciary sub-committee hearing as government censorship; in response, Democrats amended it to require that the regulations be "reasonable." They also added language making it clear that Congress and the states could ban corporations (but not "the press") from election-related spending.[7]

The final version of the proposed amendment reads:

SECTION 1. To advance democratic self-government and political equality, and to protect the integrity of government and the electoral process, Congress and the States may regulate and set reasonable limits on the raising and spending of money by candidates and others to influence elections.

SECTION 2. Congress and the States shall have power to implement and enforce this article by appropriate legislation, and may distinguish between natural persons and corporations or other artificial entities created by law, including by prohibiting such entities from spending money to influence elections.

SECTION 3. Nothing in this article shall be construed to grant Congress or the States the power to abridge the freedom of the press.[8]

Rather than focus on the dangers of "corruption," Senate Democrats commendably put the issue of political equality front and center in the debate and in the amendment's language. During some of his floor time, Reid described attending the Supreme Court's oral argument in *Baker v. Carr,* the landmark one person, one vote case, as a student in 1962, tying campaign finance to the struggle for equally weighted votes. Senator Dick Durbin compared the struggles over campaign financing to the civil rights movement, talking of the "blood, sweat, tears and even lives" Americans had given to protect the right to vote. Elizabeth Warren, Democratic senator from Massachusetts and a former Harvard law professor, declared: "When 32 people can outspend 3.7 million citizens, our democracy is in real danger. . . . We are here to fight back against a Supreme Court that says there is no difference between free speech and billions of dollars spent by the privileged few to swing elections and buy off legislators." Coming from Warren, it was a trademark populist message, though the talk of "buying off legislators" sounded like corruption hyperbole.[9]

The Senate Judiciary Committee's report, authored by Democrats, declared the measure necessary because of the inequality in spending the

Supreme Court allowed through its rulings. "As a result of the Court's decisions, a small minority of wealthy individuals and special interests have been able to, and increasingly will be able to, drown out the voices of ordinary Americans and skew both the electoral process and public policy outcomes."[10]

Despite the benefits of framing the campaign finance debate around a constitutional amendment, it was the wrong path for Democrats to take. To begin with, it was a political non-starter. A constitutional amendment requires the affirmative vote of two-thirds of each house of Congress, as well as approval from three-fourths of state legislatures. If Congress could not even pass the DISCLOSE Act, a post–*Citizens United* bill Democrats repeatedly try to pass to plug up the holes in the nation's disclosure laws, there was no way it would pass a constitutional amendment. It did not matter that 3 million people upset about the Supreme Court's ruling in *Citizens United* presented petitions urging Congress to overrule the Supreme Court. A constitutional amendment is going nowhere.[11]

Democrats should have put more efforts into proposals that could help fix campaign financing in the short term. In addition to pushing for greater disclosure through the DISCLOSE Act, they should have focused on any of several proposals for multiple matching funds for small campaign contributions. Although still an uphill battle, disclosure and voluntary public financing plans had a much greater chance of success than the quixotic attempt at constitutional amendment. Come the next campaign finance scandal, there would be an opening for such measures to pass, but there would still be insurmountable barriers to getting an amendment through Congress and the states. Better disclosure laws and small matching grants would do much more for the cause of political equality than grandstanding on a constitutional amendment.

Further, the fight over language shows the inherent difficulty of drafting the right kind of constitutional amendment to overturn *Citizens United*. Amendment drafters are stuck between two bad spots. On one hand, if the measure is drafted broadly it raises what we can call the Lorne Michaels problem: as originally drafted, the Democrats' proposed amendment could have given broad latitude not just to Congress, but also to state and even local governments, to suppress too much political speech.

The problem is exacerbated by sloppy drafting and the potential for un-

intended consequences. One of the most popular constitutional amendment proposals, for example, put forward by the group "Move to Amend,"
appears to *require* Congress, state, and local governments to adopt some (it
is not clear which) campaign finance regulations. It also does not include
a press exemption, but it does remove all constitutional rights for corporations, raising serious questions about whether a state could stop the *New
York Times* or Fox News from covering an election.[12]

Udall's original amendment provided that both Congress and the states
could impose campaign finance contribution and spending limits. But it
included a press exemption that applied only to Congress, not the states:
"Nothing in this article shall be construed to grant Congress the power to
abridge the freedom of the press." Udall no doubt intended to prevent the
states as well from abridging freedom of the press, but by mentioning the
states and Congress having power to regulate campaigns and limiting Congress's but not states' encroachment on press freedoms, his initial version
left future courts free to infer that the difference was deliberate. That problem was fixed by the final version.

On the other hand, the alternative to broad grants of power to Congress
and states to regulate campaign financing is to impose limitations on that
power. Preventing encroachment on freedom of the press is one such limitation; requiring that any spending limits be "reasonable" is another. In
adopting the reasonableness standard, the Democratic senators listened to
the recommendation of retired justice John Paul Stevens, who detailed this
approach to campaign finance in his book suggesting six amendments to
the Constitution. Justice Stevens's (overly) simple amendment reads: "Neither the First Amendment nor any other provision of this Constitution
shall be construed to prohibit the Congress or any state from imposing
reasonable limits on the amount of money that candidates for public office,
or their supporters, may spend in elections."[13]

This approach, in its vagueness, does nothing to set boundaries on court
interpretation or judicial expression. Amendments that allow only for "reasonable" limits leave the ultimate determination of reasonableness in the
Supreme Court's hands. What makes Justice Stevens or Senate Democrats
think the current Supreme Court, which finds that all of the current spending limits impinge too much on freedom of speech, would consider any
limits "reasonable" under a new amendment? Or things could work the

other way: future courts could allow *any* limits on money in politics, even those aimed at squelching political competition. That could be worse than what we have now.

The same could be said of the freedom of "the press" that appears in the Senate Democrats' proposed amendment, but not in Justice Stevens's version. Inevitably the Supreme Court would have to determine who counts as "the press." As we saw in the last chapter, there is a broad division between those who believe the First Amendment protects journalism as an industry and those who believe the protection applies to all presslike activities. A conservative majority of the Supreme Court could adopt the latter reading of the press clause in the Democrats' amendment and thus render it completely ineffectual.

Finally, all of these proposed amendments go well beyond a "reversal" of *Citizens United.* They also reverse the part of the Supreme Court's decision in *Buckley v. Valeo* that bars imposition of individual spending limits. That is a more serious step, and most of the amendments do nothing to ensure that the amendment would be read to require courts to police campaign finance rules to maintain robust political speech. Under the Democrats' proposed amendment, for example, a government could stop all corporate spending on elections, including by corporate PACs, but it does not appear that labor unions could face a parallel draconian limitation (unless a court found such a limitation "reasonable").

In short, the concern is not that Lorne Michaels faced even a remote threat of prosecution if the Senate Democrats passed their amendment. If this country ever reaches the point where someone can go to jail for political satire, that will be far from our biggest worry. It is that a constitutional amendment is not a good strategy for balancing society's interest in political equality with its interest in maintaining competitive elections and robust political speech. There is too great a risk of drafting something either ineffective or subject to abuse in the hands of a self-interested legislative body.

☑

"Embrace the irony" was the message of Professor Larry Lessig's "Mayday PAC." Dubbed "the Super PAC to end all Super PACs," Mayday's idea was to raise big money to fund independent ads supporting candidates who favored campaign finance reform. Mayday, begun for the 2014 elections, was part of a network of organizations and groups Lessig has created or backed in an effort to keep campaign finance a central issue in American politics.[14]

As a matter of marketing, Mayday PAC and Lessig's other efforts were brilliant. Lessig came to prominence as a rock-star law professor focusing on intellectual property and digital technology. His struggles to get Congress and the courts to loosen copyright restrictions to allow for freer flow of information led him to believe that moneyed interests were preventing them from addressing the issue.[15]

Mayday PAC's tactics were controversial, not because it was using big money in an attempt to defeat big money, but because of whom it was funding. Its beneficiaries included not just the usual liberal Democrats who support campaign finance reform, but some Republicans as well. It supported a long-shot Tea Party candidate who ran against Scott Brown in the 2014 Republican primary for the U.S. Senate seat from New Hampshire, and Walter Jones, a North Carolina Republican who supported campaign finance reform but also wanted to impeach President Obama.[16]

The big problem with Lessig's approach is not that his PAC reached across party lines, but that it offered unrealistic hope. Lessig seemed to have convinced himself, and then others, that the Supreme Court would embrace his "originalist" view of the meaning of the term "corruption," and on that basis reverse its decision in *Citizens United*.[17]

Once that failed to happen—given the opportunity, the Court reaffirmed the decision in a one-paragraph opinion from Montana without even holding an oral argument—Lessig shifted gears. First he dismissed concerns about the Supreme Court's view of these cases. He told an audience at Duke Law School in February 2014: "The truth is . . . I don't think the Supreme Court is the problem. I don't think the Supreme Court is the problem. You know, anybody who knows Elena Kagan knows she will eventually wrestle them to the ground, and they will be on the right side of this issue, you know, whether it's Scalia or Kennedy or the next Scalia or Kennedy. She will win that issue; we don't need to worry about that." In reality, it seems doubtful that even Justice Kagan would have that kind of power over the conservative justices.[18]

But Lessig also began to push for actions that he said could be taken consistent with the *Citizens United* decision, while leaving open the possibility of pursuing a constitutional amendment later on. He also has flirted with the idea of convening a constitutional convention in which "citizens" would decide on fundamental government reforms.[19]

Part of Lessig's legislative program is in line with my own: new voluntary congressional public financing that empowers more voters through measures such as vouchers. He has backed legislation that would provide multiple matches for campaign contributions. Although I question whether the current Supreme Court would allow such multiple matches (because they appear at least partly intended to level the playing field), an effort such as this on the congressional level is much more productive than a quixotic push for a constitutional amendment.[20]

But Lessig also continues to argue that Congress could impose limits on contributions to Super PACs consistent with *Citizens United*. This is a pipe dream. When the United States Court of Appeals for the District of Columbia Circuit in the *Speechnow.org* case held that there is a constitutional right to make unlimited contributions to independent expenditure committees, there was a reason the United States government did not appeal. It knew it would lose, and lose badly. There is no chance that the current Supreme Court would uphold a law that limits contributions to independent spending PACs. In fact, Congress passed such a law in the Federal Election Campaign Act amendments of 1974: a $5,000 individual contribution limit, which the D.C. Circuit struck down in *SpeechNow.org*. If Congress passed the same law today, the courts would strike it down.

Using a Super PAC to elect enough members of Congress to end all Super PACs is a tough job. We have seen that there is no simple linear relationship between money and election outcomes, and getting Congress to move on this issue will not be easy. And even if the group achieved success by helping elect one or two more senators or members of Congress who support stricter campaign finance rules, that is not enough of a critical mass to get anything done on this issue. We know this because at the end of the 2014 lame-duck session of Congress, as part of a must-pass package of legislation known as the "CRomnibus," Congress allowed a seven-fold increase in the amount people could contribute to political parties. This provision was not something Mitch McConnell and Senate Republicans rammed down Democrats' throats as part of a larger deal. Instead, prominent Democratic attorney Marc Elias, working with outgoing Senate majority leader (and Democrat) Harry Reid, was the force behind this provision reopening the path for party soft money and the sale of access to the parties' high rollers.[21]

✔️

Lessig and the populists supporting a constitutional amendment to overturn the Supreme Court's campaign finance cases are at least sincere in their desire to make things better. That's not true of many Democratic officeholders, beginning at the top.[22]

Bashing *Citizens United,* the Republican Supreme Court, and Republicans in Congress is good business for Democrats and helps with fundraising. President Obama has been the Basher-in-Chief, controversially criticizing the *Citizens United* decision in a State of the Union address with Supreme Court justices in attendance. When he falsely claimed that the decision allowed for foreign corporations to spend money in elections (the Court specifically reserved this issue in *Citizens United* and later—inconsistently—decided against foreign campaign spenders), cameras showed Justice Alito shaking his head and saying "not true."[23]

President Obama's progressive credentials overall are outside the scope of this book; his record on campaign finance reform, however, has been all talk and no action. He was the first general election candidate to choose not to participate in the presidential public funding program, a decision that effectively killed the program. True, the program's demise was inevitable, given its failure to keep up with the kind of fundraising available in the private market. But he promised a plan to fix the program if elected and never offered one. He promised a program to fix the Federal Election Commission, and never offered one. He has been slow to nominate the agency's commissioners. He has never presented legislative alternatives to mitigate the effects of *Citizens United,* and he has not actively led on congressional efforts to improve campaign finance disclosure.[24]

Even if his proposals would have failed in Congress because of Republican opposition, he could have put out his proposal as a marker, and an ideal for people to rally around and to strive for. He has done this in other policy areas. The best that could be said of his record is that late in his tenure he appointed Ann Ravel, someone firmly in the campaign finance reform camp, to the FEC. But he did so at a time when it was quite clear the FEC was hobbled by partisan bickering and gridlock.

In the meantime, while insisting he opposes *Citizens United*, he has taken advantage of increasing deregulation. Aside from opting out of the public funding program and aggressively using joint fundraising committees with Democratic Party organs, he has transformed his campaign organization, Obama for America, into Organizing for Action, a 501(c)(4). OFA has vastly increased the avenue for large donors to seek to curry favor with the president and the executive branch. He has blazed a fundraising trail as a president that has done great damage to the cause of campaign finance reform.[25]

Even with a Republican Congress blocking much legislation, and a Supreme Court that has limited the options on the table, there is much the president could have done. He could have led more publicly on disclosure. Some Republicans seemed interested in a deal to fix disclosure problems in exchange for raising some of the campaign contribution limits—which looks like a good deal given the alternative of less accountable money. He could have recess-appointed reformers to the Federal Election Commission. If he had proposed legislation to fix the agency it would have put pressure on congressional Republicans to do something. He could have used executive orders to require more disclosure. At the very least, he could have used his bully pulpit to present a progressive vision of what campaign finance reform in the *Citizens United* era should look like.

Perhaps the president railed so loudly against *Citizens United* to inoculate himself against criticism for the unprecedented campaign finance steps he took to fund his own two campaigns. It should be no surprise that Obama adviser David Axelrod tweeted in favor of unlimited campaign contributions to candidates. The president can proclaim a desire to fix the system, and yet make the reasonable point that rather than unilaterally disarm Democrats, he must fight political battles under the rules as they exist.

But he has done more than fight under existing rules; his actions have deregulated the system further.[26]

✔️

Arguments for constitutional amendments to "reverse" *Citizens United* often are not serious, and much of what Democrats say on campaign finance these days is lip service or worse. But a more serious argument comes from progressives Ezra Klein and Jonathan Bernstein, who have maintained in a series of blog posts and articles that the time has come to at least partially throw in the towel on campaign finance reform and move on to other issues. After all, in the first election cycle since *Citizens United,* a Democrat was reelected president and Democrats kept control of the Senate. So far there have been no revelations of scandals or threats to the integrity of our governmental system stemming from all the campaign money sloshing around (though they could emerge).[27]

Klein, a former *Washington Post* blogger who now edits the Vox website, does not call for full retreat. Pundits and campaign reformers, he writes, overrate money's role in determining the outcomes of races. Plans to harness the power of small donors, he contends, are likely to increase political polarization, as small donors tend to be ideological donors whose views will push Democrats to the left and Republicans to the right. He almost wistfully views corporate and other large funding of elections as more moderating than small-donor money.

It is not clear whether Klein offered his analysis to be deliberately provocative—he is clearly right that many overrate the importance of money in determining election outcomes—but when questioned he backed off from some of his more controversial points. In response to criticism from Mark Schmitt, Klein conceded that candidates need to obtain enough money to be taken seriously (the "money primary"). In response to criticism from Lee Drutman, he conceded that large corporate money, especially the cash now flowing into Super PACs and (c)(4)s, also tends to be polarizing, and he agreed with Drutman that providing small donor matches for in-district contributions might not be polarizing. In response to Jonathan Backer, he admitted that the problem with money in politics is not necessarily how it affects *electoral* outcomes but how it affects *legislative* outcomes. In the end,

Klein's criticism was modest, and he expressed his willingness to sign on to a campaign reform. "I'd take anything from the mild disclosure laws that Republicans filibustered in 2012 to much more aggressive public financing bills, or small-donor matching bills."[28]

Bloomberg View columnist Jonathan Bernstein goes further. Looking at the recent IRS scandal, he proposes addressing the problem of money in politics through further deregulation: "Lift the limitations on contributions. If someone wants to give a million dollars or three to a House candidate or $20M to the Republican National Committee, let 'em. No ceilings at all."

He favors better disclosure and partial public financing to provide a floor for competitors in House elections, but no limits. "Floors-not-ceilings with strong disclosure is a campaign-finance approach that can work. It's much easier to regulate than today's complex landscape, thus making future regulatory scandals less likely; it promotes accountability; and it helps ensure minimally competitive House races without hurting competitiveness of other federal elections. If big money is inherently corrupt—and I don't believe it is—then at least this plan makes that corruption visible. And it has the chance to be stable, which is good for healthy parties, and healthy parties are good for the political system."

Bernstein's proposal, however, would be a disaster for the progressive vision of campaign finance reform. The main problem of campaign money on the federal level—aside from the huge need for members of Congress to spend so much time dialing for dollars that they have little time for legislative business—is that it skews legislative priorities. As we have seen, large donors, lobbyists, and others who bundle contributions are more able than others to obtain broad access to legislators and staffers to make their case for legislative action (or inaction). Access does not guarantee legislative success, but it is usually a prerequisite. On issues with little public salience, large-donor or lobbyist support on an issue can be decisive. The political science literature on access and rent seeking especially through hired-gun lobbyists is pretty convincing.

Deregulation of campaign financing has only exacerbated this problem. Members of Congress feel compelled either to do the bidding of those who would donate millions of dollars to Super PACs and 501(c)(4)'s acting against them or to curry favor with supporters to do more fundraising (or encourage supportive outside groups to do so) to fend off the outside attack. Contrary to Bernstein, there is still virtue in keeping politicians and the money supporting them separate: to put it another way, $20 million in a Super PAC supporting Representative X is bad, but it's less bad than $20 million in Representative X's campaign account.

If members of Congress already feel beholden to large donors, bundlers, and outside money players, how much greater would the pressure be to respond to the $1 million or $20 million donors? A skewed politics would become even more skewed.

✔

If a constitutional amendment, new legislation imposing contribution limits on independent spending committees, a focus on "corruption" in Congress, lip service, and throwing in the towel are all wrong paths to fixing our broken campaign finance system, what is the right way?

9

The Last Great Hope for Reform

WHEN THE CONSERVATIVE ACTIVIST Carrie Severino was asked to describe what it will be like in the U.S. Senate and the country when it is time for the president to name a replacement for Justice Anthony Kennedy, she replied, "World War III." Replace Kennedy with another conservative, and the balance of power on the Supreme Court remains mostly the same. Replace him with a liberal like Ruth Bader Ginsburg, and the Court's views on issues from campaign finance to abortion to gun rights will almost certainly flip 180 degrees.[1]

New York Times reporter Adam Liptak similarly predicts a "battle royale" if a Democratic president gets to nominate a replacement for any of the conservative justices. Both Kennedy and Scalia will be eighty in 2016. Indeed, no matter who is president when Kennedy dies or resigns, there will be "real fireworks" over his replacement.

And it is not just the retirement of conservatives. Fireworks will also erupt if a Republican president and a Republican Senate stand ready to replace the liberal justices Ginsburg (who will be eighty-three in 2016) or Stephen Breyer (who will be seventy-eight), both of whom are old enough that it is hard to imagine both of them remaining on the Court to the end of the next two presidential terms. With four older justices unlikely to all last through the next eight years, the stakes for ideological control of the Court are high and the outcome is uncertain.[2]

Severino and many others on the right will mobilize conservative activists to push for a strong conservative replacement for Kennedy and to fight a liberal or even a moderate Republican nominee. Conservatives fought hard against even George W. Bush's nominee to replace Justice O'Connor in 2005, Harriet Miers, because they saw her as insufficiently committed to a conservative judicial philosophy. After Miers withdrew under pressure, Bush nominated Samuel Alito, who was confirmed with conservative and Republican support over the opposing votes of forty-two Democratic senators. Conservatives were "ecstatic" with the Alito nomination. "'The difference from after the Miers nomination was like being at a morgue vers[u]s being at a combination of a wedding reception, Super Bowl party and bar mitzvah,' said Jordan Lorence, a lawyer for the Christian conservative Alliance Defense Fund." The conservative celebration was justified: as we have seen, Alito provided the crucial fifth vote to overturn *Austin* and usher in the era of *Citizens United* campaign finance deregulation, and he has been reliably conservative on many other issues as well.[3]

When Justice Kennedy's time comes, groups on the left will also fight hard for a progressive nominee if there is a Democratic president, and fight to force a more moderate nominee if the president is a Republican. But in the past few decades, the left has been less organized about judicial nominations than the right. With a potential change or solidifying of the Court's balance of power, the left will need the greatest mobilization since the civil rights movement to get through a nominee it strongly favors or to block a nominee it opposes. The fight will be even fiercer if a Republican president and a Republican Senate try to replace Justice Ginsburg with a conservative nominee. In short, if a conservative justice retires at a time of unified Democratic control of the presidency and the Senate or a liberal justice retires at a time of unified Republican control, that's when we can expect "World War III."

It is these fights over Supreme Court nominees over the coming decade that will determine for the next generation whether meaningful campaign finance regulation is possible. Change the Supreme Court in a progressive direction, and campaign finance reform—even vouchers + limits enacted to promote political equality—becomes possible. Let the Supreme Court stay as it is, and no change is possible. This window will open quickly, upon the resignation or death of key justices, and then will close for up to a generation once their replacements are confirmed.

The fight for campaign reform will be political, not legal, in the battle over control of the Court: it likely will take a Democratic president nominating progressives who can be confirmed by the Senate. And that will take hard political work on the part of the progressive community and hard jurisprudential work by sympathetic scholars.

✔️

It may seem odd to promote changing the Supreme Court as the best way to achieve campaign finance reform. To begin with, it is the tail wagging the dog. A change in the balance of power on the Court would likely change so many important areas of the law—criminal defendants' rights, social issues, protection of (and from) religion, voting rights, business cases, intellectual property cases, and much more. In other words, moving the Court in a progressive direction on campaign finance would move it on much more besides. The only people who will support it to get campaign reform will be those who otherwise have a progressive agenda.

Further, it is unusual (at least for non-lawyers) to talk about constitutional change in terms of changing Supreme Court justices. If the Court has interpreted the Constitution in a way that is deeply unpopular, amending the Constitution seems the most straightforward way to fix it. The amendment process is so difficult, however, especially in these polarizing times, that it is hard to imagine any amendment on as controversial a subject as campaign finance reform actually passing. Changing justices is a cumbersome and uncertain way to change the Constitution, but in our present environment it is the only way to move this issue forward.

Many constitutional law scholars see the Constitution as having often been informally "amended" as justices reinterpreted various clauses' meanings. Yale law professor Bruce Ackerman, for example, famously wrote of the New Deal and other periods of U.S. history as times when the justices changed the scope of powers, rights, and responsibilities entrusted to Congress and the executive branch.[4]

How is informal amendment possible in a system with a written Constitution? The premise of the question is incorrect. Even though its language is static, judicial understanding of the Constitution's terms has varied widely. Its provisions are often general, aspirational, and ambiguous: to take the key example in this book, different justices have wildly different ideas about what it means to impermissibly "abridge" the "freedom of speech, or of the press," and different ideas about the meaning of the same words in different contexts, such as pornography, hate speech, or commercial speech. To the conservatives currently on the Court, campaign finance limits usually abridge First Amendment freedoms; to the Court's liberals, these usually do not.

Contrary to the stated views of a few justices—such as Justice Scalia, who believes textual examination of the written Constitution can answer most questions about its meaning—most justices take a more contextual view that calls for them to look at the Constitution's meaning through text and history, precedent, and contemporary understandings of the scope of government and individual powers, rights, and responsibilities. Those justices who profess adherence to textualism or original meaning tend to adopt conservative positions on most of the pressing ideological issues, including campaign finance. They are also inconsistent in their use of originalism.[5]

The key insight of the legal realist movement of the 1940s, as well as more recent critical theories, is that there are no neutral principles for resolving many of the deep jurisprudential and constitutional questions facing the Court. There is instead constitutional interpretation filtered through the Court's precedent and justices' philosophies and ideologies. In the past decade this ideological division among justices has gained a partisan overlay, and this is what likely will make the Supreme Court nomination battles in the next decade so fierce.

☑

Ideological polarization on the Supreme Court is nothing new. Each term, the Court issues a fair number of decisions on 5-to-4 votes, many of them divided on ideological lines. Among the issues that have been decided this way in the past few years aside from campaign finance are abortion, affirmative action, gun rights, and the treatment of enemy combatants.[6]

From 2006 through 2014, the Supreme Court issued an average of seventeen 5–4 decisions each term, with 66 percent representing a liberal-conservative ideological split and 64 percent of those resulting in a conservative victory. Justice Kennedy, as a conservative who sometimes sides with liberals, has been the most important swing voter: from the October 2007 to October 2013 term, Kennedy was in the majority in 5–4 decisions between 67 percent and 100 percent of the percent of the time. No other justice comes close.[7]

While ideological polarization at the Supreme Court is not new, what is new is how the ideological split lines up with a partisan split: all the conservative justices on the court today were nominated by Republican presidents, and all the liberal justices were nominated by Democratic presidents. George W. Bush replaced the conservative-moderate justice Sandra Day O'Connor with the strong conservative justice Samuel Alito. Justices John Paul Stevens and David Souter, the last moderate-liberals appointed by Republicans, were replaced by President Obama's appointees, Sonia Sotomayor and Elena Kagan. Byron White was the last conservative-leaning justice appointed by a Democrat to leave the Court, replaced with a strong liberal, Ruth Bader Ginsburg. Given the extraordinary tenure of Supreme Court justices, there can well be a lag between popular opinion and the Court's decisions.[8]

Recent attacks on the Supreme Court from the left have accused the five conservative justices of deciding cases to benefit Republicans politically. Such crude thinking is probably incorrect; I do not believe the justices are consciously trying to help the political party of the president who appointed them. It is more a case of honest agreement: conservative justices' free market ideology lines up with the views and interests of the Republican Party. This is also why liberal justices often vote in ways that line up with the interests of the Democratic Party.[9]

Nonetheless, the more people think of the justices as deciding cases in the same partisan way in which legislators decide on legislative actions (whether or not that is accurate), the easier it will be for senators to oppose judicial nominations on ideological and partisan grounds.

Senators have become more vocal about opposing Supreme Court nominees on ideological grounds than they have been in previous decades, in part because a nominee's ideology is more predictable. Professor Lee Epstein and her co-authors found that the "degree to which [Supreme Court nominees] share the political values of their nominating President is higher now than it was just three decades ago. And . . . although Senators of today—no less than those of yesterday—attend to the nominees' qualifications, ideological compatibility now takes precedence."[10]

Consider the statement Senator Barack Obama made in 2005 against the nomination of John Roberts to be chief justice of the United States:

> There is absolutely no doubt in my mind Judge Roberts is qualified to sit on the highest court in the land. Moreover, he seems to have the comportment and the temperament that makes for a good judge. He is humble, he is personally decent, and he appears to be respectful of different points of view. It is absolutely clear to me that Judge Roberts truly loves the law. He couldn't have achieved his excellent record as an advocate before the Supreme Court without that passion for the law, and it became apparent to me in our conversation that he does, in fact, deeply respect the basic precepts that go into deciding 95 percent of the cases that come before the Federal court—adherence to precedence, a certain modesty in reading statutes and constitutional text, a respect for procedural regularity, and an impartiality in presiding over the adversarial system. All of these characteristics make me want to vote for Judge Roberts.
>
> The problem I face—a problem that has been voiced by some of my other colleagues, both those who are voting for Mr. Roberts and those who are voting against Mr. Roberts—is that while adherence to legal precedent and rules of statutory or constitutional construction will dispose of 95 percent of the cases that come before a court, so that both a Scalia and a Ginsburg will arrive at the same place most of the time on those 95 percent of the cases— what matters on the Supreme Court is those 5 percent of cases that are truly difficult. In those cases, adherence to precedent and rules of construction and interpretation will only get you through the 25th mile of the marathon. That last mile can only be determined on the basis of one's deepest values, one's core concerns, one's broader perspectives on how the world works, and the depth and breadth of one's empathy.[11]

The shift to explicit voicing of ideological concerns and away from at least an ostensible focus on judicial competence has coincided with an increasing partisan split on votes for Supreme Court confirmations. Putting aside the contentious hearings over Robert Bork, whose nomination was voted down, and over Clarence Thomas's confirmation vote—which took place after a hearing in which he was accused of sexual harassment—Supreme Court nominees until recently enjoyed bipartisan support. Justices Scalia and Kennedy were approved on unanimous votes, and only a few votes were cast against Justices Breyer and Ginsburg.[12]

More recent votes have seen much more substantial opposition to nominees, mostly along party lines. Many of these votes played well to each senator's base. Twenty-two senators, all Democrats, voted against confirmation for Roberts, without raising any objections to his qualifications. Forty-two Democrats voted against Alito (two more than necessary for a filibuster, had Democrats decided to filibuster); only four voted in his favor. Thirty-one Republicans voted against Sotomayor versus nine in her favor. The most recent nominee, Elena Kagan, had thirty-seven Republican votes cast against her and gained only five. In none of these cases did opposing senators raise any serious questions about the nominee's qualifications.

Notably, all four Democrats who voted for Justice Alito (Senators Kent Conrad, Ben Nelson, Tim Johnson, and Robert Byrd, who died in office) have since left the Senate, as did three of the five Republicans voting for Justice Kagan (Senators Judd Gregg, Richard Lugar, and Olympia Snowe). All seven were known as moderates.

The big question is whether the increasing partisan and ideological opposition to Supreme Court nominees will lead senators to begin to consider filibustering Supreme Court nominees from the other party. The issue could come to a head when the four oldest justices leave the Court.

In recent years, both Democratic senators and Republican senators have filibustered, stalled, or put holds on lower-court nominees, especially nominees to the federal appellate courts. Senators are especially interested in filibustering young appellate court judges, such as Republican Miguel Estrada (filibustered by Democrats) or Democrat Goodwin Liu (filibustered by Republicans), who appeared to be on track for an eventual Supreme Court nomination.[13]

The fights over lower-court nominees only accelerated during the Obama administration. Democrats finally broke the logjam by eliminating the filibuster for all judicial (and other executive) nominees except for Supreme Court justices. A contentious Supreme Court nomination would certainly rile the Senate, and supporters of a nominee facing a potential filibuster will no doubt urge Senate leadership to eliminate the filibuster for these appointments as well.[14]

The battle over lower-court judicial nominations might not resemble the battle over control of the Supreme Court. Lower-court nominations are of much lower salience than Supreme Court nominations, especially one to replace a swing justice on a sharply divided court. When the moment comes to fight over control of the Supreme Court, interest groups will erupt, social media will howl, and senators from the opposition party will come under intense pressure to filibuster any nominee who is not ideologically acceptable. Some will defend the filibuster as a means of ensuring the placement of moderates on the Court. But in the past senators have not been willing to pull the trigger even when it came to controversial nominations such as Justice Thomas's and in situations in which there were more than enough votes to filibuster. With increased partisanship in the Senate and the stakes so high, I would not bet that the filibuster will last.

The coming dispute differs markedly from the fight over the Bork nomination. Although some attribute the current tensions over judicial nominees to the Bork fight, in the years following that battle the Senate easily confirmed four of the next five Supreme Court nominees (two Democrats and two Republicans) unanimously or by lopsided majorities. But the four most recently confirmed justices—all eminently well qualified jurists—got through on sharply divided votes. Something in the Senate seems to have changed fundamentally.[15]

A partisan confrontation over a Supreme Court nominee might end several ways. The president might withdraw a nomination and name a replacement candidate whom the minority threatening a filibuster sees as more moderate. Alternatively, the president and the Senate majority might hold firm on the original nominee, and simply remove the possibility of filibustering Supreme Court nominees. Senators alternatively might conclude that eliminating the filibuster in this way could have negative consequences for the Senate's conduct of business. They could strike a more radical compromise on Supreme Court nominations. For example, they might try to limit judicial terms to eighteen years, which would lower the costs of confirming an ideological justice to the Court and create more turnover on the Court.

Term limits, if imposed, could change the nature of the Court. By lowering the stakes, they should make ideological judges easier to confirm. By the same token, term limits might make it easier for presidents to nominate more ideological justices. More speculatively, they create a risk that justices will judge with future career prospects in mind. Both of these paths, to the extent that the public begins to see justices as both ideological and self-interested, suggest dangers to the Court's long-term legitimacy.

Of course, if the president is popular and has much of the Senate behind him or her, a new nominee, even a committed progressive or conservative, could make it through the confirmation process. And with a president and Senate of opposite parties, the confirmation of more moderate justices seems more likely.

The uncertainty ahead can lead to many potential outcomes, but only one of them is a new, progressive Supreme Court.

☑

Predicting the outcome of the next set of Supreme Court nomination battles is difficult, but understanding the stakes is not. Putting aside the myths about judges "finding" the law, at least in the realm of difficult constitutional questions, the best predictor of the future of whether meaningful campaign finance is achieved is the ideology of the majority on the Supreme Court. And these days the best predictor of that ideology is whether the president who gets to nominate the justice holding the ideological balance of power on the Court is a Democrat or a Republican.

One could well argue that leaving key social and political decisions in the hands of life-tenured Supreme Court justices deciding cases on ideological grounds and with scant possibility of popular constitutional amendment is not the best way to make policy. But, to paraphrase the former defense secretary Donald Rumsfeld, we fight these battles with the political and legal system we have, not with the system we might wish to have at a later time. Whether the Supreme Court should be more politically responsive, or less ideological, or whether amending the Constitution should be made easier or harder are questions that can be debated—but these issues are even more intractable than campaign finance reform.[16]

Reformers need both an immediate and a longer term strategy. To begin with, it is important to defend what remains of campaign finance law, and to continue pursuing and defending legislation within the confines of Supreme Court precedent. Consider, for example, how defenders of campaign finance law beat back attempts in a number of jurisdictions to get courts to strike down laws banning direct corporate contributions to candidates. The Supreme Court recently declined to hear one of these challenges, and at this writing, direct corporate bans remain in place.[17]

Preserving what remains of campaign finance law remains vital. Laws imposing contribution limitations on candidate elections, closing loopholes in those limitations, and improving disclosure regimes are all constitutional and must be pursued and defended. Voluntary public financing plans still are constitutional, although the Supreme Court's decision in the *Arizona* case barring additional public financing for candidates facing wealthy opponents or large outside spending campaigns makes it very difficult to design systems that are both constitutional and attractive enough to persuade candidates to participate. Creative campaign finance solutions, such as vouchers, should be defended as constitutional and should be a key part of the agenda. Progressives need to think creatively about institutional design that furthers all the goals of progressive campaign financing, from protecting robust free speech to deterring corruption and promoting equality.

In addition, there needs to be more done to fix problems with disclosure law. Disclosure is no substitute for voucher + limits or other subsidies in terms of promoting political equality and preventing corruption. But disclosure provides valuable information to busy voters (you may not follow a ballot measure election, for example, but if I tell you that one side is backed by the National Rifle Association or the National Abortion Rights Action League, that may be all you need to know to vote consistent with your views) and helps ferret out actual corrupt deals between donors and politicians. California has been a model in requiring effective disclosure. In a high-profile case, its Fair Political Practices Commission forced the disclosure of millions of dollars of secret money connected to Koch brothers organizations that was being used to fund an anti-union ballot measure campaign. The California model of aggressive disclosure should be pushed throughout the country, but disclosure thresholds should be raised so those spending small amounts on politics do not face onerous bureaucratic requirements.[18]

With federal action to fix campaign financing apparently off the table for the time being, the focus turns to the states. States are hamstrung by the Supreme Court's money-in-politics decisions, especially recent cases barring corporate and labor union spending limits, and the *Arizona* public financing decision. But states can still take important steps, such as the expansion of small-donor matching programs or voucher plans, imposition of campaign finance limits on candidates and parties, and greatly improved disclosure. Many of these measures will no doubt provoke lawsuits, and they must be carefully crafted and a strong legislative record built to allow them to sustain constitutional challenge. Even when the Court opens the window for greater reform, progressives will have to start pushing for reform on the state and local level before turning to Congress—where political obstacles will no doubt remain.

But the longer-term strategy is Supreme Court centered. Even if progressives win World War III in the Senate, however, it will not be enough. The key is returning the Court to its role of carefully balancing rights and interests in this very difficult arena.

Recall Harvard law professor Elena Kagan's skepticism, when she wrote about the *Austin* case, of the political equality rationale and incumbency protection. Reformers must demonstrate to the new Court that reasonable limits on corporate and even individual spending, when coupled with generous public financing, would not squelch competition or inhibit robust debate.

Even progressive justices like Kagan will need convincing, and they should demand it in any case: true progressive campaign finance reform does not favor suppressing debate, even (especially) from those with whom progressives disagree. Further, reformers must defend the press exemption. Allowing the exemption makes the law less coherent (though no less coherent than current law, which limits foreign spending on elections but not corporate spending). But it plays a key role in protecting democratic institutions and free debate.

In addition, scholars must do more work defining and defending governmental interests that justify reasonable campaign finance laws. One possibility (which I have resisted in this book) is to seek to expand or redefine the meaning of "corruption" the Supreme Court uses in its campaign finance balancing to its pre–*Citizens United* understanding. This would require us to hope for scandal that is outrageous enough to spur reform and judicial acceptance of reform, yet does not do significant damage.

Another possibility is that the Court can adopt political equality notions more opaquely, such as by accepting Larry Lessig's arguments about "dependence corruption" or Robert Post's "electoral integrity." Even though I am not convinced that these arguments offer something new, a progressive Supreme Court majority might accept one of these arguments as a doctrinal hook to reach a result consistent with political equality principles without formally overturning earlier precedent rejecting political equality as a permissible rationale for regulation.

Ideally, we should persuade a new progressive Supreme Court to publicly accept a political equality interest that could justify reasonable campaign finance regulation, consistent with progressive values. Justice Breyer sketched a view of what this might look like in his 2001 *Shrink Missouri* concurrence, and Judge Calabresi offered his thoughts in a concurring court of appeals opinion in 2011. This book is my main contribution to this debate. The idea is to for courts to apply strict scrutiny to campaign finance laws for pro-incumbent and anti-speech measures, but to accept political equality as a compelling interest for reform that can justify egalitarian and speech-enhancing programs. It is a tough and delicate balance.[19]

Opponents of campaign finance laws have looked at this issue with a long time horizon. Justices Scalia and Kennedy first dissented against upholding limits on corporate spending in elections in 1990, in the *Austin* case. They had to wait two decades for a reversal, and they never stopped dissenting before then in cases inconsistent with their vision. Noted campaign finance lawyer Jim Bopp had a ten-year plan for attacks on campaign laws. With a sympathetic Supreme Court he has so far gotten some, but not all, of what he wished for.[20]

Progressive campaign finance reform supporters need to be just as patient in waiting until the moment is right. That moment could come at any time, but it will almost certainly come within the next decade.

However bad the next confirmation battles are, I hope they bring us a

Supreme Court ready to accept the idea that the super-wealthy should not have an outsized influence on electoral and policy outcomes in the United States. No one in a democracy committed to basic norms of political equality should be able to contribute or spend $50 or $100 million—or, as the Koch brothers and their allies promise, $889 million—in a single election season. That is a plutocracy, not a democracy.

Principles of political equality embodied in the Supreme Court's rejection of poll taxes and its embrace of the one-person, one-vote rule should carry over to money-in-politics decisions. It is possible to impose reasonable limits on money in elections, to empower voters through campaign vouchers, and to ensure robust speech and political competition. We can do all of it if the Supreme Court allows it.

In the meantime, activists continue to keep the issue of campaign finance reform in the news. On the fifth anniversary of the *Citizens United* opinion, a group of protesters (for the second time) smuggled recording devices into the Supreme Court's majestic courtroom to record a protest over the decision. One by one, protesters with the group 99Rise (referencing the 99 percent of the "Occupy" movement) shouted slogans against the decision, and one by one, Court police removed the protesters. SCOTUSblog's Mark Walsh described the scene:

> Just after the Justices had taken the bench at 10 a.m. [on January 21, 2015], and as they were about to announce opinions, a woman stood from her seat near the back of the courtroom and said, "I rise on behalf of democracy." She continued with a mention of *Citizens United*, the 2010 ruling that removed limits on independent political expenditures by corporations and unions. Three Supreme Court police officers quickly converged on her, causing a loud commotion as they pushed through an area of the courtroom where single wooden chairs are in use, forcefully subdued her, and then removed her from the courtroom.
>
> As what at first seemed like the lone demonstrator was removed, Chief Justice John G. Roberts Jr. quipped, "Our second order of business this morning . . ." to laughs from the crowded courtroom.
>
> But before he could finish that thought, a second demonstrator[] stood and said, "One person, one vote." It was perhaps a continuation of the *Citizens United* theme, or a reference to a key phrase from the Court's voting

rights jurisprudence. As the second protestor was being approached by officers, a third and a fourth one stood and uttered similar lines.

The Chief Justice was heard to mutter, "Oh, please."[21]

"Oh, please" indeed. Chief Justice Roberts appeared miffed that the decorum of the Court had been disrupted for a few moments. The rest of us suffer with the disruption that the Court's campaign finance jurisprudence has done to our democracy for years. Nothing less than changing the Court can now fix it.

The health of our democracy depends upon winning this battle.

NOTES

Introduction: A New American Plutocracy

1. David Firestone, *The Line to Kiss Sheldon Adelson's Boots,* Taking Note, N.Y. Times, Mar. 31, 2014, http://takingnote.blogs.nytimes.com/2014/03/31/the-line-to-kiss -sheldon-adelsons-boots/.

2. Michael Barbaro, *Seeking Political Revival, Christie Joins '16 Contenders at G.O.P. Forum,* N.Y. Times, Mar. 29, 2014, www.nytimes.com/2014/03/30/us/politics/ at-republican-gathering-top-2016-contenders-bring-a-unified-message.html.

3. Firestone, *supra* note 1; Thomas B. Desalt, *The High Cost of Free Speech,* N.Y. Times, Apr. 6, 2014, www.nytimes.com/2014/04/09/opinion/the-high-cost-of -free-speech.html.

4. Matea Gold & Philip Rucker, *Billionaire Mogul Sheldon Adelson Looks for Main- stream Republican Who Can Win in 2016,* Wash. Post, Mar. 25, 2014, www.wash ingtonpost.com/politics/billionaire-mogul-sheldon-adelson-looks-for-main stream-republican-who-can-win-in-2016/2014/03/25/e2f47bb0-b3c2-11e3-8cb6 -284052554d74_story.html; Theodoric Meyer, *How Much Did Sheldon Adelson Really Spend on Campaign 2012?,* ProPublica, Dec. 20, 2012, www.propublica.org/article/ how-much-did-sheldon-adelson-really-spend-on-campaign-2012.

5. Nicholas Confessore & Jo Craven McGinty, *Obama, Romney and Their Parties on Track to Raise $2 Billion,* N.Y. Times, Oct. 25, 2012, www.nytimes.com/2012/10/26/ us/politics/obama-and-romney-raise-1-billion-each.html.

6. Ruben Navarrette, Jr., *How Meg Whitman Spent a Fortune—and Lost,* CNN, Nov. 3, 2010, www.cnn.com/2010/OPINION/11/03/navarrette.california.whitman/index .html; PunditFact, *Rare Feat: Cantor Spent More at Steakhouses Than Opponent Did on Campaign,* Jun. 11, 2014, www.politifact.com/punditfact/statements/2014/jun /11/chuck-todd/rare-feat-cantor-spent-more-steakhouses-opponent-d/; Center for Responsive Politics, Top Individuals Funding Outside Spending Groups 2014,

OpenSecrets.Org, www.opensecrets.org/outsidespending/summ.php?cycle=2014 &disp=D&type=V.

7. The website of the American Anti-Corruption Act is http://anticorruptionact.org/ (last visited Jan. 9, 2015). Represent Us is at https://represent.us/ and some of the quoted language appears on the page http://anticorruptionact.org/full-text (last visited Jan. 9, 2015).

8. I have had a long-running debate with Professor Lessig over how to characterize his "dependence corruption" argument. See note 34 in Chapter 3. On Jefferson, see Jerry Markon, *Ex-Rep. Jefferson Gets 13 Years in Freezer Cash Case,* Wash. Post (Nov. 14, 2009), http://articles.washingtonpost.com/2009-11-14/news/36786791_1_william-j-jefferson-prison-term-robert-p-trout. On Cunningham, see Bill Chappell, *Former Rep. 'Duke' Cunningham Freed After Bribery Sentence,* NPR News, Jun. 4, 2013, www.npr.org/blogs/thetwo-way/2013/06/04/188667106/former-rep-duke -cunningham-freed-after-bribery-sentence.

9. Lawrence Lessig, *Republic Lost* 8 (2011). For example, after the Supreme Court decided the *McCutcheon* case, Fred Wertheimer of Democracy 21 released a statement reading in part: "The Supreme Court majority voted in *McCutcheon* today to license the further corruption of our democracy. The Court re-created the system of legalized bribery today that existed during the Watergate days." *Fred Wertheimer Statement on McCutcheon vs. FEC,* Democracy 21, Apr. 2, 2014, www.democracy21.org/inside-the-courts/press-releases-inside-the-courts/fred -wertheimer-statement-on-mccutcheon-vs-fec/.

10. Michael Beckel, *Don't Support 'Campaign Finance Reform'? Try Combatting 'Corruption,'* The Center for Public Integrity, Dec. 3, 2013, www.publicintegrity.org/ 2013/12/03/13943/don-t-support-campaign-finance-reform-try-combating-cor ruption.

11. 424 U.S. 1 (1976).

12. *Citizens United v. FEC,* 558 U.S. 310 (2010). On the role of *Citizens United* in spawning Super PACs, see Richard L. Hasen, *The Numbers Don't Lie: If You Aren't Sure Citizens United Gave Rise to Super PACs, Just Follow the Money,* Slate, Mar. 9, 2012, www.slate.com/articles/news_and_politics/politics/2012/03/the_supreme _court_s_citizens_united_decision_has_led_to_an_explosion_of_campaign _spending_.html.

13. *McCutcheon v. FEC,* 134 S. Ct. 1434 (2014). *See* Richard Briffault, *Of Constituents and Contributors,* U. Chi. Legal F. (forthcoming 2015), *available at* http://papers .ssrn.com/sol3/papers.cfm?abstract_id=2553456.

14. See Richard L. Hasen, *Lobbying, Rent Seeking, and the Constitution,* 64 Stan. L. Rev. 191 (2012) and the sources cited therein.

15. Stephen W. Mazza et al., *Measuring Rates of Return on Lobbying Expenditures: An Empirical Case Study of Tax Breaks for Multinational Corporations,* 25 J. L. & Pol. 401 (2010).

16. On the passage of Dodd-Frank, see Robert G. Kaiser, *Act of Congress: How America's Essential Institution Works, and How It Doesn't* (2013). On what has happened since Dodd-Frank's passage, see Gary Rivlin, *How Wall Street Defanged Dodd-Frank,*

The Nation, May 20, 2013, www.thenation.com/article/174113/how-wall-street
-defanged-dodd-frank.

17. Daniel P. Tokaji and Renata E. B. Strause, *The New Soft Money: Outside Spending
in Congressional Elections*, Election Law @ Moritz Report, Jun. 18, 2014, http://
moritzlaw.osu.edu/thenewsoftmoney/wp-content/uploads/sites/57/2014/06/
the-new-soft-money-WEB.pdf.

18. Martin Gilens & Benjamin I. Page, *Testing Theories of American Politics: Elites, Interest Groups, and Average Citizens*, 12 Persp. on Pol. 564 (2014), http://journals.cam
bridge.org/download.php?file=%2FPPS%2FPPS12_03%2FS1537592714001595a
.pdf&code=3af62995a033b88315bc15f69c7fae16.

19. Lynn Vavreck, *The Power of Political Ignorance*, N.Y. Times, May 23, 2014, www.ny
times.com/2014/05/25/upshot/the-power-of-political-ignorance.html.

20. *Senate Democrats Begin Efforts to Amend Constitution*, Roll Call, Jun. 6, 2014, www
.rollcall.com/news/senate_democrats_begin_efforts_to_amend_constitution
-233618-1.html?pg=1&dczone=politics. For a list of forty-three co-sponsors, all
Democrats except for the Independents Bernie Sanders and Angus King, see
www.congress.gov/bill/113th-congress/senate-joint-resolution/19/cosponsors.

21. Aaron Blake, *Harry Reid: 'Republicans Are Addicted to Koch,'* Wash. Post, Mar. 4,
2014, www.washingtonpost.com/blogs/post-politics/wp/2014/03/04/harry-reid
-republicans-are-addicted-to-koch/; John Stanton & Kate Nocera, *Harry Reid Backs
Constitutional Amendment to Limit Koch Brothers' Influence*, BuzzFeed, May 14,
2014, www.buzzfeed.com/johnstanton/harry-reid-backs-constitutional-amend
ment-to-limit-koch-brot. On Democrats and Wall Street, see Rivlin, *supra* note 16.

22. On Democratic super PAC fundraising, see Annie Linskey & Julie Bykowicz,
Democrats Griping About False Ads Respond with Deception, Bloomberg News,
Jun. 18, 2014, www.bloomberg.com/news/2014-06-18/democrats-griping-about
-false-ads-respond-with-deception.html. On President Obama's (and other Dem-
ocrats') hypocrisy on campaign finance reform, see Richard L. Hasen, *Three
Wrong Progressive Approaches (and One Right One) to Campaign Finance Reform*, 8
Harv. L. & Pol'y Rev. 21 (2014).

23. On McCain, see John Hudson, *How McCain Flirted Then Dumped Campaign Finance Reform*, The Wire, Jul. 17, 2012, www.thewire.com/politics/2012/07/how
-mccain-flirted-and-then-dumped-campaign-finance-reform/54683/. On McConnell, see Editorial, *McConnell's Hypocrisy on Campaign Disclosure*, Lexington Herald-
Leader, Aug. 1, 2010, www.kentucky.com/2010/08/01/1372068/mcconnells-hy
pocrisy-on-campaign.html. On Cruz, see Press Release, *Sen. Cruz Files Bills to
Protect the Individual Right to Free Speech*, Press Office of Senator Ted Cruz, Jun.
3, 2014, www.cruz.senate.gov/?p=press_release&id=1320.

Chapter 1. The Corruption Distortion

1. The documents in *Bluman v. FEC* are posted on the Federal Election Commission's page at: www.fec.gov/law/litigation/bluman.shtml. The three-judge district court decision from which the facts here are drawn is at 800 F. Supp. 2d 281

(D.D.C. 2011). The Supreme Court's order without opinion summarily affirming the trial court is at 132 S. Ct. 1087 (2012).

2. As of 2015, Benjamin was working as an associate at a Vancouver law firm, Davis LLP. www.davis.ca/en/lawyer/Benjamin-Bluman/.

3. As of 2015, Steiman was listed as practicing internal medicine in Manhattan. www.healthgrades.com/physician/dr-asenath-steiman-gbyt9.

4. The *Bluman* district court decision at page 283 describes and provides citations to the congressional findings on foreign money in the 1996 elections.

5. Kenneth P. Vogel, *Lawsuit Revives Fears of Foreign Cash*, Politico, May 12, 2011, www.politico.com/news/stories/0511/54802.html.

6. Randy Boswell, *Canadians Lose Fight to Spend Money on U.S. Election Campaigns*, Nat'l Post, Jan. 19, 2012, http://news.nationalpost.com/2012/01/19/canadians -lose-fight-to-spend-money-on-u-s-election-campaigns/.

7. Most cases reach the Supreme Court through the filing of what is known as a petition for writ of certiorari, or a cert petition. Review is completely discretionary, and a decision to reject a cert petition has no precedential value—it does not mean the lower court got it right. But in a few kinds of cases, thanks to statutes passed by Congress, cases come up the Supreme Court on an "appeal." When the Court decides not to hear one of these cases and just to let it be, it does so either by affirming without an opinion (a "summary affirmance") or by dismissing the case. Either way, a decision like that *is* precedential, and stands for the proposition that the lower court got the result right (but not necessarily for the right reasons). The two most important pieces of federal legislation on campaign finance, the Federal Election Campaign Act Amendments of 1974 and the Bipartisan Campaign Reform Act of 2002, each included special jurisdictional provisions allowing some legal challenges to go straight from a three-judge court directly on appeal to the Supreme Court. The jurisdictional provision drives the Court to take many more cases than it otherwise would. *See* Richard L. Hasen, *The Supreme Court and Election Law: Judging Equality from* Baker v. Carr *to* Bush v. Gore 36–38 (2003) (discussing the reasons the Supreme Court's poll tax case, *Harper v. Virginia Bd. of Elections,* 383 U.S. 663 (1966), was decided through a full opinion and not decided through a summary affirmance and dissent); Joshua A. Douglas, *The Procedure of Election Law in Federal Courts,* 2011 Utah L. Rev. 433, 446 (2011); Michael E. Solimine, *The Three-Judge District Court in Voting Rights Litigation,* 30 U. Mich. J.L. Reform 79, 132 (1996).

8. Louis Jacobson, *Why Alito Shook His Head: Obama Exaggerates Impact of Supreme Court Ruling on Foreign Companies,* Politifact, Jan. 27, 2010 (updated Jul. 21, 2011), www.politifact.com/truth-o-meter/statements/2010/jan/27/barack-obama/obama -says-supreme-court-ruling-allows-foreign-com/. In 2011, Politifact changed its rating of President Obama's statement about *Citizens United* from "barely true" to "mostly false," part of its change of all "barely true" ratings to "mostly false" ratings.

9. Associated Press, *Justice Alito Defends High Court's 2010 Decision in Citizens*

United Case, Fox News, Nov. 17, 2012, www.foxnews.com/politics/2012/11/17/jus tice-alito-defends-high-court-2010-decision-in-citizens-united-case/. Justice Alito told the *American Spectator:* "I don't play poker. . . . Either I should take it up so that I learn to have a poker face, or it's a good thing that I don't because I'd lose a lot of money. People thought I said something. I assume that they're correct. I certainly thought it. The president said that *Citizens United* overruled a century of precedent, which just isn't true." Matthew Walther, *Sam Alito: A Civil Man,* Am. Spectator, May 2014, http://spectator.org/articles/58731/sam-alito-civil-man. Interestingly, in explaining his incredulity, Justice Alito latched onto the "century of precedent" comment rather than the foreign spending comment. Alito was correct that the president was wrong on both of these points. The corporate spending ban overturned in *Citizens United* dates to the 1940s. (It is the corporate contribution ban which dated to 1907, but that ban was not at issue in *Citizens United* and, as of 2015, still stands.)

10. Justice Stevens wrote: "If taken seriously, our colleagues' assumption that the identity of a speaker has *no* relevance to the Government's ability to regulate po- litical speech would lead to some remarkable conclusions. Such an assumption would have accorded the propaganda broadcasts to our troops by 'Tokyo Rose' during World War II the same protection as speech by Allied commanders. More pertinently, it would appear to afford the same protection to multinational cor- porations controlled by foreigners as to individual Americans: To do otherwise, after all, could 'enhance the relative voice' of some (*i.e.,* humans) over others (*i.e.,* nonhumans)." The full set of opinions is *Citizens United v. FEC,* 558 U.S. 310 (2010).

11. For a full analysis of the case and its implications, see Richard L. Hasen, Citizens United *and the Illusion of Coherence,* 109 Mich. L. Rev. 581 (2011). The next few pages draw from that analysis and the opinion itself.

12. You can watch the trailer for the movie at http://hillarythemovie.com/trailer .html.

13. For a detailed history, see Robert E. Mutch, *Campaigns, Congress, & Courts: The Making of Federal Campaign Finance Law* (1988) and Robert E. Mutch, *Buying the Vote: A History of Campaign Finance Reform* (2014). The Federal Election Commis- sion offers a brief overview of the history: www.fec.gov/info/appfour.htm.

14. The next few paragraphs draw from my history of the litigation surrounding *Buckley v. Valeo.* Richard L. Hasen, *The Nine Lives of* Buckley v. Valeo in *First Amendment Stories* (Richard Garnett & Andrew Koppelman eds., 2012).

15. *Id.*

16. On the internal drafting history of *Buckley,* see Richard L. Hasen, *The Untold Drafting History of Buckley v. Valeo,* 2 Election L.J. 241 (2003).

17. On the "incorporation" of First Amendment limits against the states, see *Gitlow v. New York,* 268 U.S. 652 (1925).

18. Eugene Volokh, *Money and Speech,* Volokh Conspiracy, Jan. 24, 2010, www.volokh .com/2010/01/24/money-and-speech-2/. Whether money is speech or not could

affect the level of scrutiny to apply. But because I argue that my voucher + limits plan is constitutional even under strict scrutiny, nothing in this book turns on resolution of this particular legal question.

19. For a general discussion of balancing and levels of scrutiny (although in the context of equal protection challenges), see Erwin Chemerinsky, *Constitutional Law: Principles and Policies* § 9.1.2 (4th ed. 2011).

20. The opinion in *Buckley v. Valeo* is at 424 U.S. 1 (1976). For full citations to these parts of *Buckley*, see Richard L. Hasen, *Legislation, Statutory Interpretation, and Election Law: Examples and Explanations* ch. 13 (2014).

21. I review these cases and the pendulum swings in *id.*, chs. 13, 14. The Court case on evidence of corruption from newspaper editorials is *Nixon v. Shrink Mo. Gov't PAC*, 528 U.S. 377 (2000).

22. *First Nat'l Bank of Bos. v. Bellotti*, 435 U.S. 765 (1978).

23. *FEC v. Mass. Citizens for Life*, 479 U.S. 238 (1986).

24. *Austin v. Mich. Chamber of Commerce*, 494 U.S. 652 (1990).

25. Elizabeth Garrett, *New Voices in Politics: Justice Marshall's Jurisprudence on Law and Politics*, 52 Howard L.J. 655, 669 (2009).

26. For the history, see *McConnell v. FEC*, 540 U.S. 93 (2003).

27. The Supreme Court discussed the Yellowtail ad in footnote 78 of the *McConnell* opinion.

28. *Shrink Mo.*, 528 U.S. 377.

29. On the history of *Citizens United* and the Court's decision not to apply the principles of constitutional avoidance, see Richard L. Hasen, *Constitutional Avoidance and Anti-Avoidance by the Roberts Court*, 2009 Sup. Ct. Rev. 181 (2009).

30. On the Souter dissent, see Jeffrey Toobin, *Money Unlimited*, The New Yorker, May 21, 2012, www.newyorker.com/reporting/2012/05/21/120521fa_fact_toobin.

31. See the transcript of the second oral argument, posted at www.supremecourt .gov/oral_arguments/argument_transcripts/08-205%5BReargued%5D.pdf.

32. *See Citizens United v. FEC*, 558 U.S. 310 (2010)

33. The Montana case is *Am. Tradition P'ship, Inc. v. Bullock*, 132 S. Ct. 2490 (2012).

34. *Bluman v. FEC*, 800 F. Supp. 2d 281 (D.D.C. 2011).

35. *SpeechNow.Org v. FEC*, 599 F.3d 686 (D.C. Cir. 2010), *cert. denied sub nom.*, *Keating v. FEC*, 131 S.Ct. 553 (2010).

36. On the Federal Election Commission decisions, see FEC Adv. Op. 2010-09 (Club for Growth); FEC Adv. Op. 2010-11 (Commonsense Ten). On the term "Super PAC," see Eliza Newlin Carney, *FEC Rulings Open Door for 'Super' PACs*, Nat'l J., Aug. 2, 2010, www.nationaljournal.com/columns/rules-of-the-game/fec-rulings -open-door-for-super-pacs-20100802.

37. On this history, see Richard L. Hasen, *Super PAC Contributions, Corruption, and the Proxy War Over Coordination*, 9 Duke J. Const. L & Pub. Pol'y 1 (2014), http:// scholarship.law.duke.edu/cgi/viewcontent.cgi?article=1085&context=djclpp.

38. On the role of these mega-donors in the 2012 elections, see Kenneth P. Vogel, *Big Money* (2014).

39. On the conflicts over 501(c)(4) political activity, see Hasen, *supra* note 20, ch. 15.3.
40. On the facts, see *McCutcheon v. FEC,* 134 S. Ct. 1434 (2014). On the critique of the reasoning, see Richard L. Hasen, *Die Another Day,* Slate, Apr. 2, 2014, www.slate .com/articles/news_and_politics/jurisprudence/2014/04/the_subtle_awful ness_of_the_mccutcheon_v_fec_campaign_finance_decision_the.html.

Chapter 2. What Does Money Buy in Politics?

1. Bradley A. Smith, *Unfree Speech: The Folly of Campaign Finance Reform* 42 (2001); George F. Will, *The Democratic Vision of Big Brother,* Wash. Post, Oct. 17, 2010, www .washingtonpost.com/wp-dyn/content/article/2010/10/15/AR2010101504201 .html ("Total spending, by all parties, campaigns and issue-advocacy groups, concerning every office from county clerks to U.S. senators, may reach a record $4.2 billion *in this two-year cycle.* That is about what Americans spend *in one year* on yogurt but less than they spend on candy in two Halloween seasons. Procter & Gamble spent $8.6 billion on advertising in its most recent fiscal year.").
2. Zach Holden, *Overview of Campaign Finances, 2011–2012 Elections,* Nat'l Inst. on Money in St. Pols., May 13, 2014, http://beta.followthemoney.org/research/insti tute-reports/overview-of-campaign-finances-20112012-elections/. Of the $7.1 billion spent on federal election activity in the 2011–12 election cycle, just under $2 billion was spent in 2011. *FEC Summarizes 2011 Campaign Activity,* FEC Press Office, May 1, 2012 (revised Apr. 3, 2014), www.fec.gov/press/press2012/ 20120501_2011YESummaries.shtml.
3. On the Gross Domestic Product data, see www.tradingeconomics.com/united -states/gdp ($15.864 trillion in 2012). On potato chip sales data, see United States Potato Board, *Sales & Utilization Estimates 2001–2010,* at 14, www.uspotatoes.com/ newsletters/downloads/2011USPB-SalesUtilizationEstimatesFINAL.pdf; United States Potato Board, *Chip-Stock—U.S. Market Long Range Plan 2012–2016,* www .uspotatoes.com/downloads/Chips_and_Chipping_Potatoes-US_Market.pdf ("Chips remain America's favorite salty snack with sales in excess of $6 billon. But as an industry that is over 150 years old, it falls well within the classification of being a 'mature' industry. Overall, sales have been relatively flat, in both pounds and dollars, over the past several years, somewhat encouraging given its maturity, the multitude of alternate snack items, and America's push to dieting and healthier eating."). In contrast to the decreasing trend in these (inflation-adjusted) numbers from the U.S. Potato Board, figures from Market Line showing market values of the U.S. potato chip market shows an average three percent growth in supermarket sales from 2000–2013. (Data from Market Line on file with the author.)
4. Joshua Tucker, *Time to Stop a Spuddering Analogy: The Differences Between Campaign Finance and Potato Chips,* The Monkey Cage, Nov. 28, 2012, http://themonkey cage.org/2012/11/28/time-to-stop-a-spuddering-analogy-the-difference-between -campaign-finance-and-potato-chips/.

5. Smith, *supra* note 1, at 227.

6. Walter Hickey, *House Candidates Who Spent More Money Won Their Elections 95% of the Time,* Bus. Insider, Nov. 9, 2012, www.businessinsider.com/congress-elec tion-money-2012-11. Center for Responsive Politics, Election Stats 2012, OpenSecrets .Org, www.opensecrets.org/bigpicture/elec_stats.php?cycle=2012 (last visited Jan. 10, 2015).

7. On the incumbent reelection rate, see *id.*

8. On Cantor versus Brat, see Russ Choma, *Dave Versus Goliath, By the Numbers,* Center for Responsive Politics, Jun. 11, 2014, www.opensecrets.org/news/ 2014/06/dave-versus-goliath-by-the-numbers/. On Brown, see Seema Mehta & Maeve Reston, *Jerry Brown Nearly Matched Meg Whitman's Campaign Spending on TV in Final Weeks of Race,* L.A. Times, Feb. 1, 2011, http://articles.latimes .com/2011/feb/01/local/la-me-governor-money-20110201.

9. *Id.* On reasons for Cantor's loss, see David Wasserman, *What We Can Learn from Eric Cantor's Defeat,* Five Thirty Eight Politics, Jun. 20, 2014, http://fivethirty eight.com/features/what-we-can-learn-from-eric-cantors-defeat/.

10. Rick Jervis, *Akin's Gaffe Helps McCaskill Retain Missouri Senate Seat,* USA Today, Nov. 7, 2012, www.usatoday.com/story/news/politics/2012/11/06/akin-mccaskill -missouri-senate/1687873/. Gail Russell Chaddock, *Claire McCaskill: 'Most Endangered Democrat' Wins Missouri Senate Race (+Video),* Christian Sci. Monitor, Nov. 7, 2012, www.csmonitor.com/USA/Elections/Senate/2012/1107/Claire-McCaskill -most-endangered-Democrat-wins-Missouri-Senate-race-video. On the McCaskill-Akin campaign figures, see Center for Responsive Politics, Total Raised and Spent, 2012 Race: Missouri Senate, OpenSecrets.Org, www.opensecrets.org/races/sum mary.php?id=MOS2&cycle=2012 and www.opensecrets.org/races/indexp.php? cycle=2012&id=MOS2&spec=N (last accessed Jul. 7, 2014).

11. Lynn Vavreck, *The Power of Political Ignorance, The Upshot,* N.Y. Times, May 23, 2014, www.nytimes.com/2014/05/25/upshot/the-power-of-political-ignorance.html. *See also* Paul Freedman et al., *Campaign Advertising and Democratic Citizenship,* 48 Am. J. Pol. Sci. 723 (2004).

12. On partisan mobilization, see Eric McGhee & John Sides, *Do Campaigns Drive Partisan Turnout?,* 33 Pol. Behavior 313 (2011), http://link.springer.com/article/ 10.1007/s11109-010-9127-8. On candidate quality and other effects on campaigns, see Henry E. Brady et al., *The Study of Political Campaigns, in* Capturing Campaign Effects 1, 12 (Henry E. Brady & Richard Johnston eds., 2006), www .press.umich.edu/pdf/0472099213-ch1.pdf. On campaigns in presidential elections, see Thomas M. Holbrook, *Do Campaigns Matter?* 145 (1996). I am focusing here on federal elections, and not everything I say will apply to state and local elections or, especially, to judicial elections, where there are additional interests at play, including public confidence in the impartiality of the judiciary. (No one expects legislators to be impartial.)

13. On the money primary, see Michael J. Goff, *The Money Primary* (2004); Corwin Smidt & Dino Christenson, *More Bang for the Buck: Campaign Spending and Fund-*

raising Success, 40 Am. Pol. Research 949 (2012). For a review of the literature and argument that the money primary violates principles of political equality, see Nathan Burroughs, *The 'Money Primary' and Political Inequality in Congressional Elections* (draft dated Apr. 16, 2003), http://papers.ssrn.com/sol3/papers.cfm?abstract_id=2251978.

14. Lawrence Lessig, *One Way Forward: The Outsider's Guide to Fixing the Republic* (Kindle Single) (Kindle Locations 582–84) (2012). On the 2012 figures, see Center for Responsive Politics, Donor Demographics 2012, OpenSecrets.Org, www.opensecrets.org/bigpicture/donordemographics.php?cycle=2012&filter=A (last visited Jan. 10, 2015).

15. Nicholas O. Stephanopoulos, *Aligning Campaign Finance Law,* 101 Va. L. Rev. (forthcoming 2015), *draft available at* http://papers.ssrn.com/sol3/papers.cfm?abstract_id=2511079 (footnotes omitted).

16. Adam Bonica et. al, *Why Hasn't Democracy Slowed Rising Inequality?,* 27 J. Econ. Perspectives 103, 113 (2013) ("there appears to be a growing reliance on the top 0.01 percent of donors. Democrats as well as Republicans rely on big donors. . . . The Democrats have come to rely, increasingly, on contributions from individuals, particularly big money. Contributions from organized labor, never dominant, have fallen in importance. . . . While Republicans had a slight advantage in fundraising from the top 0.01 percent during the 1980s, this trend had reversed by the mid-1990s, with Democrats raising more than Republicans from the top 0.01 percent in six out of eight election cycles between 1994 and 2008. Only in the last two election cycles did Republicans regain the advantage in fundraising from the top 0.01 percent.").

17. On the general point, see Jennifer A. Steen, *Self-Financed Candidates in Congressional Elections* (2006).

18. Philip Bump, *No Recent Candidate Has Benefited from Outside Money as Much as Chris McDaniel, The Fix,* Wash. Post, Jun. 24, 2014, www.washingtonpost.com/blogs/the-fix/wp/2014/06/24/no-recent-candidate-has-benefited-from-outside-money-as-much-as-chris-mcdaniel/.

19. On the debate over when outside spending began to rise, see Richard L. Hasen, *The Numbers Don't Lie: If You Aren't Sure Citizens United Gave Rise to Super PACs, Just Follow the Money,* Slate, Mar. 9, 2012, www.slate.com/articles/news_and_politics/politics/2012/03/the_supreme_court_s_citizens_united_decision_has_led_to_an_explosion_of_campaign_spending_.html; Matt Bai, *How Much Has Citizens United Changed the Political Game?,* N.Y. Times Magazine, Jul. 17, 2012, www.nytimes.com/2012/07/22/magazine/how-much-has-citizens-united-changed-the-political-game.html?_r=1&pagewanted=all; Rick Hasen, *What Matt Bai's Missing in His Analysis of Whether Citizens United is Responsible for the Big Money Explosion,* Election Law Blog, Jul. 18, 2012, http://electionlawblog.org/?p=37108.

20. Blair Bowie & Adam Lioz, *Billion Dollar Democracy: The Unprecedented Role of Money in the 2012 Elections,* Demos (Jan. 17, 2013), www.demos.org/publication/

billion-dollar-democracy-unprecedented-role-money-2012-elections; Matea Gold & Tom Hamburger, *In 2016, the Lament of the Not Quite Rich Enough*, Wash. Post, Mar. 25, 2015, www.washingtonpost.com/politics/in-2016-campaign-the-lament-of-the-not-quite-rich-enough/2015/03/24/f0a38b18-cdb4-11e4-8a46-b1dc9be5a8ff_story.html.

21. Gary C. Jacobson, *The Effects of Campaign Spending on Congressional Elections*, 72 Am. Pol. Sci. Rev. 469 (1978); Gary C. Jacobson, *Enough Is Too Much: Money and Competition in House Elections*, in Elections in America 173 (Kay Lehman Schlozman ed., 1987); Gary C. Jacobson, *The Effects of Campaign Spending in House Elections: New Evidence for Old Arguments*, 34 Am. J. Pol. Sci. 334 (1990). *See also* Alan I. Abramowitz, *Incumbency, Campaign Spending, and the Decline of Competition in U.S. House Elections*, 53 J. Pol. 34 (1991).

22. Donald P. Green & Jonathan S. Krasno, *Salvation for the Spendthrift Incumbent: Reestimating the Effects of Campaign Spending in House Elections*, 34 Am. J. Pol. Sci. 884 (1988); Donald P. Green & Jonathan S. Krasno, *Rebuttal to Jacobson's "New Evidence for Old Arguments,"* 34 Am. J. Pol. Sci. 363 (1990); Alan Gerber, *Estimating the Effects of Campaign Spending on Senate Election Outcomes Using Instrumental Variables*, 92 Am. Pol. Sci. Rev. 401 (1998).

23. Gerber, *supra* note 22, at 410.

24. Smith, *supra* note 1, at 127.

25. *See* Frank J. Sorauf, *Money in American Elections* 316 (1988); Stephen Ansolabehere et al., *Why Is There So Little Money in U.S. Politics?*, 17 J. Econ. Perspectives 105 (2003).

26. Kenneth P. Vogel, *Big Money* xii (2014).

27. John M. Glionna, *Casino Magnate Sheldon Adelson Leads Charge Against Online Gambling*, L.A. Times, May 20, 2014, www.latimes.com/nation/la-na-adv-adelson-online-gambling-20140521-story.html; Michael Barber, *Ideological Donors, Contribution Limits, and the Polarization of American Legislatures* (Jan. 30, 2015) (unpublished manuscript), *available at* http://static1.squarespace.com/static/51841c73e4b04fc5ce6e8f15/t/54d24adae4b092c13f8d35c6/1423067866936/Limits_Revised.pdf.

28. Jennifer Jacobs, *Conservative Group Americans for Prosperity Targets Iowa*, Des Moines Register, Jul. 6, 2014, www.desmoinesregister.com/story/news/politics/2014/07/06/conservative-group-americans-prosperity-targets-iowa/12262325/; Nicholas Confessore, *Koch Brothers' Budget of $889 Million for 2016 Is on Par with Both Parties' Spending*, N.Y. Times, Jan. 26, 2015, www.nytimes.com/2015/01/27/us/politics/kochs-plan-to-spend-900-million-on-2016-campaign.html.

29. Daniel P. Tokaji & Renata E. B. Strause, *The New Soft Money: Outside Spending in Congressional Elections* 82–83 (2014), http://moritzlaw.osu.edu/thenewsoftmoney/.

30. Smith, *supra* note 1, at 127 n.15 ("But cf. Richard Hall and Frank Wayman, 'Buying Time: Moneyed Interests and the Mobilization of Bias in Congressional Committees,' 810: 'If money does not necessarily buy votes or change minds . . . it can buy members time.'"); *McConnell v. FEC*, 540 U.S. 93 (2003).

31. From the Supreme Court's *McConnell* opinion at 540 U.S. 150–52:

> The record in the present cases is replete with similar examples of national party committees peddling access to federal candidates and officeholders in exchange for large soft-money donations. As one former Senator put it:
>
>> Special interests who give large amounts of soft money to political parties do in fact achieve their objectives. They do get special access. Sitting Senators and House Members have limited amounts of time, but they make time available in their schedules to meet with representatives of business and unions and wealthy individuals who gave large sums to their parties. These are not idle chit-chats about the philosophy of democracy. . . . Senators are pressed by their benefactors to introduce legislation, to amend legislation, to block legislation, and to vote on legislation in a certain way. (quoting declaration of former Sen. Warren Rudman ¶ 7)
>
> So pervasive is this practice that the six national party committees actually furnish their own menus of opportunities for access to would-be soft-money donors, with increased prices reflecting an increased level of access. For example, the DCCC offers a range of donor options, starting with the $10,000-per-year Business Forum program, and going up to the $100,000-per-year National Finance Board program. The latter entitles the donor to bimonthly conference calls with the Democratic House leadership and chair of the DCCC, complimentary invitations to all DCCC fundraising events, two private dinners with the Democratic House leadership and ranking Members, and two retreats with the Democratic House leader and DCCC chair in Telluride, Colorado, and Hyannisport, Massachusetts. . . . [S]ee also [*McConnell v. FEC*, 251 F. Supp. 2d 176, 506 (D.D.C. 2003) (describing records indicating that DNC offered meetings with President in return for large donations); *id.* (describing RNC's various donor programs); *id.* (same for NRSC); *id.* (same for DSCC); *id.* (same for NRCC). Similarly, "the RNC's donor programs offer greater access to federal office holders as the donations grow larger, with the highest level and most personal access offered to the largest soft money donors." *Id.* (finding, further, that the RNC holds out the prospect of access to officeholders to attract soft-money donations and encourages officeholders to meet with large soft-money donors).

Some citations omitted and altered.

32. Fred Schulte et al., *Obama Rewards Big Bundlers with Jobs, Commissions, Stimulus Money, Government Contracts and More*, Center for Public Integrity, Jun. 15, 2011 (Updated May 19, 2014), www.publicintegrity.org/2011/06/15/4880/obama -rewards-big-bundlers-jobs-commissions-stimulus-money-government-con tracts-and; Fredreka Schouten, *Mitt Romney Declining to Disclose Names of Campaign Bundlers*, USA Today, May 25, 2012, http://usatoday30.usatoday.com/news/ politics/story/2012-05-25/mitt-romney-bundlers/55202324/1.

33. *Washington's Open Secret: Profitable PACs*, 60 Minutes, Oct. 21, 2013, www.cbs

news.com/news/washingtons-open-secret-profitable-pacs/. As the television program explained, "Over time the leadership PACs that were created as a way for congressional leaders of both parties, to raise money and distribute it to their members, have evolved into something different. Today, nearly every congressman and senator has a leadership PAC, not just the leaders. And they are used to solicit contributions from friends and supporters in order to advance their political agendas, their careers and, in many cases, their lifestyle."

The Sunlight Foundation's "Party Time" blog chronicles the big-ticket fundraisers for members of Congress, the president, and others. *See* http://blog.polit icalpartytime.org/category/congressional-leadership/.

34. Juliet Eilperin, *Obama Ambassador Nominees Prompt an Uproar with Bungled Answers, Lack of Ties*, Wash. Post, Feb. 14, 2014, www.washingtonpost.com/politics/ obama-ambassador-nominees-prompt-an-uproar-with-bungled-answers-lack-of -ties/2014/02/14/20fb0fe4-94b2-11e3-83b9-1f024193bb84_story.html.

35. Justin Grimmer & Eleanor Neff Powell, *Congressmen in Exile: The Politics and Consequences of Involuntary Committee Removal,* 75 J. Pol. 907 (2013), http://jour nals.cambridge.org/action/displayAbstract?fromPage=online&aid=9030307& fileId=S0022381613000704.

36. Joshua L. Kalla & David E. Broockman, *Campaign Contributions Facilitate Access to Congressional Officials: A Randomized Field Experiment,* Am. J. Pol. Sci. (forthcoming 2015), *available at* www.ocf.berkeley.edu/~broockma/kalla_broockman _donor_access_field_experiment.

37. The next few paragraphs draw from my article on lobbying, Richard L. Hasen, *Lobbying, Rent Seeking, and the Constitution,* 64 Stan. L. Rev. 191 (2012), www.stan fordlawreview.org/print/article/lobbying-rent-seeking-and-constitution.

38. Richard L. Hall & Alan V. Deardorff, *Lobbying as Legislative Subsidy,* 100 Am. Pol. Sci. Rev. 69 (2006); John M. de Figueiredo & Brian S. Silverman, *Academic Earmarks and the Returns to Lobbying,* 49 J.L. & Econ. 597 (2006).

39. Jeffery H. Birnbaum & Alan S. Murray, *Showdown at Gucci Gulch: Lawmakers, Lobbyists, and the Unlikely Triumph of Tax Reform* (1987); Frank M. Baumgartner et al., *Lobbying and Policy Change: Who Wins, Who Loses, and Why* 239–40 (2009); Eric Lichtblau, *Industry Lobbying Imperils Obama Overhaul of Student Loans,* N.Y. Times, Feb. 5, 2010, at A1, *available at* www.nytimes.com/2010/02/05/us/poli tics/05loans.html; Peter Baker & David M. Herszenhorn, *Obama Signs Overhaul of Student Loan Program,* N.Y. Times, Mar. 31, 2010, at A14, *available at* www.ny times.com/2010/03/31/us/politics/31obama.html.

40. Baumgartner, *supra* note 39, at 120–21; Birnbaum & Murray, *supra* note 39, at 236–37, Edward Wyatt & Eric Lichtblau, *A Finance Overhaul Fight Draws a Lobbying Swarm,* N.Y. Times, Apr. 20, 2010, at A1, *available at* www.nytimes.com/ 2010/04/20/business/20derivatives.html; Binyamin Appelbaum, *On Finance Bill, Lobbying Shifts to Regulations,* N.Y. Times, Jun. 27, 2010, at A1, *available at* www.nytimes.com/2010/06/27/business/27regulate.html?pagewanted=all.

41. Gene M. Grossman & Elhanan Helpman, *Special Interest Politics* 11 (2001);

Thomas M. Susman, *Private Ethics, Public Conduct: An Essay on Ethical Lobbying, Campaign Contributions, Reciprocity, and the Public Good*, 19 Stan. L. & Pol'y Rev. 10, 15–17 (2008); Lloyd Hitoshi Mayer, *What Is This "Lobbying" That We Are So Worried About?*, 26 Yale L. & Pol'y Rev. 485, 524 (2008); Robert G. Kaiser, *So Damn Much Money: The Triumph of Lobbying and the Corrosion of American Government* 297 (2009); Larry Makinson, *What Money Buys, in* Shades of Gray: Perspectives on Campaign Ethics 171, 181 (Candice J. Nelson et al. eds., 2002) .

42. *See* Kaiser, *supra* note 41, at 80, 105–6, 185, 272. Senator Chuck Hagel described how both Democrats and Republicans looking to raise $20 million to $25 million for House and Senate campaign committees "go to a committee of twenty-five lobbyists, a steering committee. And you say, Okay, you guys each have to come up with a million dollars." *Id.* at 291. *See also* Jonathan Martin, *The Cash-for-Speaker Program*, Politico (Jul. 29, 2010), www.politico.com/news/stories/0710/40380.html; Eric Lipton, *G.O.P. Leader Tightly Bound to Lobbyists*, N.Y. Times, Sept. 12, 2010, at A1, *available at* www.nytimes.com/2010/09/12/us/politics/12boehner.html?pagewanted=all ("[Lobbyists and former aides] have contributed hundreds of thousands of dollars to [Boehner's] campaigns, provided him with rides on their corporate jets, socialized with him at luxury golf resorts and waterfront bashes and are now leading fund-raising efforts for his Boehner for Speaker campaign, which is soliciting checks of up to $37,800 each, the maximum allowed. [¶] Some of the lobbyists readily acknowledge routinely seeking his office's help—calling the congressman and his aides as often as several times a week—to advance their agenda in Washington. And in many cases, Mr. Boehner has helped them out.").

43. George Packer, *The Empty Chamber: Just How Broken Is the Senate?*, New Yorker, Aug. 9, 2010, at 38, *available at* www.newyorker.com/reporting/2010/08/09/100809fa_fact_packer; Christopher Lee, *Daschle Moving to K Street: Dole Played a Key Role in Recruiting Former Senator*, Wash. Post, Mar. 14, 2005, at A17, *available at* www.washingtonpost.com/wp-dyn/articles/A32604-2005Mar13.html; Susan Crabtree, *PMA's Fallout Shines Spotlight on Revolving Door of Lobbyists*, The Hill (Jun. 22, 2009), http://thehill.com/homenews/news/47250-pmas-fallout-shines-spotlight-on-revolving-door-of-lobbyists; Manu Raju & John Bresnahan, *Sen. Richard Shelby Steers Cash to Ex-Aides*, Politico, www.politico.com/news/stories/0710/40388.html (Jul. 29, 2010); Marianne Bertrand et al., *Is It Whom You Know or What You Know? An Empirical Assessment of the Lobbying Process* 18–20 (Feb. 2011) (unpublished manuscript), *available at* http://ssrn.com/abstract=1748024.

44. Andrew Zajac, *Congressional Staffers Turn Lobbyists: Health Care Lobby Drafts Army of Insiders to Help Fight Overhaul*, Chi. Trib. (Dec. 20, 2009), http://articles.chicagotribune.com/2009-12-20/news/0912190289_1_health-care-lobbyists-insiders; Jordi Blanes i Vidal et al., *Revolving Door Lobbyists* 102 Amer. Econ. Rev. 3731 (2012).

45. Grossman & Helpman, *supra* note 41, at 5–6; Kevin M. Esterling, *Buying Expertise: Campaign Contributions and Attention to Policy Analysis in Congressional*

Committees, 101 Am. Pol. Sci. Rev. 93, 93 (2007); Baumgartner et al., *supra* note 39, at 88, 110–11, 124; Hall & Deardorff, *supra* note 38; Stephen Ansolabehere et al., *Why Is There So Little Money in U.S. Politics?*, 17 J. Econ Perspectives 105, 126 (2003).

46. Martin Gilens & Benjamin I. Page, *Testing Theories of American Politics: Elites, Interest Groups, and Average Citizens,* 12 Perspectives on Pol. 564, 565 (2014), http:// journals.cambridge.org/download.php?file=%2FPPS%2FPPS12_03%2FS15375 92714001595a.pdf&code=bfb2be66cee17b44ead73b8e039e5e6c.

47. *Id.* at 572.

48. Larry M. Bartels, *Unequal Democracy: The Political Economy of the New Gilded Age* (2008).

49. Lynda W. Powell, *The Influence of Campaign Contributions in State Legislatures: The Effects of Institutions and Politics* (2012).

50. Timothy Werner & John Coleman, *Assessing the Potential Effects of* Citizens United: *Policy and Corporate Governance in the States* (Feb. 2013), http://users.polisci.wisc .edu/coleman/wernercolemanpcs2013.pdf.

51. This paragraph first appeared in Richard L. Hasen, *Super PAC Contributions, Corruption, and the Proxy War over Coordination,* 9 Duke J. Const. L. & Pub. Pol'y 1, 3–4 (2014), http://papers.ssrn.com/sol3/papers.cfm?abstract_id=2383452.

52. John Herzfeld, *Jury Convicts N.Y. State Legislator on Charges of Trading Favors for Bribes,* Bloomberg BNA Money & Pol. Report (Jan. 15, 2014), http://news.bna .com/mpdm/MPDMWB/split_display.adp?fedfid=39901945&vname=mpebu lallissues&fn=39901945&jd=39901945. On the relative rates of bribery in Congress compared to different states, and the potential role of media scrutiny in deterring corruption, see Richard L. Hasen, *Why Isn't Congress More Corrupt? A Preliminary Inquiry,* Fordham L. Rev. (forthcoming 2015), *draft available at* http:// papers.ssrn.com/sol3/papers.cfm?abstract_id=2585260. *See* also Adriana Cordis & Jeffrey Milyo, *Measuring Public Corruption in the United States: Evidence from Administrative Records of Federal Prosecutions* 34 fig.1 (2013) (unpublished manuscript), *available at* http://economics.missouri.edu/working-papers/2013/WP13 22_milyo.pdf.

53. For background, see David G. Savage, *When Is a Campaign Contribution a Bribe?,* L.A. Times, Jun. 2, 2012, http://articles.latimes.com/2012/jun/02/nation/la-na -siegelman-bribery-20120603; David G. Savage, *Court Refuses to Hear Former Alabama Governor's Challenge to Bribery Conviction,* L.A. Times Jun. 5, 2012, http:// articles.latimes.com/2012/jun/05/nation/la-na-court-bribes-20120605.

54. On the problem of prosecutorial discretion in political cases, see Richard L. Hasen, *Let John Edwards Go!,* Slate, Apr. 23, 2012, www.slate.com/articles/news _and_politics/jurisprudence/2012/04/john_edwards_should_not_be_prose cuted_for_campaign_finance_violations_.html.

55. *McCutcheon v. FEC,* 134 S. Ct. 1434, 1468 (2014) (Breyer, J., dissenting):

That is also why the Court has used the phrase "subversion of the political process" to describe circumstances in which "[e]lected officials are influenced to act contrary to their obligations of office by the prospect of financial gain to themselves or infusions of money into their campaigns." See generally R. Post, Citizens Divided: Campaign Finance Reform and the Constitution 7–16, 80–94 (forthcoming 2014) (arguing that the efficacy of American democracy depends on "electoral integrity" and the responsiveness of public officials to public opinion).

Some citations omitted; Rick Hasen, *Perhaps for the First Time, Justice Breyer's McCutcheon Dissent Cites Unavailable Forthcoming Scholarship,* Election Law Blog Apr. 19, 2014, http://electionlawblog.org/?p=60645.

Post said the question of how the book ended up being cited before being published should be directed to Justice Breyer. He explained that Justice Breyer was present when Post presented a version of his lectures and the text of the lectures was available online. "Justice Breyer evidently liked the thesis of the lectures, and, knowing that the book was about to be published . . . , must have requested (and received) an advance copy of the published version. Cite checkers at the Court evidently determined the correct page numbers." Ronald Collins, *Ask the Author: Robert Post—Citizens Divided,* SCOTUSblog (Aug. 11, 2014), www.scotus blog.com/2014/08/ask-the-author-robert-post-citizens-divided/; *see also* Richard L. Hasen, *Response: "Electoral Integrity," "Dependence Corruptions," and What's New Under the Sun,* 89 NYU L. Rev. Online Symp. 87 (2014), www.nyulawreview .org/issues/volume-89-online-symposium/response-electoral-integrity-depend ence-corruption-and-whats-new.

56. Robert Post, *Citizens Divided: Campaign Finance Reform and the Constitution* 87–88 (2014) (footnotes omitted).

57. *See id.* at 88–89.

58. Frank J. Sorauf, *Politics, Experience, and the First Amendment: The Case of American Campaign Finance,* 94 Colum. L. Rev. 1348, 1349–50 (1994); *Buckley v. Valeo,* 424 U.S. 1, 27 (1976) (internal quotations omitted).

59. Pamela S. Karlan, *Citizens Deflected: Electoral Integrity and Political Reform, in* Post, *supra* note 56, at 141–51.

60. Nathaniel Persily & Kelli Lammie, *Perceptions of Corruption and Campaign Finance: When Public Opinion Determines Constitutional Law,* 153 U. Pa. L. Rev. 119 (2004); Jeff Milyo, *Do State Campaign Finance Reforms Increase Trust and Confidence in State Government?,* paper presented at the annual meetings of the Midwest Political Science Association in Chicago, Ill. (April 2012), *available at* http://web .missouri.edu/~milyoj/PERL/pdf/PERL_CFR and trust.pdf; Megan Thee-Brenan, *Polls Show Broad Support for Campaign Spending Caps,* N.Y. Times, Apr. 2, 2014, www.nytimes.com/2014/04/03/us/politics/polls-show-broad-support-for-cam paign-spending-caps.html; Rebecca Shabad, *Public Lacks Confidence in Government, Poll Shows,* article in *Briefing Room,* The Hill, Jan. 2, 2014, http://thehill.com/ blogs/blog-briefing-room/news/194230-poll-public-lacks-confidence-in-govern ment.

61. On campaign advertising as educating voters, see Samuel L. Popkin, *The Reasoning Voter: Communication and Persuasion in Presidential Campaigns* (1994); John

Geer & Lynn Vavreck, *Negativity, Information, & Candidate Position Taking*, 31 Pol. Comm. 218 (2014), www.tandfonline.com/doi/abs/10.1080/10584609.2013.828 140. On the claim that negative advertising can demobilize voters, see Stephen Ansolabehere & Shanto Iyengar, *Going Negative: How Attack Ads Shrink and Polarize the Electorate* (1995). For a critique, see Martin P. Wattenberg & Craig Leonard Brians, *Negative Campaign Advertising: Demobilizer or Mobilizer?*, 93 Am. Pol. Sci. Rev. 891 (1999). On the rise in negative advertising, driven much by outside groups, see Matea Gold, *Big Spending By Parties, Independent Groups Drowns Airwaves in Negative Attacks*, Wash. Post, Oct. 22, 2014, www.washingtonpost.com/politics/big-spending-by-parties-independent-groups-drowns-airwaves-in-negative-attacks/2014/10/21/b4447f66-593c-11e4-b812-38518ae74c67_story.html.

62. On the common mistakes journalists and others usually make about campaign financing and politics, see Kenneth R. Mayer, *Hey, Wait a Minute: The Assumptions Behind the Case for Campaign Finance Reform*, in *A User's Guide to Campaign Finance Reform* ch. 4 (Gerald C. Lubenow ed., 2001).

Chapter 3. The Voting Lottery

1. Many scholars have proposed or criticized the proposal for lotteries to replace voting. *See* Bruce A. Ackerman, *Social Justice in the Liberal State* 285–89, 298 (1980) (concluding that one argument that favors a "responsive lottery"—a weighted lottery for resolving disputes—is that "it gives the egalitarian minority at least some chance of determining the political outcome"); Akhil Reed Amar, *Choosing Representatives By Lottery Voting*, 93 Yale L.J. 1283 (1984); Akhil Reed Amar, *Lottery Voting: A Thought Experiment*, 1995 U. Chi. Legal F. 193 (1995); Benjamin R. Barber, Strong Democracy: Participatory Politics for a New Age 291–92 (1984) (proposing filling local offices by lot); John Burnheim, *Is Democracy Possible? The Alternative to Electoral Politics* 9–12, 110–19 (1985) (proposing a lottery system for choosing public officials to ensure "a representative sample of the people concerned"); Brian D. Feinstein, *Congressional Government Rebooted: Randomized Committee Assignments and Legislative Capacity*, 7 Harv. L. & Pol'y Rev. 139 (2013); Bruce Chapman, *Chance, Reason, and the Rule of Law*, 50 Univ. of Toronto L.J. 469 (2000) (reviewing Duxbury); Neil Duxbury, *Random Justice: On Lotteries and Legal Decision-Making* (1999) (proposing randomized resolution of majority-minority divisions on occasion); Jon Elster, *Solomonic Judgments: Studies in the Limitations of Rationality* 97–98 (1989) (proposing stratified random sampling); Alexander Guererro, *The Lottocracy*, Aeon Magazine, Jan. 23, 2014, *available at* http://aeon .co/magazine/living-together/forget-elections-lets-pick-reps-by-lottery/; Hélène Landemore, *Deliberation, Cognitive Diversity, and Democratic Inclusiveness: An Epistemic Argument for the Random Selection of Representatives*, 190 Synthese 1209 (2012); Alan A. Lockard, *Decision by Sortition: A Means to Reduce Rent-Seeking*, 116 Pub. Choice 435 (2003); Bernard Manin, *The Principles of Representative Government* 8–84 (1997); John P. McCormick, *Contain the Wealthy and Control the*

Magistrates: Restoring Elite Accountability to Popular Government, 100 Am. Political Sci. Rev. 147 (2006); Dennis C. Mueller et al., *Representative Democracy Via Random Selection,* 12 Pub. Choice 57, 60–61 (1972) (advocating a system of random selection of representatives); Ben Saunders, *Democracy, Political Equality, Majority Rule,* 121 Ethics 148 (2010); Peter Stone, *The Logic of Random Selection,* 37 Pol. Theory 375 (2009); Richard H. Thaler, *Illusions and Mirages in Public Policy,* 73 Pub. Int. 60, 72 (1983) (proposing that congressional committees be assigned randomly to avoid the problems associated with self-selection); Robert Weissberg, *Collective vs. Dyadic Representation in Congress,* 72 Am. Pol. Sci. Rev. 535, 544 (1978) ("If one's constitutional goal were simply the best institutional representation of mass opinions, the optimal solution is clearly a random sample of about 1500 citizens. . . ."); Richard Zeckhauser, *Majority Rule with Lotteries on Alternatives,* 83 Q. J. Econ. 696 (1969) (discussing the use of lotteries on alternatives as potential choices in the context of a majoritarian system).

2. On the incentives created by baseball arbitration, see Daniel R. Marburger, *Arbitrator Compromise in Final Offer Arbitration: Evidence from Major League Baseball,* 42 Econ. Inquiry 60 (2004).

3. *Harper v. Va. State Bd. of Elections,* 383 U.S. 663 (1966).

4. *Lassiter v. Northampton Cnty. Bd. of Elections,* 360 U.S. 45 (1959); Richard L. Hasen, *Legislation, Statutory Interpretation, and Election Law: Examples and Explanations* 211–12 (2014).

5. On conservatives' current views on voting, see Richard L. Hasen, *The New Conservative Assault on Early Voting,* Slate, Feb. 10, 2014, www.slate.com/articles/news _and_politics/politics/2014/02/the_new_conservative_assault_on_early_voting _more_republicans_fewer_voters.html; *A Year After the President's Testimony, Fox's Hannity and Colmes,* Fox News Network, Aug. 17, 1999, *transcript available at* www .lexisnexis.com/lnacui2api/auth/checkbrowser.do?ipcounter=1&cookieState =0&rand=0.6328511700829144&bhcp=1 (Voter ignorance about whether the House of Representatives impeached President Clinton is "why I think there should be a literacy test and a poll tax for people to vote"); Media Matters for America, *Fox News Asks if It's "Time to Revisit" Voter Literacy Test Requirements,* Apr. 15, 2015, http://mediamatters.org/video/2015/04/15/fox-news-asks-if-its-time-to-revisit -voter-lite/203289 (including video of Coulter comments supporting literacy tests). In 2011, Newt Gingrich remarked: "But maybe we should also have a voting standard that says to vote, as a native born American, you should have to learn American history." Newt Gingrich, *Georgia Republican Party Convention,* C-SPAN (May 13, 2011), www.c-span.org/video/?299462-1/newt-gingrich-remarks &start=764. In 2011, Tom Tancredo remarked that President Obama was elected because "we do not have a civics, literacy test before people can vote in this country." Kevin Hechtkopf, *Tom Tancredo Tea Party Speech Slams "Cult of Multiculturalism,"* CBS News (February 5, 2010), www.cbsnews.com/news/tom-tancre do-tea-party-speech-slams-cult-of-multiculturalism/.

6. J. Douglas Smith, *On Democracy's Doorstep* 16 (2014).

7. *Reynolds v. Sims*, 377 U.S. 533, 562–63 (1964).

8. See, for example, the defense of the Electoral College by Robert Goldwin. Robert A. Goldwin, *Defending the Constitution*, Am. Enter. Inst., Dec. 27, 2002, www .aei.org/article/defending-the-constitution/ (reviewing Robert A. Dahl, *How Democratic Is the American Constitution?* (2002)).

9. On Justice Alito's older views on the one person, one vote rule, see Richard L. Hasen, *One Person, One Filibuster? Justice Alito's Controversial Comment on a Supreme Court Voting Rights Case*, Findlaw, Nov. 30, 2005, http://writ.news.findlaw .com/commentary/20051130_hasen.html. For the statements at his confirmation hearing, see Rick Hasen, *Justice Alito States What He Meant By One Person, One Vote Criticism in 1985 Job Application*, Election Law Blog, Jan. 10, 2006, http://electionlawblog.org/archives/004716.html. At issue in the *Evenwel* case, *infra* note 15, is how to implement the standard, not the standard itself.

10. For an extended discussion of the relationship between campaign finance, rent seeking, and lobbying, see Richard L. Hasen, *Lobbying, Rent Seeking, and the Constitution*, 64 Stan. L. Rev. 191 (2012).

11. For an argument that it is compelled, see Jamin Raskin & John Bonifaz, *The Constitutional Imperative and Practical Superiority of Democratically Financed Elections*, 94 Colum. L. Rev. 1160 (1994).

12. Jordan Ellenberg, *The Summer's Most Unread Book Is . . .* , Wall St. J., Jul. 3, 2014, http://online.wsj.com/articles/the-summers-most-unread-book-is-1404417569 ("Mr. Piketty's book is almost 700 pages long, and the last of the top five popular highlights appears on page 26."); Thomas Piketty, *Capital in the Twenty-First Century* (2014).

13. Maria Tadeo, *Unrepentant Tom Perkins Apologises for 'Kristallnacht' Remarks But Defends War on the Rich Letter*, Indep, Jan. 28, 2014, www.independent.co.uk/news/ business/news/unrepentant-tom-perkins-apologises-for-kristallnacht-remarks -but-defends-war-on-the-rich-letter-9091226.html.

14. *Ognibene v. Parkes*, 671 F.3d 174 (2d Cir. 2011) (Calabresi, J., concurring).

15. Among other things, the "one person, one vote" rule is undertheorized in that it does not specify who exactly deserves equality: voters or people. *See* Sanford Levinson, *One Person, One Vote: A Mantra in Need of Meaning*, 80 N.C. L. Rev. 1269 (2002); Joseph Fishkin, *Weightless Votes*, 121 Yale L.J. 1888 (2012). The Supreme Court will soon consider the standard in *Evenwel v. Perry*, 135 S. Ct. 2349 (probable jurisdiction noted May 26, 2015). I premise the argument in the text on the idea that it is permissible for the people to favor a system and to pass laws promoting equality of voters, even though there are other contested meanings of political equality and those other meanings could lead to favoring different campaign finance systems.

16. *Austin v. Mich. Chamber of Commerce*, 494 U.S. 652, 659–60 (1990).

17. I explored this barometer equality rationale first in Richard L. Hasen, *The Supreme Court and Election Law* 111–14 (2003).

18. Douglas W. Rae, *Equalities* (1981).

19. On the demise of the public financing system, see Richard L. Hasen, *The Transformation of the Campaign Financing Regime for US Presidential Elections, in The Funding of Political Parties: Where Now?* 225–242 (Keith Ewing et al., eds, 2011).

20. Daniel H. Lowenstein, *On Campaign Finance Reform: The Root of All Evil is Deeply Rooted,* 18 Hofstra L. Rev. 301 (1989).

21. Charles R. Beitz, *Political Equality: An Essay in Democratic Theory* 201 (1990).

22. *Id.*

23. For an argument from the progressive perspective for an interest in "political opportunity," which aligns with level-up political equality, see Mark Schmitt, Brennan Ctr. for Justice, *Political Opportunity: A New Framework for Democratic Reform* (2015), *available at* www.brennancenter.org/publication/political-opportunity-new-framework-democratic-reform.

24. *Id.* at 209. Perhaps for this reason, Professor Beitz, writing in 1989 well before the rise of Super PACs and the explosion of outside money, expressed support for the equality of political opportunity concept, stating his preference for a campaign finance system promoting *adequacy of access* to the political arena rather than full equality: "What a doctrine of political fairness must require is that the system of political finance ensure *adequate* access to the public arena; it is a criterion of sufficiency, not necessarily of equality." *Id.* I discuss Professor Beitz's equality of campaign resources argument further in the next chapter.

25. John Rawls, *Political Liberalism* 360 (expanded ed. 2005).

26. Cass R. Sunstein, *Political Equality and Unintended Consequences,* 94 Colum. L. Rev. 1390, 1399 (1994).

27. *Ognibene v. Parkes,* 671 F. 3d, at 198–99.

28. *Nixon v. Shrink Mo. Gov't PAC,* 528 U.S. 377, 397–403 (2000) (Breyer, J., concurring).

29. Stephen Breyer, Active Liberty: Interpreting Our Democratic Constitution 44 (2005). See also my discussion of Justice Breyer's views in Richard L. Hasen, Buckley *Is Dead, Long Live* Buckley: *The New Campaign Finance Incoherence of* McConnell v. Federal Election Commission, 153 U. Pa. L. Rev. 31, 60–67 (2004), from which part of this discussion is drawn.

30. *McCutcheon v. FEC,* 134 S. Ct. 1434, 1467–68 (2014) (Breyer, J., dissenting).

31. *Buckley v. Valeo,* 424 U.S. 1, 26–27, 49 (1976) (*per curiam*).

32. Hasen, *supra* note 17, at 113–14; Elizabeth R. Garrett, *New Voices in Politics: Justice Marshall's Jurisprudence on Law and Politics,* 52 How. L. J. 655, 669 (2009); *Citizens United v. FEC,* 558 U.S. 310, 381 (2010) (Roberts, C.J. concurring) ("The First Amendment theory underlying *Austin*'s holding is extraordinarily broad. *Austin*'s logic would authorize government prohibition of political speech by a category of speakers in the name of equality—a point that most scholars acknowledge (and many celebrate), but that the dissent denies"). Other cases aside from *Austin* and *Buckley* rejecting the equality rationale include *Davis v. FEC,* 554 U.S. 724 (2008) and *Ariz. Free Enter. Club's Freedom PAC v. Bennett,* 131 S. Ct. 2806 (2011).

33. This paragraph is drawn from Richard L. Hasen, *"Electoral Integrity," "Dependence*

Corruption," and What's New Under the Sun, 89 NYU L. Rev. Online Symp. 87 (2014),
www.nyulawreview.org/issues/volume-89-online-symposium/response-electoral
-integrity-dependence-corruption-and-whats-new.

34. Richard L. Hasen, *Fixing Washington*, 126 Harv. L. Rev. 550 (2012) (reviewing
Lawrence Lessig, *Republic, Lost* (2011) and Jack Abramoff, *Capitol Punishment*
(2011)); Lawrence Lessig, *A Reply to Professor Hasen*, 126 Harv. L. Rev. Online
61 (2012); Richard L. Hasen, *Is "Dependence Corruption" Distinct from a Political Equality Argument for Campaign Finance Laws? A Reply to Professor Lessig*, 12
Election L.J. 315 (2013); Lawrence Lessig, *What an Originalist Would Understand
"Corruption" to Mean*, 102 Cal. L. Rev. 1 (2014); *see also* Robert A. Post, *Citizens
Divided* 52–53 (2014). Professor Lessig initially protested that his argument is not
based on political equality, but instead is about something else. I have written
extensively on this point and will not belabor it here; I would just point readers
to Professor Lessig's keynote at Stetson University Law School in which he analo-
gizes the money primary to the white primary, which prohibited non-whites from
voting in primaries in Texas. Lawrence Lessig, *Keynote from Symposium at Stetson
Law School*, Mar. 1, 2014, http://lessig.tumblr.com/post/78203377963/keynote
-from-symposium-at-stetson-law-school. In his most recent writings, Lessig has
argued that the problem of money in campaign finance implicates both corruption and equality concerns. Lawrence Lessig, *Corrupt and Unequal, Both*, Fordham L. Rev. (forthcoming 2015), *draft available at* http://papers.ssrn.com/sol3/
papers.cfm?abstract_id=2587018.

35. Deborah Hellman, *Defining Corruption and Constitutionalizing Democracy*, 111
Mich. L. Rev. 1385 (2013); Yasmin Dawood, *Classifying Corruption*, 9 Duke J. Const.
L. & Pub. Pol'y 102 (2014), http://papers.ssrn.com/sol3/papers.cfm?abstract_id=
2401297; Zephyr Teachout, *Corruption in America* (2014).

36. *McCutcheon*, *supra* note 30, at 1441.

37. Bruce C. Cain, *Moralism and Realism in Campaign Finance Reform*, 1995 U. Chi.
Legal F. 111 (1995); David A. Strauss, *What Is the Goal of Campaign Finance Reform?*, 1995 U. Chi. Legal F. 141 (1995); Daniel H. Lowenstein, *Campaign Contributions and Corruption: Comments on Strauss and Cain*, 1995 U. Chi. Legal F. 163,
171–72. Compare Teachout, *supra* note 35, at 283–84 (suggesting equal dollars per
voter could still lead to corruption) with *id.* at 300 (supporting concept of public
financing through vouchers).

Chapter 4. Level Up, Level Down

1. *Ariz. Free Enter. Club's Freedom PAC v. Bennett*, 131 S. Ct. 2806 (2011) [hereinafter
Arizona].

2. *Id.* at 2813–14.

3. *McComish v. Bennett*, 611 F.3d 510, 528 (9th Cir. 2010) (Kleinfeld, J., concurring),
rev'd, Arizona, 131 S. Ct. 2806 (2011).

4. *Arizona*, 131 S. Ct. at 2818 (internal quotation marks omitted). The *Arizona* case
built upon the Supreme Court's earlier decision in *Davis v. FEC*, 554 U.S. 724

(2008), a case that struck down a portion of the McCain-Feingold law, which allowed federal candidates to raise additional contributions when they faced large spending from a wealthy opponent or outside group. The Court held the limit was not justified on anticorruption grounds, and reiterated that political equality was an impermissible interest for campaign finance regulation.

5. The oral argument transcript from the *Arizona* case dated March 28, 2011, is posted at: www.supremecourt.gov/oral_arguments/argument_transcripts/10-238.pdf. The chief justice's remark is on page 48. The opening brief for the Arizona Free Enterprise Club first noted the election commission's statement. Brief of Petitioners, *Arizona*, 131 S. Ct. 2806 (Nos. 10-238, 10-239), 2011 WL 1209127, at 10 n.3.

6. *Arizona*, 131 S. Ct. at 2825 n.10 (internal quotations and citations omitted).

7. *Id.* at 2843–44 (Kagan, J., dissenting).

8. *Id.* at 2845 (Kagan, J., dissenting).

9. Richard L. Hasen, *The Big Ban Theory: Does Elena Kagan Want to Ban Books? No, and She Might Even Be a Free-Speech Zealot*, Slate, May 24, 2010, www.slate.com/ articles/news_and_politics/jurisprudence/2010/05/the_big_ban_theory.html; Robert Barnes, *In Elena Kagan's Work as Solicitor General, Few Clues to Her Views*, Wash. Post, May 13, 2010, at A3, www.washingtonpost.com/wp-dyn/content/arti cle/2010/05/12/AR2010051205049_pf.html ("In the *Citizens United* case, Kagan asked the court to uphold a 1990 precedent that said government could restrict corporations from using their general treasuries to advocate for or against candidates. But she did not rely on the logic behind the decision, advancing other arguments. . . . Interestingly, though, the argument that Kagan did not advance in the court is the one Obama makes when he criticizes the *Citizens United* decision —that corporations will use their wealth to distort the political process"); Elena Kagan, *Private Speech, Public Purpose: The Role of Governmental Motive in First Amendment Doctrine*, 63 U. Chi. L. Rev. 413, 472 (1996) ("The harsh treatment of laws directed at correcting distortion, even when these laws are framed in content -neutral language, arises from the fear that if the usual standards of review applied, legislators would use these laws as a vehicle for improper motive, and courts would bless what the First Amendment proscribes.").

10. *Buckley v. Valeo*, 424 U.S. 1, 48–49 (1976).

11. On the majority's evidence of a deterrent effect of the extra matching funds, see *Arizona*, 131 S. Ct. at 2813, 2818. On Justice Kagan's response, see *id.* at 2836–39 & nn. 5–6. On the Arizona legislature's attempt to repeal the public financing program, see Howard Fischer, *Lawmakers to Ask Voters for Repeal of Clean Elections*, KNAU Public Radio, Jan. 6, 2014, http://knau.org/post/lawmakers-ask-voters-repeal-clean-elections.

12. Michael J. Malbin et al., *Small Donors, Big Democracy: New York City's Matching Funds as a Model for the Nation and States*, 11 Election L.J. 3 (2012); Eliza Newlin Carney, *Sarbanes Bill Aims to Draw in Small Donors*, article in *Beltway Insiders*, Roll Call, Feb. 4, 2014, http://blogs.rollcall.com/beltway-insiders/sarbanes-bill-aims -to-draw-small-donors/.

13. *McCutcheon v. FEC*, 134 S. Ct. 1434, 1458 (2014) ("A final point: It is worth keeping

in mind that the *base limits* themselves are a prophylactic measure. As we have explained, restrictions on direct contributions are preventative, because few if any contributions to candidates will involve *quid pro quo* arrangements. The aggregate limits are then layered on top, ostensibly to prevent circumvention of the base limits. This prophylaxis-upon-prophylaxis approach requires that we be particularly diligent in scrutinizing the law's fit.") (internal citations and quotations omitted).

14. Senator Lee Metcalf proposed a voucher plan in 1967. *See* Richard L. Hasen, *Clipping Coupons for Democracy: An Egalitarian/Public Choice Defense of Campaign Finance Vouchers*, 84 Cal. L. Rev. 1, 20 (1996). My *Clipping Coupons* article proposes a detailed voucher plan. Other notable proposals include Professor Bruce Ackerman's and Professor Larry Lessig's. *See* Bruce Ackerman, *Crediting the Voters: A New Beginning for Campaign Finance*, 4 Am. Prospect 71, 78–79 (1993), *available at* http://prospect.org/article/crediting-voters-new-beginning-campaign -finance (a proposal he expanded upon in Bruce Ackerman & Ian Ayres, *Voting with Dollars: A New Paradigm for Campaign Finance* (2004)); Lawrence Lessig, Republic, Lost 265–271 (2011).

   Professor Lessig at one point supported limits on independent expenditures for both corporations and individuals. Lawrence Lessig, *An Open Letter to the Citizens Against* Citizens United, Atlantic (Mar. 23, 2012), www.theatlantic. com/politics/archive/2012/03/an-open-letter-to-the-citizens-against-citizens -united/254902/2/. But in his most recent writings, Professor Lessig emphasizes only "level up" measures, such as campaign finance vouchers, putting limits and constitutional change on the back burner. Lawrence Lessig, *What's So Bad About a Super PAC?*, Medium, Jun. 4, 2014, https://medium.com/@lessig/whats-so-bad -about-a-superpac-c7cbcf617b58 ("So these constitutional changes may well make sense. They may well be necessary, at least ultimately. But right now, we can make enormous progress in a much easier way—through statutes that would change the way campaigns are funded."); Lawrence Lessig, *#Escapethe1990s*, Lessig Blog, V.2 (Aug. 1, 2014), http://lessig.tumblr.com/post/93500567957/escapethe1990s (defending vouchers and tax credits on grounds that they do not restrict speech).

15. Melanie Mason & Matea Gold, *'Super PAC' Leaders Profit from Lack of Oversight*, L.A. Times, Feb. 22, 2012, http://articles.latimes.com/2012/feb/22/nation/la-na -superpac-spending-20120223.

16. Heather K. Gerken & Alex Tausanovitch, *A Public Finance Model for Lobbying: Lobbying, Campaign Finance, and the Privatization of Democracy*, 13 Election L.J. 75 (2014). Professor Gerken specifically explained how the proposal is one to "Level Up." Heather K. Gerken, *Gerken: Leveling Up: A Public Finance Analog for Lobbying*, Election Law Blog, Feb. 10, 2011, http://electionlawblog.org/archives/018736 .html.

17. Charles R. Beitz, *Political Equality: An Essay in Democratic Theory* 201 (1990); Bradley A. Smith, *Unfree Speech: The Folly of Campaign Finance Reform* 204 (2001); *see also id.* at 71, 79–83, 179, 203.

18. Burt Neuborne, *Is Money Different?*, 77 Texas L. Rev. 1609 (1999).

19. *Kim Kardashian, Despite Being a Fan of Rick Santorum, Says She's a Democrat,* N.Y. Daily News, May 2, 2012, www.nydailynews.com/entertainment/gossip/kim-kar dashian-fan-rick-santorum-democrat-article-1.1070930.

20. On the extent to which the National Rifle Association relies upon contributions from gun manufacturers rather than rank-and-file gun owners and Second Amendment supporters, see Jordan Weissmann, *Whom Does the NRA Really Speak For?*, Atlantic, Dec. 18, 2012, www.theatlantic.com/business/archive/2012/12/ whom-does-the-nra-really-speak-for/266373/ ("In 2010, [the NRA] received $71 million in contributions, up from $46.3 million in 2004. Some of that money came from small-time donors, who've received a barrage of fundraising appeals warning of President Obama's imminent plot to gut the Second Amendment and confiscate Americans' firearms. But around 2005, the group began systematically reaching out to its richest members for bigger checks through its 'Ring of Freedom' program, which also sought to corral corporate donors. Between then and 2011, the Violence Policy Center estimates that the firearms industry donated as much as $38.9 million to the NRA's coffers. The givers include 22 different gun makers, including famous names like Smith & Wesson, Beretta USA, SIGARMS, and Sturm, Ruger & Co. that also manufacture so-called assault weapons.").

21. Michael Beschloss, *Money and Politics Go Hand-in-Hand,* ABC News (May 23— no year indicated), http://abcnews.go.com/Politics/story?id=121651.

22. On the pluralist case for campaign finance reform, see Bruce E. Cain, *Democracy More or Less: America's Political Reform Quandary* 138–43 (2014).

23. One subsidiary question is which entities get to make contributions or spend in elections? Under my proposal, domestic corporations, labor unions, and other such entities would be able to spend, but we will need to have rules in place to assure that individuals do not create sham corporations or other artificial entities as conduits for their own contributions. Anti-conduit rules are already familiar under existing law, *see* 52 U.S.C.A § 30122 (2014), and would need to be expanded under my proposal.

There are other arguments aside from equality and corruption prevention for limiting corporate political spending. One often-raised concern is the protection of shareholders, an interest the Court recognized in *Austin v. Mich. Chamber Commerce,* 494 U.S. 652 (1990), but rejected in *Citizens United v. FEC,* 558 U.S. 310 (2010). This shareholder protection argument seems disingenuous, one more about coming up with ways of limiting corporations (for other reasons, such as promoting political equality or preventing corruption) than protecting shareholders. As the Court noted in *First National Bank of Boston v. Bellotti,* 435 U.S. 765, 792–93 (1978), the shareholder rationale is underinclusive, in that it allows corporations to spend all kinds of money on potentially wasteful political activities so long as they do not count as election spending under the relevant election rules.

24. *Nixon v. Shrink Mo. Gov't PAC,* 528 U.S. 377, 398 (2000) (Stevens, J., concurring)

("In response to [Justice Kennedy's] call for a new beginning, therefore, I make one simple point. Money is property; it is not speech. [¶] Speech has the power to inspire volunteers to perform a multitude of tasks on a campaign trail, on a battleground, or even on a football field. Money, meanwhile, has the power to pay hired laborers to perform the same tasks. It does not follow, however, that the First Amendment provides the same measure of protection to the use of money to accomplish such goals as it provides to the use of ideas to achieve the same results.") (footnote omitted).

25. *Nixon v. Shrink Mo. Gov't PAC*, 528 U.S. 377, 402 (2000) (Breyer, J., concurring).

26. *Buckley*, 424 U.S. at 19–20, n.20. The information on the newspaper in question and the newspaper rates appears on page 32 of Volume II, Part A of the joint appendix, available at http://galenet.galegroup.com/servlet/SCRB?uid=0&srcht-p=a&ste=14&rcn=DW3901979745.

27. Jim Geraghty, *The Tactic of 2012 . . . Full-Page Newspaper Ads?*, Nat'l Rev. Online, Jan. 5, 2012, www.nationalreview.com/campaign-spot/287259/tactic-2012-full-page-newspaper-ads ("According to the advertising department of the *New Hampshire Union Leader*, the ad ran in black & white in the print edition and cost $4,624.20. If a similar full-page ad runs in the Sunday edition, it will cost $4,907.70; adding color as in the version above would cost $615 beyond the listed fees."); David Streitfeld, *Plot Thickens as 900 Writers Battle Amazon*, N.Y. Times, Aug. 7, 2014, www.nytimes.com/2014/08/08/business/media/plot-thickens-as-900-writers-battle-amazon.html (reporting cost of full-page ad in Sunday *New York Times* in 2014 as $104,000).

28. On the changing nature of political campaigns thanks to social media, see Diana Owen, *New Media and Political Campaigns*, in Kate Kenski and Kathleen Hall Jamieson, *The Oxford Handbook of Political Communication* (forthcoming), *draft available at* https://blogs.commons.georgetown.edu/cctp-505-fall2011/files/Owen.New-Media-and-Campaigns.pdf. On the continued use of direct mail, see Dan Eggen, *Direct Mail Still a Force in Campaigns*, Wash. Post, Oct. 12, 2012, www.washingtonpost.com/politics/decision2012/direct-mail-still-a-force-in-Campaigns/2012/10/12/24f6f830-0bf9-11e2-bb5e-492c0d30bff6_story.html.

29. Aaron Blake, *The Most Interesting Political Stat of the Day*, The Fix, Wash. Post, Feb. 18, 2015, www.washingtonpost.com/blogs/the-fix/wp/2015/02/18/the-most-interesting-political-stat-of-the-day/ ("while the amount of money flowing into elections is bigger than ever, the number of total donors is actually shrinking").

30. Ronald Collins & David Skover, *When Money Speaks: The McCutcheon Decision, Campaign Finance Laws and the First Amendment* 1–2 (2014).

31. Tami Luhby, *Median Income Falls, But So Does Poverty*, CNN Money, Sept. 12, 2012, http://money.cnn.com/2012/09/12/news/economy/median-income-poverty/ ("Median household income fell to $50,054 in 2011, down 1.5% from a year earlier"); Kevin McCormally, *Where Do You Rank as a Taxpayer?*, Kiplinger, Jan. 17, 2014, www.kiplinger.com/article/taxes/T054-C000-S001-where-do-you-rank

-as-a-taxpayer.html ("The latest numbers from the IRS—based on just released data from 2011 tax returns—show what it takes to be among the top 1% of income earners: adjusted gross income of $388,905 or more.").

32. John S. Shockley, *Money in Politics: Judicial Roadblocks to Campaign Finance Reform*, 10 Hastings Const. L.Q. 679, 695–96 (1983).

33. Frederick Schauer & Richard H. Pildes, *Electoral Exceptionalism and the First Amendment*, 77 Texas L. Rev. 1803, 1805 (1999) (footnotes omitted).

34. Cass R. Sunstein, *Political Equality and Unintended Consequences*, 94 Colum. L. Rev. 1390, 1398–99 (1994).

35. Ronald Collins, *Ask the Author: Robert Post*—Citizens Divided, SCOTUSblog (Aug. 11, 2014), www.scotusblog.com/2014/08/ask-the-author-robert-post-citizens-divided/; Robert Post, *Citizens Divided: Campaign Finance Reform and the Constitution* (2014).

36. On the analogy to oral argument time before the Supreme Court, see Jessica A. Levinson, *The Original Sin of Campaign Finance Law: Why* Buckley v. Valeo *Is Wrong*, 47 U. Richmond L. Rev. 881, 908 (2013); Paul Bender, *The Constitutionality of Campaign Finance Legislation: After* Buckley v. Valeo, 34 Ariz. St. L.J. 1105, 1110 (2002) ("Consider, for example, the traditional town meeting where, after a debate on the issue or candidacy under consideration a vote is taken to decide the matter. Does anyone think that it is unconstitutional for a town governed through town meetings to allocate equal amounts of pre-vote debate time to competing candidates, and to refuse to sell extra debate time to a side or candidate that can afford to buy it? To take another example, is it unconstitutional for legislatures to divide floor debate time equally between those supporting and opposing a bill under consideration, rather than to allocate that time on the basis of ability of debating legislators to pay? And, I suspect, no one thinks that courts violate the spirit of the First Amendment by equally dividing, rather than selling, oral argument time or the number of pages the contending sides in a case are entitled to include in their written briefs.").

Chapter 5. Censorship

1. The transcript of the original oral argument before the Supreme Court in *Citizens United v. FEC*, dated March 24, 2009, is posted at: www.supremecourt.gov/oral_arguments/argument_transcripts/08-205.pdf. The Wisconsin case is *FEC v. Wis. Right to Life, Inc.*, 551 U.S. 449 (2007).

2. On the decision to rehear the oral argument, and the many paths the Supreme Court could have taken in *Citizens United* but did not, see Richard L. Hasen, *Constitutional Avoidance and Anti-Avoidance by the Roberts Court*, 2009 Sup. Ct. Rev. 181 (2010).

3. Rick Hasen, Citizens United: *Of Book Banning, Kindles, and the Corporate PAC Requirement*, Election Law Blog (Mar. 24, 2009), http://electionlawblog.org/archives/013276.html.

4. Adam Liptak, *Justices Seem Skeptical of Scope of Campaign Law,* N.Y. Times, Mar. 25, 2009, at A16, *available at* www.nytimes.com/2009/03/25/washington/25sco tus.html.

5. Jeffrey Toobin, *Money Unlimited: How Chief Justice Roberts Orchestrated the Citizens United Decision,* New Yorker, May 21, 2012, www.newyorker.com/magazine/ 2012/05/21/money-unlimited; Adam Liptak, *Sidebar: Justice Stevens Suggests Solution for 'Giant Step in the Wrong Direction,'* N.Y. Times, Mar. 21, 2014, www.ny times.com/2014/04/22/us/politics/justice-stevenss-prescription-for-giant-step -in-wrong-direction.html.

6. Richard L. Hasen, *The Big Ban Theory: Does Elena Kagan Want to Ban Books? No, and She Might Even Be a Free-Speech Zealot,* Slate, May 24, 2012, www.slate.com/ articles/news_and_politics/jurisprudence/2010/05/the_big_ban_theory.html; Robert Barnes, *In Elena Kagan's Work as Solicitor General, Few Clues to Her Views,* Wash. Post, May 13, 2010, at A3, *available at* www.washingtonpost.com/wp-dyn/con tent/article/2010/05/12/AR2010051205049_pf.html; *Full Transcript of Bryan A. Garner's Interview with Elena Kagan,* ABA J., Sept. 1, 2012, www.abajournal.com/ magazine/article/full_transcript_of_bryan_a._garners_interview_with_elena _kagan/.

7. The transcript of the September 9, 2009, argument is posted at www.supreme court.gov/oral_arguments/argument_transcripts/08-205%5BReargued%5D .pdf. Kagan began to address the issue on page 64 of the transcript.

8. Marcia Coyle, *The Roberts Court: The Struggle for the Constitution* 272 (2012).

9. *Citizens United v. FEC,* 558 U.S. 310, 337 (2010).

10. Bryan A. Garner, *Garner's Dictionary of Legal Usage* 144 (3d ed. 2011). The book he co-authored with Justice Scalia is Antonin Scalia & Bryan A. Garner, *Reading Law: The Interpretation of Legal Texts* (2012). The text of the Sedition Act appears at http://memory.loc.gov/cgi-bin/ampage?collId=llsl&fileName=001/llsl001.db& recNum=719. For additional background and primary source documents, see Alien and Sedition Acts, Primary Documents in American History, Library of Congress Web Guides, www.loc.gov/rr/program/bib/ourdocs/Alien.html (last visited Jan. 9, 2015).

11. For some of Abrams's most notable writings on the First Amendment, see Floyd Abrams, *Friend of the Court: On the Front Lines with the First Amendment* (2013).

12. A video of the March 5, 2012 debate is posted at http://web.law.umich.edu/flash media/public/Default.aspx?mediaid=2105/. The excerpted transcript below appears in the video at the 36:28 minute mark.

13. Bradley A. Smith, *Unfree Speech: The Folly of Campaign Finance Reform* (2001).

14. Brad Smith, *Bluman v. FEC and the Infield Fly Rule,* Ctr. for Competitive Politics Blog (Jan. 9, 2012), www.campaignfreedom.org/2012/01/09/bluman-v-fec-and -the-infield-fly-rule/.

15. Posting of James Bopp to the Election Law Listserv (Jan. 9, 2012), http://depart ment-lists.uci.edu/pipermail/law-election/2012-January/002277.html (quoted with the permission of the author).

16. Posting of James Bopp to the Election Law Listserv (Jan. 9, 2012), http://depart ment-lists.uci.edu/pipermail/law-election/2012-January/002283.html (quoted with the permission of the author).

17. Eugene Volokh, *Why Buckley v. Valeo Is Basically Right*, 34 Ariz. St. L.J. 1095 (2002).

18. Eugene Volokh, *Supreme Court Upholds Ban on Candidate Campaign Contributions and Expenditures by Non-Permanent-Resident Foreign Citizens*, The Volokh Conspiracy (Jan. 10, 2012), www.volokh.com/2012/01/10/supreme-court-upholds -ban-on-candidate-campaign-contributions-and-expenditures-by-non-perma nent-resident-foreign-citizens/.

19. Garner, *supra* note 10 (emphasis omitted).

20. Theodoric Meyer, *How Much Did Sheldon Adelson Really Spend on Campaign 2012?*, ProPublica, Dec. 20, 2012, www.propublica.org/article/how-much-did-sheldon -adelson-really-spend-on-campaign-2012; Ronald Collins & David Skover, *When Money Speaks: The McCutcheon Decision, Campaign Finance Laws and the First Amendment* 1–2 (2014); Center for Responsive Politics, Top Individuals Funding Outside Spending Groups 2014, OpenSecrets.Org, www.opensecrets.org/out sidespending/summ.php?cycle=2014&disp=D&type=V.

21. Richard Briffault, *The Return of Spending Limits: Campaign Finance After* Landell v. Sorrell, 32 Fordham Urb. L.J. 399, 405–6 (2005) ("Albuquerque had adopted spending limits in 1974 and, amazingly enough, despite *Buckley* those limits remained on the books and were apparently enforced through 1995. The limits were temporarily enjoined in 1997, but restored and amended in 1999. When a mayoral candidate sought to enjoin their enforcement in the 2001 race, Judge Vazquez denied the plaintiff's request for a preliminary injunction, concluding that the plaintiff had shown neither a likelihood of success on the merits nor that the public interest would benefit from an injunction") (footnotes omitted).

22. *Homans v. City of Albuquerque*, 160 F. Supp. 2d 1266, 1269 (D.N.M. 2001), *rev'd*, 264 F.3d 1240 (10th Cir. 2001) (preliminary injunction granted); *Homans v. City of Albuquerque*, 217 F. Supp. 2d 1197 (D.N.M. 2002), *aff'd*, 366 F.3d 900 (10th Cir. 2004), *cert. denied*, 543 U.S. 1002 (2004).

23. *Randall v. Sorrell*, 548 U.S. 230 (2006); Briffault, *supra* note 21.

24. For information and analysis of the British system, see Lisa E. Klein, *On the Brink of Reform: Political Party Funding in Britain*, 31 Case W. Res. J. Int'l L. 1, 17 (1999) ("The 1883 Act imposed ceilings on candidate expenditures, limited the type of permissible expenditures, and imposed liability on candidates.") (citing H.F. Rawlings, *Law and the Electoral Process* 136–37 (1988)); Keith D. Ewing, *Promoting Political Equality: Spending Limits in British Electoral Law*, 2 Election L. J. 499, 501 (2003); Keith D. Ewing and Jacob Rowbottom, *The Role of Spending Controls: New Electoral Actors and New Campaign Techniques, in* The Funding of Political Parties: Where Now? 77–91 (Keith D. Ewing et al. eds., 2012); Jacob Rowbottom, *Democracy Distorted: Wealth, Influence and Democratic Politics* (2010).

25. *Harper v. Canada* (Attorney General), [2004] 1 S.C.R. 827, 2004 SCC 33 (Can.). For overviews of the Canadian system, see Lisa Young, *Regulating Campaign Fi-*

nance in Canada: Strengths and Weaknesses, 3 Election L.J. 444 (2004); Robert Boatright, *Interest Groups and Campaign Finance Reform in the United States and Canada* (2011); Mark Rush, Book Review, *A Study of Interest Groups and Campaign Finance Reform in the United States and Canada,* 11 Election L.J. 267 (2012). For an overall look at Canadian campaign finance jurisprudence, see Yasmin Dawood, *Democracy and the Right to Vote: Rethinking Democratic Rights Under the Charter,* 51 Osgoode Hall L.J. 251, 281–90 (2013), *available at* http://papers.ssrn.com/sol3/papers.cfm?abstract_id=2396199.

26. Freedom House, 2014 Freedom in the World, https://freedomhouse.org/report -types/freedom-world—.VLDABVr3qoY (last visited Jan. 9, 2014).

27. Daniel P. Tokaji, Commentary, *Reviving Equality: What the United States Can Learn from Canada,* ACSblog (Jan. 28, 2011), www.acslaw.org/acsblog/reviving-equality -what-the-united-states-can-learn-from-canada; Daniel P. Tokaji, *The Obliteration of Equality in America Campaign Finance Law: A Trans-Border Comparison,* 5 J. Parliamentary & Pol. L. 381 (2011), *available at* http://papers.ssrn.com/sol3/papers .cfm?abstract_id=1746868; Yasmin Dawood, *Democracy and the Freedom of Speech: Rethinking the Conflict between Liberty and Equality,* 26 Can. J. L. & Juris. 293, 307–9 (2013).

Chapter 6. The (New) Media

1. *Austin v. Mich. Chamber of Commerce,* 494 U.S. 652, 679–80 (1990) (Scalia, J., dissenting).

2. *Id.* at 691.

3. *Id.*

4. Richard L. Hasen, *Campaign Finance Laws and the Rupert Murdoch Problem,* 77 Tex. L. Rev. 1627 (1999). Some of the material in this part of the chapter draws from my discussion in that article.

5. L. A. Powe, Jr., *Commentary: Boiling Blood,* 77 Tex. L. Rev. 1667 (1999); 147 Cong. Rec. 5152 (2001) (quoting Sen. McConnell and reproducing Stuart Taylor, Jr., *The Media Should Beware of What It Embraces,* Nat'l J., Jan. 1, 2000, www.national journal.com/magazine/legal-affairs-the-media-should-beware-of-what-it-em braces-20000101).

6. John Paul Stevens, *Six Amendments: How and Why We Should Change the Constitution* 57–80 (2014).

7. Adam Liptak, *Justice Stevens Suggests Solution for 'Giant Step in the Wrong Direction,'* N.Y. Times, Apr. 21, 2014, at A14, www.nytimes.com/2014/04/22/us/politics/ justice-stevenss-prescription-for-giant-step-in-wrong-direction.html.

8. A video of the March 5, 2012, debate between Abrams and me is posted at http:// web.law.umich.edu/flashmedia/public/Default.aspx?mediaid=2105/; Jacob Rowbottom, *How Campaign Finance Laws Made the British Press So Powerful,* New Republic, Jul. 25, 2011, www.newrepublic.com/article/world/92507/campaign -finance-united-kingdom-news-corporation.

9. A closer look at the media exception's legislative history reveals that it was some-what of an afterthought, or perhaps a way to protect union access to the press. The House Report states that the media exception and other exceptions to the definition of expenditure "underscore and reaffirm the principles" stated in an amendment proposed by Representative Orval Hansen. H.R. Rep. No. 93-129 at p. 4 (1974). But Hansen's amendment, found at 117 Cong. Rec. 41,869 (1971), contained only these other exceptions and not the media exception. The floor de-bate surrounding Hansen's amendment makes clear that it was offered to ensure that unions could engage in get-out-the-vote drives and send communications to union members and their families. See 117 Cong. Rec. 43,381–91 (1971). Section 308 of the same bill, which exempts media corporations from reporting as politi-cal committees, also appears to have been motivated by a desire to protect unions. *See* 120 Cong. Rec. 34,374 (1974) (remarks of Rep. Cannon).

10. *Austin v. Mich. Chamber of Commerce*, 494 U.S. 652, 667–68.

11. *Citizens United v. FEC*, 558 U.S. 310, 417 (2010) (Stevens, J., dissenting); Rob-ert Post, *Citizens Divided: Campaign Finance Reform and the Constitution* 72 n.* (2014).

12. Alexander Dyck et al., *Media Versus Special Interests*, 56 J. L. & Econ. 521 (2013). Recent analyses demonstrate that newspaper endorsements do not appear to influence the outcome of presidential elections. The same is probably true for Senate and House elections, which also tend to be of high salience. The evidence on the effect of newspaper endorsements is ambiguous even as to low-salience races, where the free-rider problem appears most acute. *See, e.g.*, James E. Gregg, *Newspaper Editorial Endorsements and California Elections, 1948–62*, 42 Journal-ism Q. 532, 538 (1965) (finding newspaper endorsements had the greatest influ-ence at local levels and on the ballot); Dick Morris, *Times Machine: How the Paper Picks Winners*, N.Y. Mag., Sept. 29, 1997, at 15–16 (discussing the importance of *New York Times* endorsements in a city council primary race); John E. Mueller, *Choosing Among 133 Candidates*, 34 Pub. Opinion Q. 395, 399–400 (1970) (find-ing that newspaper endorsements affected the outcome of an election with 133 candidates for a junior college board of trustees); Howard A. Scarrow & Steve Borman, *The Effects of Newspaper Endorsements on Election Outcomes: A Case Study*, 43 Pub. Opinion Q. 388, 391–92 (1979) (finding significant the effect of a news-paper endorsement on the election of a county district attorney); *see also* Maxwell McCombs, *Editorial Endorsements: A Study of Influence*, 44 Journalism Q. 545, 545 (1967) (criticizing Gregg's methodology for failing to use individual voter data). *But see* Philip L. Dubois, *Voting Cues in Nonpartisan Trial Court Elections: A Multivariate Assessment*, 18 Law & Soc'y Rev. 395, 422 (1984) (examining non-partisan trial judge elections and finding that "receiving the endorsement of the local newspaper, while helpful, is not as valuable as campaign spending or being included in the voters' pamphlet"); John E. Mueller, *Voting on the Propositions: Ballot Patterns and Historical Trends in California*, 63 Am. Pol. Sci. Rev. 1197, 1206 (1969) (noting that "it seems quite likely that there is no major impact of news-

paper recommendation on proposition voting, especially over a series of ballot items") (emphasis omitted); Paul Raymond, *The American Voter in Nonpartisan Urban Elections,* 20 Am. Pol. Q. 247, 255 (1992) (finding newspaper endorsements had no effect on voters' evaluations of candidates in nonpartisan city council race).

13. *See* Hasen, *supra* note 4, at 1642–43 (reviewing literature); Dorothy Giobbe, *Dole Wins . . . In Endorsements,* Editor & Publisher, Oct. 26, 1996, at 7 (noting that more newspapers supported Democrats than Republicans in only the 1964 and 1992 elections). Interestingly, chain newspapers "were not more likely than non-chains to endorse" the Republican candidate. John C. Busterna & Kathleen A. Hansen, *Presidential Endorsement Patterns by Chain-Owned Papers, 1976–84,* 67 Journalism Q. 286, 290 (1990). Almost 70% of newspapers failed to endorse a candidate in the 1996 presidential election. *See* Stacy Jones, *Declining Endorsements,* Editor & Publisher, Oct. 26, 1996, at 12. That figure was only 13.4% in 1940. *See id.*

14. Chun-Fang Chian & Brian Knight, *Media Bias and Influence: Evidence from Newspaper Endorsements,* 78 Rev. Econ. Stud. 795, 817 (2011), http://restud.oxfordjour nals.org/content/early/2011/03/02/restud.rdq037.full.pdf+html ("Our primary finding is that endorsements are influential in the sense that voters are more likely to support the recommended candidate after publication of the endorsement. The degree of this influence, however, depends upon the credibility of the endorsement. In this way, endorsements for the Democratic candidate from left-leaning newspapers are less influential than are endorsements from neutral or right-leaning newspapers and likewise for endorsements for the Republican candidate. Endorsements are also more influential among moderate voters and those more likely to be exposed to the endorsement. Taken together, these results suggest that voters are sophisticated and attempt to filter out any bias in media coverage of politics."); Agustín Casas et al., *Surprise Me If You Can: Influence of Newspaper Endorsements in U.S. Presidential Elections* (UC3M Working papers, Economics No. 14–16, July, 2014), http://e-archivo.uc3m.es/bitstream/ handle/10016/19205/we1416.pdf?sequence=1; Riccardo Puglisi & James M. Snyder Jr., *The Balanced U.S. Press,* J. European Econ. Ass'n (forthcoming), http:// onlinelibrary.wiley.com/doi/10.1111/jeea.12101/full.

15. I review the mixed evidence of media bias in reporting in Hasen, *supra* note 4, at 1660–61. On the profoundly changed media landscape and potential bias, see *New Directions in Media and Politics* (Travis N. Ridout, ed., 2013). On Justice Scalia, see Jennifer Senior, *In Conversation: Antonin Scalia,* N.Y. Mag., Oct. 6, 2013, http://nymag.com/news/features/antonin-scalia-2013-10/.

16. Paul Fahri, *Charting the Years-Long Decline of Local News Reporting,* Wash. Post, Mar. 26, 2014, www.washingtonpost.com/lifestyle/style/charting-the-years-long -decline-of-local-news-reporting/2014/03/26/977bf088-b457-11e3-b899-20667 de76985_story.html.

17. On media concentration and political equality, see Rowbottom, *supra* note 8;

C. Edwin Baker, *Media Concentration and Democracy: Why Ownership Matters* (2006).

18. Of course, providing quick and reliable Internet access furthers modern democracy as well. But Comcast does not need an exemption from regularly applicable campaign finance laws to fulfill this function.

19. A. J. Liebling, *The Press* 30 (rev. ed. 1964).

20. *Citizens United v. FEC*, 558 U.S. 310, 352 (quoting Justice Scalia's dissenting opinion in *Austin v. Mich. Chamber of Commerce*, 494 U.S. 652, 691) (internal quotation marks omitted); Post, *supra* note 11, at 71 n.*; Randall P. Bezanson, *Whither Freedom of the Press?*, 97 Iowa L. Rev. 1259, 1263 (2012).

21. *Minneapolis Star v. Minn. Comm'r*, 460 U.S. 575 (1983), Post, *supra* note 11, at 71–72 n.*; Bezanson, *supra* note 20, at 1263. In support of this statement, Professor Bezanson cites: "See, e.g., *Bartnicki v. Vopper*, 532 U.S. 514 (2001) (finding an illegally obtained recording of a telephone conversation given to the press (in this case, a radio station) was privileged with respect to publication by the press); *Minneapolis Star & Tribune Co. v. Minn. Comm'r of Revenue*, 460 U.S. 575, 592–93 (1983) (striking down a tax 'that single[d] out the press'); *Gertz v. Robert Welch, Inc.*, 418 U.S. 323 (1974) (providing privilege for media libels); see also C. Edwin Baker, *The Independent Significance of the Press Clause Under Existing Law*, 35 Hofstra L. Rev. 955 (2007)." *Id.* at 1263 n.16.

22. *Mills v. Alabama*, 384 U.S. 214, 220 (1966); *see also* Sonja R. West, *The Stealth Press Clause*, 48 Ga. L. Rev. 729 (2014) (tracing cases in which the Supreme Court recognized special constitutional protection for the press as an industry).

23. *Mills*, *supra* note 22, at 219.

24. *Miami Herald Pub'g Co. v. Tornillo*, 418 U.S. 241, 256, 258 (1974). *Tornillo* is in obvious tension with *Red Lion Broadcasting v. FCC*, 395 U.S. 367, 395–96 (1969), where the Court upheld the constitutionality of the similar federal "fairness doctrine" that applies to broadcasters. For favorable commentary on *Tornillo* and a recognition of the tension between the newspaper and broadcasting cases, see L. A. Powe, Jr., *Mass Communications and the First Amendment: An Overview*, 55 Law & Contemp. Probs. 53, 67–71 (1992).

25. Eugene Volokh, *Freedom for the Press as an Industry, or for the Press as a Technology? From the Framing to Today*, 160 U. Pa. L. Rev. 459, 483–84, 522–23 (2012); Michael W. McConnell, *Reconsidering* Citizens United *as a Press Clause Case*, 123 Yale L.J. 412 (2013).

26. Paul Horwitz, *First Amendment Institutions* 146–47, 152 (2013) (citing Brian C. Murchison et al., *Sullivan's Paradox: The Emergence of Judicial Standards of Journalism*, 73 N.C. L. Rev. 7 (1994)); *First Nat'l Bank of Boston v. Bellotti*, 435 U.S. 765, 796 (1978) (Burger, C.J., concurring).

27. Sonja West, *The 'Press,' Then and Now*, Ohio St. L.J. (forthcoming 2016), *draft available at* http://papers.ssrn.com/sol3/papers.cfm?abstract_id=2579687; Bezanson, *supra* note 20; *see id.* at 1261 ("Professor Volokh, of course, is exactly right when judged by the spare and spartan doctrine of textualism and originalism.

There was no organized press—I dare not say 'institutional'—at the time of the founding, or indeed for many years after. There were not even, Volokh implies, any culturally and historically grounded values, such as commitment to truth, public need for information, or processes of selection and judgment. Of course, there was no air force then either; no automatic rifles or pistols."); *id.* ("The text of the First Amendment guarantees freedom of speech 'or' of the press, employing a disjunction, not a conjunction. To read 'or' out as a flyspeck of linguistic indifference is hard to imagine. And even for one who reads 'speech' and 'press' as being the same thing, or as just subsets of a larger universe, it is still necessary to explain why 'press' was included—was it just assurance of coverage?—and what 'press' meant. To define the term as no more than technology—the distributive means of speech—is to accuse the drafters of gross ambiguity and deception, especially given the commonplace and ardent political discussions of freedom of the press that were then and thereafter in the air. Could it be that without 'the press' as technology of distribution, the freedom of speech would have required that one keep one's views to oneself?"). The debate over originalism as a means of constitutional interpretation is well beyond the scope of this book. For a forceful argument against originalism as the sole methodology for interpreting the Constitution, see David A. Strauss, *The Living Constitution* (2010).

28. Paul Horwitz, *Institutional Actors in* New York Times v. Sullivan, 48 Ga. L. Rev. 809, 839 (2014).

29. Bezanson, *supra* note 20; *see also* Sonja R. West, *Press Exceptionalism*, 127 Harv. L. Rev. 2434, 2446 (2014). ("Members of the press also have unique needs for protection").

30. Professor McConnell writes: "Reportedly, billionaire George Soros contributed $5 million during the last election cycle to research and develop new ways to get Democratic-leaning voting groups to the polls. Expenditures of this sort are not exercises of the freedom of the press, and there is no apparent reason why they should not be as regulated (or unregulated) as contributions to candidates." McConnell, *supra* note 25, at 453. While I agree this is not press-like activity, it is hard to see how this is a contribution to a candidate if done independent of the candidate.

31. Bezanson, *supra* note 20; Horwitz, *supra* note 26, ch. 6; West, *supra* note 29. Justice Stewart's classic article on press protection is J. Potter Stewart, *"Or of the Press,"* 26 Hastings L.J. 631, 633 (1975) ("[T]he Free Speech Clause extends protection to an institution. The publishing business is, in short, the only organized private business that is given explicit constitutional protection.").

32. Horwitz, *supra* note 26, at 155. The chapter at pages 147–51 traces the rise of modern journalistic norms.

33. Nancy Watzman, *NRA Fights Campaign Finance Reform, Disclosure,* Sunlight Found. Blog (Jan. 15, 2013, 9:10 AM), http://sunlightfoundation.com/blog/2013/01/15/nra-fights-campaign-finance-reform-disclosure/.

34. The fourth question presented in the NRA's brief filed in the Supreme Court

asked: "Whether Congress violated the Equal Protection guarantee of the Fifth Amendment by granting a special exemption in Section 201 of BCRA for political speech by corporations that own broadcast facilities, as opposed to all other corporations whose identical speech constitutes forbidden electioneering communications." The brief is posted at http://findlawimages.com/efile/supreme/briefs/02-1675/02-1675.mer.apt.nra.pdf. On the emergence of NRA News, see Sharon Theimer, *NRA Seeks Status as News Outlet*, Wash. Post, Dec. 7, 2003.

35. Terri L. Brooks, *Campaign Finance Changes Highlight Election Rules for Tax-Exempt Organizations*, 16 Taxation of Exempts 35, 38 (2004) ("Already seeking to use the exception for bona fide news stories, the National Rifle Association recently announced that it is creating an 'NRA news' company to produce an Internet talk show, own and operate a radio station, and engage in television broadcasting. The NRA will, according to the statute, be free to spread its gun-rights messages using soft money contributions. While not all special interest groups have the resources to take advantage of this loophole, expect the ones that do to take full advantage, at least until this loophole is closed in a later revision of the law. Print media and Internet advertising are excluded from the definition of 'electioneering communication.'"); Bob Bauer, *Election Law and the Question of Distinctions*, More Soft Money Hard Law Blog (Jul. 26, 2004) ("The NRA has established a 'news media' organization to avoid the electioneering prohibitions of the new campaign finance law"). This posting is no longer available online, although an archived copy appears at: https://web.archive.org/web/20040807005331/http://www.moresoftmoneyhardlaw.com/other/index.htm. A copy also is on file with the author.

36. West, *supra* note 29, at 2462.

37. *Citizens United v. FEC*, 558 U.S. 310, 364.

38. West, *supra* note 29, at 2437–38; Horwitz, *supra* note 26, ch. 6.

39. 11 C.F.R. § 100.132 (2006). Even when the news facility is owned by a candidate or party, costs associated with the news story will not count as an expenditure

> (a) That represents a *bona fide* news account communicated in a publication of general circulation or on a licensed broadcasting facility; and
> (b) That is part of a general pattern of campaign-related news account that give reasonably equal coverage to all opposing candidates in the circulation or listening area. . . .

Id. (emphasis added). *See also* 52 U.S.C. § 30101(9)(B)(i) (2002).

40. West, *supra* note 29, at 2456.

41. *Id.* at 2445.

42. David A. Anderson, *The Press and Democratic Dialogue*, 127 Harv. L. Rev. F. 331, 333–34 (2014), http://harvardlawreview.org/2014/06/the-press-and-democratic-dialogue/.

43. *See* Jason A. Martin & Anthony L. Fargo, *Rebooting Shield Laws*, 24 U. Fla. J.L. & Pub. Pol'y 47, 53–65 (2013); *see also* 23 Wright & Graham, *Federal Practice and*

Procedure: Evidence § 5426 (2014) (describing scope of various press shields). The Free Flow of Information Act, S. 448, 111th Cong. (2009), initially provided that a person "engaged in journalism" was covered by a reporter's privilege. The bill defined journalism as: "the regular gathering, preparing, collecting, photograph-ing, recording, writing, editing, reporting, or publishing of news or information that concerns local, national, or international events or other matters of public interest for dissemination to the public." When the bill was amended in commit-tee, it instead provided the privilege for a person who:

(i) with the primary intent to investigate events and procure material in order to disseminate to the public news or information concerning local, national, or international events or other matters of public interest, regularly gathers, prepares, collects, photographs, records, writes, edits, reports or publishes on such matters by—

(I) conducting interviews;
(II) making direct observation of events; or
(III) collecting, reviewing, or analyzing original writings, statements, communications, reports, memoranda, records, transcripts, documents, photographs, recordings, tapes, materials, data, or other information whether in paper, electronic, or other form;

(ii) has such intent at the inception of the process of gathering the news or information sought; and

(iii) obtains the news or information sought in order to disseminate the news or information by means of print (including newspapers, books, wire services, news agencies, or magazines), broadcasting (including dissemination through networks, cable, satellite carriers, broadcast stations, or a channel or programming service for any such media), mechanical, photographic, elec-tronic, or other means.

This definition is incomplete in that it does not include those engaged in regular commentary and analysis, who were entitled to the current media exemption under pre–*Citizens United* campaign finance law and should be entitled to an exemption under any new press exemption.

44. Martin & Fargo, *supra* note 43, at 54.
45. Sam Hananel & Mark Sherman, *Supreme Court Notebook: SCOTUSBlog Denied Press Credential*, Assoc. Press, Feb. 10, 2015, http://hosted.ap.org/dynamic/stories/U/US_SUPREME_COURT_INFLUENTIAL_BLOG?SITE=AP&SECTION=HOME&TEMPLATE=DEFAULT.
46. United States Supreme Court, Requirements and Procedures for Issuing Su-preme Court Press Credentials (Feb. 2015), www.supremecourt.gov/publicinfo/press/Media_Credential_Commentary_February_2015_mod.pdf (last visited Feb. 11, 2015).
47. Eugene Volokh, *Cheap Speech and What It Will Do*, 104 Yale L.J. 1805 (1995).
48. Elizabeth Wilner, *On Points: Local Broadcast TV Ad Spend: Starting to Settle?*, Cook

Pol. Rep. (Sept. 9, 2014), http://cookpolitical.com/story/7784 (seeing slowdown in television advertising but being cautious about predicting future trends).

49. *Austin v. Mich. Chamber of Commerce*, 494 U.S. 652, 691 (Scalia, J., dissenting).

Chapter 7. (Un)Intended Consequences

1. Theodore B. Olson, *Harry Reid Rewrites the First Amendment*, Wall St. J., Sept. 7, 2014, http://online.wsj.com/articles/theodore-olson-harry-reid-rewrites-the-first -amendment-1410124101.

2. The next few paragraphs draws from my history of the *Buckley v. Valeo* litigation. Richard L. Hasen, *The Nine Lives of* Buckley v. Valeo, *in First Amendment Stories* 345 (Richard W. Garnett & Andrew Koppelman eds., 2012). On Buckley's and McCarthy's campaigns, see *id.* at 355-56. See also Judge Buckley's memoir, James L. Buckley, *Gleanings from an Unplanned Life: An Annotated Oral History* (2006).

3. Hasen, *supra* note 2, at 356-57.

4. *McConnell v. FEC*, 540 U.S. 93, 249 (2003) (Scalia, J., dissenting); *id.* at 306 (Kennedy, J., dissenting); *see also id.* at 260 (Scalia, J., dissenting) ("But let us not be deceived. While the Government's briefs and arguments before this Court focused on the horrible 'appearance of corruption,' the most passionate floor statements during the debates on this legislation pertained to so-called attack ads, which the Constitution surely protects, but which Members of Congress analogized to 'crack cocaine,' 144 Cong. Rec. 1601 (1998) (remarks of Sen. Daschle), 'drive-by shooting[s],' *id.*, at 1613 (remarks of Sen. Durbin), and 'air pollution,' 143 Cong. Rec. 20505 (1997) (remarks of Sen. Dorgan). There is good reason to believe that the ending of negative campaign ads was the principal attraction of the legislation.")

5. Hasen, *supra* note 2, at 348-53.

6. Dan Nowicki, *Keating Five Scandal Still Dogs McCain, 25 Years Later*, Ariz. Republic, Apr. 6, 2014, www.azcentral.com/story/azdc/2014/04/06/keating-five-scan dal-dogs-mccain/7328163/.

7. *Id.*

8. Peter Overby, *Decade Brought Change to Campaign Finance*, NPR, Dec. 25, 2009, www.npr.org/templates/story/story.php?storyId=121872329; Michael Tackett, *Finance Reform Fueled by Pre-Enron Scandals*, Chi. Trib., Feb. 15, 2002, http://ar ticles.chicagotribune.com/2002-02-15/news/0202150245_1_soft-money-finance -reform-largely-unregulated-contributions. On Enron's history, see Kurt Eichenwald, *Enron Founder, Awaiting Prison, Dies in Colorado*, N.Y. Times, Jul. 6, 2006, www.nytimes.com/2006/07/06/business/06enron.html.

9. *McConnell v. FEC*, 540 U.S. at 262 (Scalia, J., dissenting).

10. On the history of McCain-Feingold's passage, see Anthony Corrado, *The Legislative Odyssey of BCRA*, in *Life After Reform: When the Bipartisan Campaign Reform Act Meets Politics* 21-39 (Michael J. Malbin ed., 2003), www.cfinst.org/pdf/books-re ports/LAR/LAR_ch2.pdf; Paul S. Herrnson, *The Bipartisan Campaign Reform*

Act and Congressional Elections, in Congress Reconsidered 107–34 (Lawrence C. Dodd & Bruce I. Oppenheimer eds., 8th ed. 2005). www.mit.edu/~17.261/herrnson.pdf. Professor Pildes argues that the Supreme Court made the right call in upholding the major provisions of McCain-Feingold, because its support from outside reform groups demonstrated that most of its provisions were not "impermissible self-entrenchment" but rather were justified as "permissible expression of democratic disaffection through ongoing experimentation with the design of democratic institutions." Richard H. Pildes, *The Constitutionalization of Democratic Politics,* 118 Harv. L. Rev. 28, 141 (2004).

11. On the 60–40 Senate vote for McCain-Feingold, see Corrado, *supra* note 10, at 37. On the 98–0 vote for the 2006 Voting Rights Act renewal, see Adam Liptak, *On the Bench and Off, the Eminently Quotable Justice Scalia,* N.Y. Times, May 11, 2009, at A13, www.nytimes.com/2009/05/12/us/12bar.html. Justice Scalia criticized the 98–0 Voting Rights Act vote as well, as Liptak reports:

> Expressing skepticism about the significance of the 98–0 vote by which the Senate reauthorized the Voting Rights Act, Justice Scalia said, "The Israeli supreme court, the Sanhedrin, used to have a rule that if the death penalty was pronounced unanimously, it was invalid, because there must be something wrong there."
>
> It was as an offhand reference to an ancient court, and Justice Scalia was not announcing a universal principle. Indeed, he almost certainly does not think that every unanimous legislative act is problematic.
>
> In 1986, for instance, the Senate approved Justice Scalia's nomination to the Supreme Court by a vote of 98 to 0.

12. On Republican support for regulation of labor unions' campaign financing in the 1940s, see Robert E. Mutch, *Buying the Vote: A History of Campaign Finance Reform* 106–14 (2014). On Republican support for improved disclosure for 527 organizations, see Justin Elliott, *When the GOP Tried to Ban Dark Money,* ProPublica, Mar. 8, 2012, www.propublica.org/article/when-the-gop-tried-to-ban-dark-money. On current Republican opposition to improved campaign finance disclosure, see Paul Blumenthal, *DISCLOSE Campaign Spending Act Blocked by Senate Republicans,* Huffington Post, Jul. 16, 2012, www.huffingtonpost.com/2012/07/16/disclose-act-senate-campaign-spending_n_1678055.html. The 2012 election saw conservative nondisclosing 501(c) groups spend $265.5 million with undisclosed contributions, compared to liberal nondisclosing 501(c) groups spending $33.6 million with undisclosed contributions, according to data collected by the Center for Responsive Politics. *See 2012 Outside Spending, By Group,* Ctr. for Responsive Pol., www.opensecrets.org/outsidespending/summ.php?cycle=2012&chrt=V&disp=O&type=U (last visited Feb. 12, 2015). In 2014, conservative 501(c) groups spent $124 million compared to $34.7 million by liberal 501(c)s. *2014 Outside Spending, By Group,* Ctr. for Responsive. Pol., www.opensecrets.org/

outsidespending/summ.php?cycle=2014&chrt=V&disp=O&type=U (last visited Feb. 12, 2015).

13. Megan Thee-Brenan, *Polls Show Broad Support for Campaign Spending Caps*, N.Y. Times, Apr. 2, 2014, www.nytimes.com/2014/04/03/us/politics/polls-show-broad -support-for-campaign-spending-caps.html; David Primo, *Public Opinion and Campaign Finance: Reformers Versus Reality*, VII Indep. Rev. 207, 210 (2002). *See also* Lydia Saad, *Half in U.S. Support Publicly Financed Federal Campaigns*, Gallup Politics, Jun. 24, 2013, www.gallup.com/poll/163208/half-support-publicly-financed -federal-campaigns.aspx ("Over the years, Gallup has consistently found Americans dissatisfied with the way campaigns are financed, but not especially eager for Congress to make addressing it a high priority.").

14. David M. Primo et al., *State Campaign Finance Reform, Competitiveness, and Party Advantage in Gubernatorial Elections*, in *The Marketplace of Democracy* 268–85 (Michael P. McDonald & John Samples eds., 2006).

15. Michael G. Miller, *Subsidizing Democracy: How Public Funding Changes Elections and How It Can Work in the Future* 80–107 (2013); Kenneth T. Mayer, Timothy Werner & Amanda Williams, *Do Public Funding Programs Enhance Electoral Competition?*, in *The Marketplace of Democracy, supra* note 14, at 245–67.

16. Cass R. Sunstein, *Political Equality and Unintended Consequences*, 94 Colum. L. Rev. 1390 (1994).

17. I trace these developments in Chapter 2, where full citations to the cases cited are available.

18. *Presidential Ads 70 Percent Negative in 2012, Up from 9 Percent in 2008*, Wesleyan Media Project (May 2, 2012), http://mediaproject.wesleyan.edu/releases/ jump-in-negativity-2/ (In 2012, outside interest groups had 86% negative ads, compared to 52% negative ads for candidates and 2% for political parties).

19. Thomas E. Mann & Anthony Corrado, *Party Polarization and Campaign Finance*, Brookings Inst. Ctr, for Effective Pub. Mgmt. (July 2014) [hereinafter Mann & Corrado, *Party Polarization*], www.brookings.edu/~/media/research/files/papers/ 2014/07/polarization%20and%20campaign%20finance/mann%20and%20 corrad_party%20polarization%20and%20campaign%20finance.pdf; Ray LaRaja & Brian Schaffner, *Want to Reduce Polarization? Give Parties More Money*, Wash. Post, Monkey Cage Blog (July 21, 2014), www.washingtonpost.com/blogs/mon key-cage/wp/2014/07/21/want-to-reduce-polarization-give-parties-more-money/; Richard Pildes, *How to Fix Our Polarized Politics? Strengthen Political Parties*, Wash. Post, Monkey Cage Blog (Feb. 6, 2014) [hereinafter Pildes, *Strengthen Political Parties*], www.washingtonpost.com/blogs/monkey-cage/wp/2014/02/06/ how-to-fix-our-polarized-politics-strengthen-political-parties/; Thomas Mann & Anthony Corrado, *Don't Expect Campaign Finance Reform to Reduce Polarization*, Wash. Post, Monkey Cage Blog (Jul. 23, 2014) [hereinafter Mann & Corrado, *Don't Expect*], www.washingtonpost.com/blogs/monkey-cage/wp/2014/07/23/dont-ex pect-campaign-finance-reform-to-reduce-polarization/; Richard Pildes, *Can Polit-*

ical Party Super-PACs Reduce Polarization?, Wash. Post, Monkey Cage Blog (Sept. 26, 2014), www.washingtonpost.com/blogs/monkey-cage/wp/2014/09/26/can -political-party-super-pacs-reduce-polarization/; Paul Blumenthal, *Citizens United, McCain-Feingold, Fueled Congress' Shutdown Politics,* Huffington Post Blog (Oct. 16, 2013), www.huffingtonpost.com/2013/10/16/citizens-united-shutdown_n_41082 52.html; Fred Wertheimer, *Citizens United Decision Is the Problem, Not McCain-Feingold Law,* Huffington Post Blog (Oct. 25, 2013), www.huffingtonpost.com/ fred-wertheimer/citizens-united-decision-_b_4164407.html; Eliza Newlin Carney, *Did Soft Money Ban Kill Political Parties? / Rules of the Game,* Roll Call (May 6, 2014), http://blogs.rollcall.com/beltway-insiders/did-soft-money-ban-kill-poli tical-parties/.

20. Samuel Issacharoff & Pamela S. Karlan, *The Hydraulics of Campaign Finance Reform,* 77 Tex. L. Rev. 1705 (1999); *McConnell v. FEC,* 540 U.S. 93, 224 (2003).

21. On the decline of corporate money in federal elections after McCain-Feingold but before *Citizens United,* see Stephen R. Weissman & Ruth Hassan, *BCRA and the 527 Groups,* in *The Election After Reform* 79, 90 (Michael J. Malbin ed., 2006), www.cfinst.org/pdf/books-reports/EAR/EAR_ch5.pdf ("On the other hand, business donations (meaning those not of individual businessmen but of corporations, trade associations, and individual incorporated entities like lawyers' and doctors' practices) declined from $32 million to $30 million (actually to $26 million if one omits a large contribution by the 'Sustainable World Corporation,' widely regarded as a nonfunctioning business representing Linda Pritzker, a member of one of the world's wealthiest families). So business contributions to 527s in no way made up for the $216 million in soft money that business entities had given to national parties in the 2002 cycle. The biggest change though came in donations by individuals which rocketed from a mere $37 million to $256 million.") (citations and footnotes omitted). The amicus brief of the Committee for Economic Development and others filed in the *McConnell* case is posted at: www.campaignlegalcenter.org/attachments/BCRA_MCCAIN_FEINGOLD/Mc Connell_v_FEC_District_Court/887.pdf (last visited Jan. 18, 2015).

22. Daniel Hays Lowenstein, *On Campaign Finance Reform: The Root of All Evil Is Deeply Rooted,* 18 Hofstra L. Rev. 301 (1989); *see also* Pildes, *Strengthen Political Parties, supra* note 19, making similar arguments to channel outside money through the parties.

23. Christine Pelisek, *The Fall of Democratic Campaign Treasurer Kinde Durkee,* Daily Beast, Mar. 28, 2012, www.thedailybeast.com/articles/2012/03/28/the-fall-of-cal ifornia-democratic-campaign-treasurer-kinde-durkee.html; Julie Patel, *Super PAC Leaders Score Perks from Political Donations,* Ctr. for Pub. Integrity (Apr. 15, 2014), www.publicintegrity.org/2014/04/15/14537/super-pac-leaders-score-perks-po litical-donations; Eliza Newlin Carney, *Democracy Has Become a Cash Cow,* CQ Weekly, Feb. 2, 2015, www.cq.com/doc/weeklyreport-4613788.

24. *See* Richard L. Hasen, *Lobbying, Rent Seeking, and the Constitution,* 64 Stan. L. Rev. 191 (2012).

25. Richard L. Hasen, *Political Dysfunction and Constitutional Change*, 61 Drake L. Rev. 989 (2013), http://students.law.drake.edu/lawReview/docs/lrVol61-4-hasen.pdf.

26. Adam Bonica, *Small Donors and Polarization*, Boston Rev., Jul. 22, 2011, www.bostonreview.net/bonica-small-donors-polarization; Adam Bonica, *Mapping the Ideological Marketplace*, 58 Am. J. Pol. Sci. 367 (2014). *But see* Michael J. Malbin, *Small Donors: Incentives, Economies of Scale, and Effects*, 11 Forum 385 (2013). *See also* Mann & Corrado, *Party Polarization, supra* note 19; Mann & Corrado, *Don't Expect, supra* note 19; LaRaja & Schaffner, *supra* note 19; Pildes, *Strengthen Political Parties, supra* note 19.

27. Mann & Corrado, *Party Polarization, supra* note 19 (footnotes omitted).

28. Michael Barber, *Ideological Donors, Contribution Limits, and the Polarization of American Legislatures* (unpublished draft dated Jan. 30, 2015), *draft available at* http://static1.squarespace.com/static/51841c73e4b04fc5ce6e8f15/t/54d24adae4b092c13f8d35c6/1423067866936/Limits_Revised.pdf.

Chapter 8. Wrong Paths

1. 160 Cong. Rec. S5417–18 (daily ed. Sept. 9, 2014) (statement of Sen. Cruz).

2. 160 Cong. Rec. S5468–69 (daily ed. Sept. 10, 2014) (statement of Sen. T. Udall).

3. Louis Jacobson, *Ted Cruz Says SNL's Lorne Michaels Could Be Jailed Under Democratic Backed Amendment*, Politifact (Sept. 11, 2014), www.politifact.com/truth-o-meter/statements/2014/sep/11/ted-cruz/ted-cruz-says-snls-lorne-michaels-could-be-jailed-/.

4. 160 Cong. Reg. S5350 (daily ed. Sept. 8, 2014) (statement of Sen. Reid).

5. 160 Cong. Reg. S5399 (daily ed. Sept. 9, 2014) (statement of Sen. Hatch); Carl Hulse & John Holusha, *Amendment on Flag Burning Fails on One Vote in Senate*, N.Y. Times, Jun. 27, 2006, www.nytimes.com/2006/06/27/washington/27cnd-flag.html ("Senator Orrin Hatch, Republican of Utah and the chief sponsor of the amendment, predicted before the vote that those who opposed the amendment would be penalized by the voters if it was again defeated."). *See also* Ronald K. L. Collins, *FAN 30.2 (First Amendment News): This Evening: Vote on Proposed Amendment to First Amendment*, Concurring Opinions (Sept. 8, 2014), www.concurringopinions.com/archives/2014/09/fan-30-2-first-amendment-news-this-evening-vote-on-proposed-amendment-to-first-amendment.html (noting Sen. Hatch's positions); Press Release, *Allowing Lower Court Rulings on Same-Sex Marriage to Stand is 'Tragic and Indefensible' and 'Judicial Activism at Its Worst,'* Press Office of Senator Ted Cruz, Oct. 2, 2014, www.cruz.senate.gov/?p=press_release&id=1777 ("Marriage is a question for the States. That is why I have introduced legislation, S. 2024, to protect the authority of state legislatures to define marriage. And that is why, when Congress returns to session, I will be introducing a constitutional amendment to prevent the federal government or the courts from attacking or striking down state marriage laws.").

6. The final roll call vote appears at: www.senate.gov/legislative/LIS/roll_call_lists/

roll_call_vote_cfm.cfm?congress=113&session=2&vote=00261. In addition to all of the Democrats voting, Independent senators Bernie Sanders of Vermont and Angus King of Maine voted in favor of the measure. The four senators not voting were Coburn, Cruz, Gillibrand, and Murkowski. www.senate.gov/legis lative/LIS/roll_call_lists/roll_call_vote_cfm.cfm?congress=113&session=2& vote=00261#position. It is not clear why Senator Cruz missed the vote. Katie Singh, *Hypocrite Ted Cruz Too Scared to Vote with Fellow Republicans to Keep Citizens United*, Burnt Orange Report (Sept. 24, 2014), www.burntorangereport.com/ diary/18221/hypocrite-ted-cruz-scared-vote-fellow-republicans-keep-citizens -united ("And yet, despite his constant fearmongering around the issue, Ted Cruz did not actually vote with his fellow Republicans on the constitutional amendment last week. Instead, he skipped the vote entirely. You would think that if the entire future of the First Amendment was really at risk, Cruz would make the time to be on the Senate floor to vote to protect it. Instead, he evidently had something better to do. (Perhaps he's gone fishing with Dan Patrick? Or maybe there was something going on in Iowa that was too important for him to miss?)"). The night before, he gave the speech praising Israel which gained extensive media coverage. Leigh Ann Caldwell, *Ted Cruz Booed at Christian Unity Dinner*, CNN (Sept. 11, 2014), www.cnn.com/2014/09/11/politics/cruz-booed-off-stage/.

7. The original amendment, Senate Joint Resolution 19, proposed by Senator Tom Udall, read:

SECTION 1. To advance the fundamental principle of political equality for all, and to protect the integrity of the legislative and electoral processes, Congress shall have power to regulate the raising and spending of money and in-kind equivalents with respect to Federal elections, including through setting limits on—

(1) the amount of contributions to candidates for nomination for election to, or for election to, Federal office; and

(2) the amount of funds that may be spent by, in support of, or in opposition to such candidates.

SECTION 2. To advance the fundamental principle of political equality for all, and to protect the integrity of the legislative and electoral processes, each State shall have power to regulate the raising and spending of money and in-kind equivalents with respect to State elections, including through setting limits on—

(1) the amount of contributions to candidates for nomination for election to, or for election to, State office; and

(2) the amount of funds that may be spent by, in support of, or in opposition to such candidates.

SECTION 3. Nothing in this article shall be construed to grant Congress the power to abridge the freedom of the press.

SECTION 4. Congress and the States shall have power to implement and enforce this article by appropriate legislation.

The text of the original version of the proposed amendment is available at www.congress.gov/bill/113th-congress/senate-joint-resolution/19/text/107139. The full history of the proposed amendment is available at www.congress.gov/ bill/113th-congress/senate-joint-resolution/19/actions.

On Senator Durbin's amendments, including the addition of the word "reasonable" to the constitutional amendment's language, see Stephen Dinan, *Democrats Draft Amendment to Curb Election Spending,* Wash. Times, Jun. 18, 2014, www.wash ingtontimes.com/news/2014/jun/18/democrats-draft-amendment-to-curb-elec tion-spendin/?page=all.

8. The final text of the amendment appears at: www.congress.gov/113/bills/sjres19/ BILLS-113sjres19rs.xml.

9. 160 Cong. Rec. S5355–56 (daily ed. Sept. 8, 2014) (statement of Senator Durbin); 160 Cong. Rec. S5355 (daily ed. Sept. 8, 2014) (statement of Senator Warren); 160 Cong. Rec. S5350 (daily ed. Sept. 8, 2014) (statement of Senator Reid).

10. S. Rep. 113-223, at 2 (2014), www.congress.gov/congressional-report/113th-congress/ senate-report/223/1.

11. Carissa Miller, *Three Million Petition Signatures to Overturn Citizens United Delivered to Congress,* Daily Kos (Sept. 9, 2014), www.dailykos.com/story/2014/09/ 09/1328331/-PHOTOS-3-000-000-petition-signatures-to-overturn-Citizens-United -delivered-to-Congress.

12. Here is the proposed constitutional amendment from Move to Amend:

Section 1. [Artificial Entities Such as Corporations Do Not Have Constitutional Rights]

The rights protected by the Constitution of the United States are the rights of natural persons only.

Artificial entities established by the laws of any State, the United States, or any foreign state shall have no rights under this Constitution and are subject to regulation by the People, through Federal, State, or local law.

The privileges of artificial entities shall be determined by the People, through Federal, State, or local law, and shall not be construed to be inherent or inalienable.

Section 2. [Money is Not Free Speech]

Federal, State, and local government shall regulate, limit, or prohibit contributions and expenditures, including a candidate's own contributions and expenditures, to ensure that all citizens, regardless of their economic status, have access to the political process, and that no person gains, as a result of their money, substantially more access or ability to influence in any way the election of any candidate for public office or any ballot measure.

Federal, State, and local government shall require that any permissible contributions and expenditures be publicly disclosed.

The judiciary shall not construe the spending of money to influence elections to be speech under the First Amendment.

The text appears at https://movetoamend.org/wethepeopleamendment.

13. John Paul Stevens, *Six Amendments: How and Why We Should Change the Constitution* 79 (2014). For my critique, see Richard L. Hasen, *Change the Constitution in Six Easy Steps? It Won't Be That Simple, Justice Stevens,* Daily Beast (Apr. 20, 2014), www.thedailybeast.com/articles/2014/04/20/change-the-constitution-in-six-easy-steps-it-won-t-be-that-simple-justice-stevens.html. The following few paragraphs draw from this critique. *See also* Noah Bierman, *John Paul Stevens Reaffirms Dissent on Campaign Finance,* Boston Globe, May 1, 2014, www.bostonglobe.com/news/nation/2014/04/30/john-paul-stevens-taking-another-run-putting-his-imprint-constitution/RkBFe4veWWMk0AiT3Pon5I/story.html (describing Justice Stevens' testimony before a Senate committee).

14. Evan Osnos, *Embrace the Irony: Lawrence Lessig Wants to Reform Campaign Finance. All He Needs Is Fifty Billionaires,* The New Yorker, Oct. 13, 2014, www.newyorker.com/magazine/2014/10/13/embrace-irony.

15. See Chapter 3, footnote 34, for links to my critiques of Lessig and Lessig's responses.

16. DocDawg, *MayDay and the Myth of the Republican Reformer,* Daily Kos (Diary) (Aug. 11, 2014), www.dailykos.com/story/2014/08/11/1320599/-Mayday-and-the-myth-of-the-Republican-reformer#.

17. Corbin Hiar, *Lawrence Lessig on Campaign Finance Reform: Overturning 'Citizens United' Isn't Enough,* The Ctr. for Pub. Integrity (Feb. 29, 2012), www.publicintegrity.org/2012/02/29/8278/lawrence-lessig-campaign-finance-reform-overturning-citizens-united-isnt-enough. Lawrence Lessig, *What an Originalist Would Understand "Corruption" to Mean,* 102 Calif. L. Rev. 1 (2014); Brief Amicus Curiae of Professor Lawrence Lessig in Support of Appellee, *McCutcheon v. FEC,* 134 S. Ct. 1434 (2014) (No. 12-536); Lawrence Lessig, *Originalists Making It Up Again: McCutcheon and 'Corruption,'* Daily Beast (Apr. 2, 2014), www.thedailybeast.com/articles/2014/04/02/originalists-making-it-up-again-mccutcheon-and-corruption.html.

18. The video of Professor Lessig's lecture as keynote speaker for a conference sponsored by the *Duke Journal of Constitutional Law and Public Policy* is posted at www.youtube.com/watch?v=8YsS9x39B5k. He makes the quoted comments at the 59:20 minute mark.

19. Lawrence Lessig, *An Open Letter to the Citizens Against* Citizens United, The Atlantic (March 23, 2012), www.theatlantic.com/politics/archive/2012/03/an-open-letter-to-the-citizens-against-citizens-united/254902/2/; Lawrence Lessig, *Why a Democratic Tea Party Is the Best Hope for Fixing Corrupt Government,* Atlantic (Dec. 6, 2012), www.theatlantic.com/politics/archive/2012/12/why-a-democratic-tea-party-is-the-best-hope-for-fixing-corrupt-government/265992/.

20. The MayDay website (as of January 2015) endorsed both public financing through vouchers or multiple small matching grants and new legislation to limit contributions to committees making independent expenditures. *The Plan to Get Democracy Back,* MaydayPAC, https://mayday.us/the-plan/ (last visited Jan. 21, 2015) ("it is not yet clear that constitutional reform will even be necessary. It is unlikely,

without a change in the composition of the Court, that either Citizens United or Buckley will be reversed. But the case establishing the freedom to contribute unlimited amounts to independent political action committees was not reviewed by the Supreme Court. Because the Court has treated the standard governing the regulation of contributions differently from expenditures, we believe it is still possible for the Court to uphold the power of Congress to limit contributions to independent political action committees (thereby eliminating so called 'super-PACs'). Given the relatively small role that independent expenditures—unrelated to superPACs—play in the current system, that change alone may be enough to secure—with the correct system of public funding—a Congress no longer pathologically dependent on large funders.").

21. Kenneth P. Vogel, *The Man Behind the Political Cash Grab: A Powerful Democratic Lawyer Crafted the Campaign Finance Deal*, Politico, Dec. 12, 2014, www.politico.com/story/2014/12/democratic-lawyer-crafted-campaign-finance-deal-113549.html.

22. The remainder of this chapter is based upon Richard L. Hasen, *Three Wrong Progressive Approaches (and One Right One) to Campaign Finance Reform*, 8 Harv. L. & Pol'y Rev. 21 (2014).

23. *Bluman v. FEC*, 132 S. Ct. 1087 (2012) (mem.), *aff'g* 800 F. Supp. 2d 281 (D.D.C. 2011) (three-judge panel); *Why Alito Shook His Head: Obama Exaggerates Impact of Supreme Court Ruling on Foreign Companies*, Politifact (Jan. 27, 2010), www.politifact.com/truth-o-meter/statements/2010/jan/27/barack-obama/obama-says-supreme-court-ruling-allows-foreign-com/ (rating President Obama's statement "mostly false").

24. Justin Elliott, *Obama's Flip-Flops on Money in Politics: A Brief History*, Pro Publica (Jan. 30, 2013), www.propublica.org/article/obamas-flip-flops-on-money-in-politics-a-brief-history; Eliza Newlin Carney, *Rules of the Game: Obama's Ethics Agenda Backfires*, Roll Call (Jan. 20, 2013), www.rollcall.com/news/rules_of_the_game_obamas_ethics_agenda_backfires-220898-1.html.

25. Frank James, *Watchdogs Not Celebrating Obama Group's Switch on Big Donors*, NPR, It's All Politics (Mar. 7, 2013), www.npr.org/blogs/itsallpolitics/2013/03/07/173748542/watchdogs-not-celebrating-obama-groups-switch-on-big-donors.

26. David Axelrod, Twitter post, Feb. 20, 2013, https://twitter.com/davidaxelrod/status/304258408058601472 ("Campaign finance system is a mess. Limits have just created a cottage industry for lawyers who devise schemes to circumvent them. 1/3"); https://twitter.com/davidaxelrod/status/304258430296813568 ("Too much money in politics. But if it's inevitable, let it flow directly to candidates and demand full disclosure, with stiff penalties.2/3"); https://twitter.com/davidaxelrod/status/304258450307833856 ("And end the SuperPac and faux SuperPac game that too often allows donors to elude detection and candidates to deny responsibility. 3/3.").

27. Ezra Klein, *We Got Way Too Excited Over Money in the 2012 Elections*, Wash. Post, Wonkblog (May 6, 2013); www.washingtonpost.com/blogs/wonkblog/wp/2013/05/06/we-got-way-too-excited-over-money-in-the-2012-elections/; Ezra Klein, *Big Money*

Corrupts Washington; Small Donors Polarize It, Wash. Post, Wonkblog (May 10, 2013), www.washingtonpost.com/blogs/wonkblog/wp/2013/05/10/big-money-corrupts-washington-small-donors-polarize-it/. Jonathan Bernstein, *How to Stop the Next IRS Scandal*, Am. Prospect (May 17, 2013), http://prospect.org/article/how-stop-next-irs-scandal.

28. Ezra Klein, *Did I Get the Money-and-Politics Debate All Wrong?* Wash. Post, Wonkblog (May 28, 2013), www.washingtonpost.com/blogs/wonkblog/wp/2013/05/28/did-i-get-the-money-and-politics-debate-all-wrong/. Mark Schmitt, *Now We Are Way Too Excited About Campaign Finance Skepticism*, Next New Deal (May 13, 2013), www.nextnewdeal.net/now-we-are-way-too-excited-about-campaign-finance-skepticism; Lee Drutman, *What Ezra Klein Gets Wrong About Big vs. Small Money in Politics*, Sunlight Found. Blog (May 10, 2013), http://sunlightfoundation.com/blog/2013/05/10/big-vs-small-money-in-politics/; Jonathan Backer, *Why Big Money Still Won in 2012*, Huffington Post (May 8, 2013), www.huffingtonpost.com/jonathan-backer/why-big-money-still-won-i_b_3237762.html; Jonathan Bernstein, *No, Campaign Money Isn't the Root of All Evil*, A Plain Blog About Politics (May 9, 2013), http://plainblogaboutpolitics.blogspot.com/2013/05/no-campaign-money-isnt-root-of-all-evil.html.

Chapter 9. The Last Great Hope for Reform

1. Tony Mauro, *The Supreme Court 'What-If' Game: Who Could Be Confirmed in This Political Climate?*, Nat'l L.J., Sept. 1, 2014, www.nationallawjournal.com/id=1202668526644/The-Supreme-Court-WhatIf-Game.

2. Liptak made his remarks at a conference, Is America Governable?, held at the University of Texas at Austin on January 26, 2013. The video of the event is posted at www.youtube.com/watch?v=_EzFHFbOjHk&feature=youtu.be and Liptak's specific comment appears around the 1:03:15 mark.

3. David Stout & Timothy Williams, *Miers Ends Supreme Court Bid After Failing to Win Support*, N.Y. Times, Oct. 27, 2005, www.nytimes.com/2005/10/27/politics/politicsspecial1/27cnd-scotus.html?pagewanted=all; Elisabeth Bumiller & Carl Hulse, *Bush Picks Appeals Court Judge to Succeed O'Connor on Court*, N.Y. Times, Oct. 31, 2005, www.nytimes.com/2005/10/31/politics/politicsspecial1/31cnd-court.html?pagewanted=all.

4. Bruce Ackerman: *We the People, Vol. II: Transformations* (2000).

5. For a tart critique of Justice Scalia's textualist and originalist methodology, see Richard A. Posner, *The Incoherence of Antonin Scalia*, New Republic, Aug. 24, 2012, www.newrepublic.com/article/magazine/books-and-arts/106441/scalia-garner-reading-the-law-textual-originalism. There is a rich literature criticizing and defending originalism as a constitutional methodology. There is also a rich literature on legal realism and more recent critical jurisprudential theories. While fascinating, these debates are well beyond the scope of this book.

6. For examples see *Schuette v. Coal. to Defend Affirmative Action*, 134 S. Ct. 1623

(2014) (affirmative action); *McDonald v. City of Chicago*, 561 U.S. 742 (2010) (gun rights); *Boumediene v. Bush*, 553 U.S. 723 (2008) (enemy combatants); *Gonzalez v. Carhart*, 550 U.S. 124 (2007) (abortion).

Much of this portion of this chapter is drawn from Richard L. Hasen, *End of the Dialogue? Political Polarization, the Supreme Court, and Congress*, 86 S. Cal. L. Rev. 205, 242–50 (2013).

7. These statistics come from the "Statpack" of SCOTUSblog covering the end of the 2013 Supreme Court term. The specific statistics on 5–4 splits appears at http://sblog.s3.amazonaws.com/wp-content/uploads/2014/07/SCOTUSblog _5-4_cases_OT13.pdf.

8. Supreme Court Nominations, Present–1789, U.S. Senate, www.senate.gov/page-layout/reference/nominations/Nominations.htm; *see generally* Richard H. Pildes, *Is the Supreme Court a "Majoritarian" Institution?*, 2010 Sup. Ct. Rev. 103, 139–42 (noting the lag-time issue).

9. Timothy K. Kuhner, *Capitalism v. Democracy: Money in Politics and the Free Market Constitution* (2014) (tying campaign finance jurisprudence to free market ideology).

10. Lee Epstein et al., *The Increasing Importance of Ideology in the Nomination and Confirmation of Supreme Court Justices*, 56 Drake L. Rev. 609, 610 (2008).

11. 151 Cong. Rec. 21,032 (2005) (statement of Sen. Barack Obama), *available at* www .gpo.gov/fdsys/pkg/CREC-2005-09-22/pdf/CREC-2005-09-22-pt1-PgS10365.pdf.

12. Nancy Gibbs, *Hill vs. Thomas: An Ugly Circus*, Time Mag., Oct. 21, 1991, available at www.time.com/time/magazine/article/0,9171,974074,00.html. Senate rejections of Supreme Court nominees have fluctuated over time. The Senate rejected three nominees besides Bork in the twentieth century, and Justice Fortas withdrew his nomination to be chief justice after a filibuster. Supreme Court Nominations, Present–1789, *supra* note 8. Nonetheless, the vast majority of Supreme Court nominees in the last century were confirmed. In the twenty-first century, so far only one nominee, Harriet Miers, withdrew her nomination. None have been filibustered. Justice Scalia was approved on a 98–0 vote and Justice Kennedy on a 97–0 vote. Justice Thomas's vote was 52 to 48, but the nomination became embroiled in controversy over sexual harassment allegations. Justice Ginsburg was approved on a 96–3 vote, and Justice Breyer, 87–9. All the figures in this and the next paragraph appear at www.senate.gov/pagelayout/reference/nominations/ Nominations.htm.

13. John Steele Gordon, *A Filibuster That Goes Around Comes Around*, Commentary, May 20, 2011, www.commentarymagazine.com/2011/05/20/filibuster-that-goes -around-comes-around/; Meredith Shiner, *Senate GOP Filibusters Goodwin Liu*, Politico, May 19, 2011 (updated May 20, 2011), www.politico.com/news/stories/ 0511/55320.html.

14. Paul Kane, *Reid, Democrats Trigger 'Nuclear' Option; Eliminate Most Filibusters on Nominees*, Wash. Post, Nov. 21, 2013, www.washingtonpost.com/politics/senate -poised-to-limit-filibusters-in-party-line-vote-that-would-alter-centuries-of-prece dent/2013/11/21/d065cfe8-52b6-11e3-9feo-fd2ca728e67c_story.html.

15. *See* Lee Epstein et al., *The Changing Dynamics of Senate Voting on Supreme Court Nominees*, 68 J. Pol. 296 (2006) ("[E]xplor[ing] the extent to which the Bork nomination has affected the decisions of U.S. Senators."). For a skeptical view of the importance of the Bork controversy on more recent judicial nomination battles, see Sarah A. Binder & Forrest Maltzman, *Advice & Dissent: The Struggle to Shape the Federal Judiciary* 7–9 (2009).

16. In 2004, during the Iraq War, Rumsfeld said, "You go to war with the army you have, not the army you might want or wish to have at a later time." Eric Schmitt, *Iraq-Bound Troops Confront Rumsfeld over Lack of Armor*, N.Y. Times, Dec. 8, 2004, www.nytimes.com/2004/12/08/international/middleeast/08cnd-rumsfeld.html.

    The remainder of this chapter draws from Richard L. Hasen, *Three Wrong Progressive Approaches (and One Right One) to Campaign Finance Reform*, 8 Harv. L. & Pol'y Rev. 21 (2014).

17. Rick Hasen, *A Tale of Two Campaign Finance Appeals at SCOTUS: Why No Push to Allow Corporate Contributions to Candidates?*, Election Law Blog (Apr. 11, 2014), http://electionlawblog.org/?p=60392.

18. Jessica Calefati, *'Dark Money': California Political Watchdog Slaps Conservative Groups with Historic Penalties*, San Jose Mercury News, Oct. 24, 2013, www.mercurynews.com/ci_24380009/californias-political-watchdog-slaps-conservative-groups-historic-penalties.

19. *Nixon v. Shrink Mo. Gov't PAC*, 528 U.S. 377, 401–3 (2000) (Breyer, J., concurring); *Ognibene v. Parkes*, 671 F.3d 174, 197–201 (2d Cir. 2011) (Calabresi, J., concurring). See also Stephen J. Breyer, *Active Liberty: Interpreting Our Democratic Constitution* (2005).

20. David D. Kirkpatrick, *A Quest to End Spending Rules for Campaigns*, N.Y. Times, Jan. 24, 2010, www.nytimes.com/2010/01/25/us/politics/25bopp.html ("'We had a 10-year plan to take all this down,' [Bopp] said in an interview. 'And if we do it right, I think we can pretty well dismantle the entire regulatory regime that is called campaign finance law.'").

21. Mark Walsh, *View from the Courtroom: Disruption from the Gallery on the Fifth Anniversary of Citizens United (Updated 4:00 p.m.)*, SCOTUSblog, Jan. 21, 2015, www.scotusblog.com/2015/01/view-from-the-courtroom-disruption-from-the-gallery-on-5th-anniversary-of-citizens-united/; *see also* Adam Liptak, *One by One, Protestors Interrupt Supreme Court*, N.Y. Times, Jan 21, 2015 ("When all of the protesters had been removed, Chief Justice Roberts said, 'We will now continue with our tradition of having open court in the Supreme Court building.'").

INDEX